P9-EMP-139

Lancaster Central Market

# COOKBOOK

May 25, 2018

Dear Peggy and Don,

We hope this little bit of
Lancaster will remind you
of a wonderful ten years
you spent here. We wish
you all the best in your
new home. We will
miss you in the neighborhood!

Love,
Adam

Carl Anthony

# Lancaster Central Market

# COOKBOOK

*25th Anniversary Edition*

## Phyllis Good

### Historical Sketches about the Market by Stephen Scott

New York, New York

Copyright © 2015 by Phyllis Good

All rights reserved. No part of this book may be reproduced in any manner without the express written consent of the publisher, except in the case of brief excerpts in critical reviews or articles. All inquiries should be addressed to Good Books, 307 West 36th Street, 11th Floor, New York, NY 10018.

Good Books books may be purchased in bulk at special discounts for sales promotion, corporate gifts, fund-raising, or educational purposes. Special editions can also be created to specifications. For details, contact the Special Sales Department, Good Books, 307 West 36th Street, 11th Floor, New York, NY 10018 or info@skyhorsepublishing.com.

Good Books is an imprint of Skyhorse Publishing, Inc.®, a Delaware corporation.

Visit our website at www.goodbooks.com.

10 9 8 7 6 5 4 3 2 1

Library of Congress Cataloging-in-Publication Data is available on file.

Print ISBN: 978-1-68099-066-9
Ebook ISBN: 978-1-68099-104-8

Cover design by Cliff Snyder
Cover photo by Jeremy Hess

Printed in China

Photo credits, by insert page number:
1: Courtesy of Lancaster Central Market's office; 2–3, 5–6, 8–9, 11–16: Jeremy Hess; 4: LancasterHistory.org; 7, 10 (top): Michelle Johnsen; 10 (bottom): Michelle Lynn

Limit of Liability/Disclaimer of Warranty: The publisher and author have made their best effort in preparing this book with care and accuracy, and it is presented in good faith. But they make no representations or warranties with respect to the completeness or accuracy of the contents of this book. Sales representatives may not create or extend any warranty either verbally or in sales materials about this book. The advice and strategies contained in these materials may not be suitable for your situation. Consult with a professional where appropriate. Neither the author nor the publisher shall be liable for any commercial damages or loss of profit, including but not limited to special, consequential, or incidental damages.

# Contents

# How This Book
## Came to Be

I love Lancaster Central Market! It is the place to go for fresh vegetables, fruits, cheese, baked goods, seafood, and meats. And good chance you'll be buying from the farmer or baker or cheesemaker who grew or produced what you'll take home.

My first job was working on market. And now I shop there once or twice nearly every week. I go for the food, but I also go for the people and the atmosphere. Recently I asked standholders why they think Lancaster Central Market has operated for so many years and has such staunchly loyal customers today.

"The people who shop here and work here are a community," they each said, one by one. As Earl Groff, a second-generation standholder, reflected, "Market is not just a place to buy and sell things. It's a place to visit, to share ideas, to talk about weather—and government!"

Twenty-five years ago, Viv Hunt, another second-generation standholder, began writing down favorite recipes of the food she sold at her stand. She urged other standholders to do the same. Many did not cook from written recipes.

In some cases, they wrote down recipes that until then had been passed along only by watching their mothers and grandmothers prepare them. Other recipes were translated from German to English for the first time. Still other recipes were so familiar and traditional to Lancaster County that standholders weren't sure they merited recording.

Viv asked us at Good Books to join them in organizing the gathering of the recipes so that the final collection would represent the current flavor of Lancaster Central Market. We asked standholders to submit three categories of recipes for the new book—a food they sell at their stand, or one made with ingredients sold at their stand; a traditional Lancaster County dish, or one from their own tradition, that they particularly enjoy; and then a personal favorite. In so doing we hoped to capture the regional rootings of the Market, as well as its current multi-cultural flavor. That spread was in that book, as it is every Tuesday, Friday, and Saturday on Lancaster Central Market.

Now, 25 years later, the original *Central Market Cookbook* is out of print. But standholders—and booksellers across the country—heard frequent requests for "that book with those choice recipes!"

This 25th Anniversary edition of the *Lancaster Central Market Cookbook* contains the best of the recipes from the original book, plus dozens of new recipes from today's standholders.

This *Cookbook* represents the work of many: first, the standholders who wrote recipes amid tending their truck farms, baking breads and pastries, butchering, curing, and making salads. Many of the standholders also tested recipes. That step brought questions from some of the best cooks—why test recipes when we know they work? It was not their quality or tastiness that we doubted; it was that we wondered if these people, who cook with as little effort as they breathe, would record all the steps needed for the uninitiated!

The *Lancaster Central Market Cookbook: 25th Anniversary Edition* has been a cooperative venture from its very beginning. Now that it's complete, we invite you to join us in Lancaster Central Market's tradition of good eating.

Phyllis Good

# The Wonder of Lancaster Central Market

Lancaster Central Market may be an historic site, but it is a vitally active place of commerce and friendship every Tuesday, Friday, and Saturday.

Today's market building, built in 1889, is old. Older still is the habit of going to market in Lancaster. When Andrew and James Hamilton planned the town site in 1730, they provided three lots for a market place. The 120-foot square lay at the northwest corner of King and Queen Streets adjoining the Centre Square.

When Lancaster was incorporated as a borough in 1742, its charter from George II of England established the market tradition: "And we do further grant for us, our heirs and successors . . . to have, hold and keep . . . two markets in each week." Already in 1744, a visitor in the town remarked, "They have a good market in this town, well filled with provisions of all kinds and prodigiously cheap." A few decades later in 1776, a British officer paroled in Lancaster remarked, "Food is very plentiful. The markets abound with most excellent cyder and provisions."

The city's interest in the market has protected its integrity and the pristine quality of the food and goods sold there. It was so from the beginning. The City Council ruled that no "chapmen" (itinerant peddlers) were permitted to sell door-to-door in the city or set up stands except at fairs. Effort was also made to establish high standards of quality for the foodstuffs sold at market: there were rules that concerned the freshness of meat and that stipulated that meat not be inflated with air to make it appear more substantial.

The first Lancaster farmers' market was an open-air affair, but by 1757 a market house had been constructed, most likely a rather primitive structure. In 1763, part of the market house was reserved for the storage of three fire engines.

In 1795, Lancaster City Hall was built on the grounds of the market. Adjoining the west end of that building, a new market house was constructed in 1798. This was a dual-purpose building consisting of brick pillars and arches surrounding an open market place on the first floor and headquarters for a Masonic lodge on the second floor. The Masons shared in the construction cost of the building. The new market officially opened on January 30, 1799. There were 24 stalls, 14 of which were occupied by butchers. The yearly rent was three pounds. This building is still standing, but the first floor has been enclosed and is now occupied by a number of shops.

The relatively small space in the 1798 building was not adequate for long, and an addition was built on the north side of it in 1815. Supplemental market space was also provided by the curb market stands on adjacent streets.

The need to expand the market was considered in 1835, but no property could be purchased at that time. Another unsuccessful attempt was made to buy more space in 1845. Finally, in 1854, several properties were purchased for $32,850. The existing buildings were cleared off, and several open-sided pavilions were erected.

The market record books from 1856 to 1875 show four market houses named A, B, C, and D, plus the Old Market House. These structures contained from 43 to 53 market stalls each (a total of 180 stalls). An 1875 map shows four long, narrow structures in the market area.

No doubt the city felt considerable pressure to erect a more substantial facility for the Central Market. Four very prominent brick market houses were built in Lancaster by the private sector between 1872 and 1888. Finally, in 1889, an all new, commodious Central Market was erected by the city of Lancaster.

## Major Renovations

Very little change was made to the Central Market house until 1973. Then, as part of an urban renewal project, the city began major restoration work on the structure. Funding came partly from a $402,000 grant provided by the Department of Housing and Urban Development, available because the market was now listed on the National Register of Historic Places. Matching funds were supplied by the city.

Under the direction of architect S. Dale Kaufman, stands were relocated to provide more aisle space, and a new underground electrical system and sewers were installed. Despite considerable inconvenience to the standholders and shoppers, the mayor announced that the Market would stay open during the whole renovation process in order to keep a two-century-old tradition alive. The refurbished market house was officially dedicated on March 21, 1975.

Most stalls or units were now six feet long with a few being nine feet or an irregular length. In the new arrangement, the stands requiring plumbing facilities for cleanup (fresh meat, fish, etc.) were limited to the rows along three of the walls and rows B and C on the west side.

One long-standing tradition changed in the remodeled market house, with the relocation of the fish stands to the inside of the building. Previously fish was sold only outside at stands along the north side of the market house. Adequate ventilation in the new Central Market took care of a potential odor problem.

A tiny restaurant that occupied the southeast corner of the market was done away with during the remodeling. City Council wished to retain the marketplace character of Central Market, rather than having it become an eating place. However, one sandwich stand was permitted, intended mainly for the convenience of the standholders who wished to eat at the Market.

In 2005, the Central Market Trust raised over $7 million to upgrade electrical and plumbing systems, replace all interior lighting and the heating system, upgrade the bathrooms for customers and standholders, replace or repair broken windows and doors, and repoint the exterior brick walls and replace bricks as needed.

Ultimately, the goal of this renovation, completed in 2011, was to restore the building to its original look in 1889. Dormer windows that had been sealed shut during the 1970s were made functional. Windows that were covered on the south wall were revealed. And the ceiling structure is now highlighted with beautiful up-lighting. The Trust is now raising funds to replace the roof, so that it can once again be slate.

Soon a *street scape* project will begin, replacing and enhancing all the streets and alleys adjacent to the Market.

There is no doubt that Lancaster Central Market has become one of the area's main destinations for visitors. For the benefit of locals and out-of-towners alike, City Council has made a concentrated effort to keep the Market a true farmers market. The regulations specify that the stands "be used solely for the sale of food products and farm produced goods. ... " Several stands established before the ruling went into effect continued to sell craft and souvenir-type items in 1989. No new stands will be granted this privilege.

## Market Days and Hours

An early ordinance established that the Market be held on Wednesdays and Saturdays from daybreak to 10:00 AM. This schedule continued until 1855, when the

Market began opening also on Tuesday and Friday evenings. In the late 1940s, the Market changed its hours and days of business to 7:30 AM until 5:30 PM on Tuesdays and Fridays.

When the city of Lancaster closed the Southern Market in 1985, its remaining standholders were offered stands at Central Market. In order to accommodate this influx, Saturday hours were added to the schedule. Currently (in 2015) Lancaster Central Market is open from 6:00 AM to 4:00 PM on Tuesdays and Fridays and from 6:00 AM to 2:00 PM on Saturdays.

## Market Auctions and Rents

The City of Lancaster owns Lancaster Central Market. The Central Market Trust, a nonprofit 501(c)3 organization that was formed in 2005, manages the Market, including making selections of new standholders.

Anyone interested in having a stand at Market completes an application, which is a mini-business plan. When a stand becomes available, a subcommittee of the Trust (the Standholder Review Committee) reviews current applicants. Making the final selection depends on a number of factors: an interview; whether or not the business seems like a good fit for Market; the available space's size and location; and whether or not the new stand will help balance the Market's product mix.

Standholders sign year-long leases. If a standholder wants to sell his or her business or pass it to the next generation, a meeting is held with the current owner, the potential new owner, and the Standholder Review Committee.

The Central Market Trust is responsible for making certain there is a good mix of businesses at Market and that all these businesses can be successful.

## The Market Manager

The man with the keys used to be called the Market Master. It was his responsibility to see that all ran smoothly within the market. That position is now called the Market Manager, and it is currently occupied by a woman.

In the early days, the overseer of the market place was called the Market Clerk. He settled disputes between buyers and sellers and enforced the official rules of the market, including compliance with standard weights and measures. He was to examine all butter and lard and measure all firewood for sale, making allowances for crooked and uneven sticks. The clerk also oversaw the town fairs.

In 1870, a city ordinance was passed that stated, ". . . The Mayor shall appoint a Market Master, whose duty it shall be to attend the market during market hours, and such other times as shall be necessary . . .; he shall prevent the sale of or exposing to sale all unsound and unwholesome provisions . . . ." The responsibility of keeping the market clean and the removal snow were also given to the Market Master.

## Lancaster Central Market Today

That Lancaster Central Market has retained its vitality for more than 250 years is due to a cooperative effort between the city and the standholders. The city has protected the Market; the standholders have demonstrated resiliency by providing the traditional along with the novel. It is that mix of old favorites and the experimental that characterizes Lancaster Central Market—chow chow residing comfortably near tarragon chicken pasta, sticky buns sharing the aisle with brioches, cup cheese sitting only stands away from Brie.

The Market belongs to and reflects the Lancaster community. The quality that is Lancaster Central Market is expressed not only in the magnificent building that houses it but also in the food and wares that are sold there—much of it home-grown and home-prepared from Lancaster's truck farms, home bakeries, and butcher shops. May it continue as it was designated in the City of Lancaster's charter: "to have, hold and keep . . . market . . . in every week of the year forever"!

When Lancaster was incorporated as a borough in 1742, its charter from George II of England established the market tradition: "And we do further grant for us, our heirs and successors . . . to have, hold and keep . . . two markets in each week."

———— ❧ ————

# APPETIZERS, SNACKS, AND BEVERAGES

## Broiled Cheesy Appetizers

FRANCES KIEFER, KIEFER'S MEAT AND CHEESE

*Makes 20 servings*
*Prep. Time: 20 minutes*
*Baking Time: 1–2 minutes*

1 cup shredded medium sharp
cheddar cheese

⅓ cup bacon bits

¼ cup mayonnaise

2 Tbsp. chopped onion

20 slices round party rye bread

1. Mix all ingredients except bread.

2. Spread about 1 Tbsp. mixture on each slice of bread.

3. Set broiler at 550°.

4. Place broiler tray at least 4 inches from heat.

5. Broil 1-2 minutes or until cheese melts.

NOTE

*Our family traditionally serves these on Christmas Eve.*

# Baked Cheese-Filled Pastry

DOROTHY KOTH, HABIBI'S

*Makes 15 rolls*
*Prep. Time: 30 minutes*
*Baking Time: 25-30 minutes*

½ lb. feta cheese, crumbled, *or* mozzarella cheese, shredded

¼ cup finely chopped flat-leaf parsley

8-10 Tbsp. margarine *or* butter, melted

15 sheets phyllo pastry

1. Mix cheese and parsley together.

2. Using a pastry brush, brush melted butter on one side of a sheet of pastry. Fold sheet in half to make a long rectangle. Brush the outside edges with butter.

3. Place 1 Tbsp. of cheese mixture on one short-sided end of pastry.

4. Fold long edges toward the center about ½ inch on each side.

5. Starting at the short end with cheese mixture, roll pastry up into a tight cylinder. Repeat process with each piece of phyllo pastry.

6. Place rolls into greased 7"x10" baking pan with seam side down.

7. Bake at 350° for 25-30 minutes or until golden brown.

# A Greek Delicacy

SAM NEFF, S. CLYDE WEAVER, INC.

*Makes 12–20 appetizer servings, or 8 main dish servings*
*Prep. Time: 30 minutes*
*Cooking/Baking Time: 1 hour*

3 Tbsp. + 1 cup (2 sticks) butter, melted, *divided*

½ cup flour

4 cups milk

1¼ lbs. feta cheese, crumbled

1 cup grated Asiago cheese

6 eggs, lightly beaten

1 lb. phyllo dough

1. Melt 3 Tbsp. butter in saucepan. Add flour and blend, browning slightly. Add milk and cook mixture until thick. Cool.

2. To cooled mixture add crumbled feta, grated Asiago, and beaten eggs.

3. Line a 9"x13" baking dish with 3 layers of phyllo dough and paint with butter. Add 3 more layers of dough and paint with butter.

4. Pour liquid cheese mixture over phyllo dough. Top with 3 more layers of dough and paint with butter. Continue to alternate 3 layers of phyllo dough, painting with butter each time, until entire pound of dough has been used.

5. Bake 45 minutes at 300°.

NOTE

*This recipe was given to us by a Greek friend whose family was from Northern Greece.*

# Cabbage Centerpiece for Appetizer

DORIS SHENK, DONEGAL GARDENS

*Prep. Time: 30 minutes*

head of cabbage
cherry tomatoes
olives
radishes
mushrooms
pickles
pepper strips
baby carrots
broccoli florets
cauliflower florets

1. Trim bottom of the cabbage head so it will sit level on a plate.

2. Put assortment of vegetables on round toothpicks.

3. Arrange vegetables on the cabbage by pushing toothpicks into the cabbage head.

4. After party, use the cabbage for slaw.

# Chipped Beef Spread

DEBBIE BUHAY, SHENK'S CHEESE CO.

*Makes 2-3 cups*
*Prep. Time: 10 minutes*

Chilling Time: overnight
2 8-oz. pkgs. cream cheese, softened
½ lb. schmierkase
½ lb. dried beef, chopped
1 small green bell pepper, chopped
1 small onion, chopped
¼ cup chopped English walnuts
½-1 tsp. seasoned salt

1. Put all ingredients into blender or food processor and mix well.

2. Refrigerate overnight.

3. Serve with assorted crackers and fresh vegetables.

### VARIATION

*Substitute sour cream for schmierkase.*

# Blue Cheese Dip or Dressing

SAM NEFF, S. CLYDE WEAVER, INC.

*Makes 8 servings*
*Prep. Time: 10 minutes*

I lb. blue cheese, *divided*
2 cups sour cream
I small onion, chopped
½ cup chopped parsley
¼ cup capers, drained
salt and pepper to taste

1. Blend half of blue cheese with all other ingredients. Crumble remaining blue cheese into mixture and mix gently by hand.

2. If using as a dip, garnish with extra parsley.

3. If using as a dressing, thin to desired consistency with milk or cream.

### VARIATION

*Add a bit of dry mustard or garlic powder.*

# Carrot Dip

ETHEL STONER, JOHN R. STONER VEGETABLES

*Makes about 1½ cups*
*Prep. Time: 10 minutes*

8-oz. pkg. cream cheese, softened
I Tbsp. milk
I Tbsp. mayonnaise
I Tbsp. sour cream
I pkg. George Washington seasoning and broth mix
I tsp. chopped chives
I small onion, grated
I carrot, grated

1. Cream softened cream cheese. Add milk, mayonnaise, sour cream, seasoning, and chives.

2. Stir in onions and carrots, and mix well.

3. Serve with a variety of fresh, raw vegetables.

### VARIATION

*Substitute onion soup mix for George Washington seasoning.*

# Baked Figs and Goat Cheese

ANDREW AND MARY MELLINGER, LINDEN DALE FARMS

*Makes 4–6 servings*
*Prep. Time: 15 minutes*
*Baking Time: 15 minutes*

8 oz. Linden Dale goat cheese

4 fresh fig leaves, *optional*

10 ripe figs, stems on, halved lengthwise

salt and pepper

1 tsp. chopped fresh thyme *or* rosemary

3 Tbsp. olive oil

1. Separate goat cheese into 6 thick pieces. Line an 8"x12" earthenware baking dish with fig leaves (if using).

2. Arrange goat cheese in center of dish and surround with fig halves. Season lightly with salt and pepper, then sprinkle with thyme or rosemary. Drizzle with olive oil.

3. Bake uncovered for 15 minutes at 400°, until both cheese and figs are softened. Run under broiler for 1 minute to brown. Let cool slightly before serving.

# Fruit Dip for Fresh Fruit

MARILYN DENLINGER, IRWIN S. WIDDERS PRODUCE

*Prep. Time: 10 minutes*

8-oz. pkg. cream cheese, softened

7-oz. jar marshmallow cream

6 Tbsp. orange *or* lemon juice

1. Blend all ingredients for dip together. Mix until smooth.

2. Serve on tray with fruit (apples, strawberries, melon balls, grapes, kiwi slices, pineapple chunks, etc.). Colored toothpicks help make this party food more attractive.

NOTE

*A simple, yet favorite, tray for a party.*

# Pan Con Tomate, Rooster-Street Style

TONY PAGE, ROOSTER STREET PROVISIONS

*Makes 4 servings* ❧ *Prep. Time: 10 minutes* ❧ *Cooking Time: 5 minutes*

1 crusty baguette

2 cloves garlic, cut in half

2 Tbsp. + 2 tsp. first cold-press extra-virgin olive oil, *divided*

1 small heirloom tomato, cut in half

1 large ball buffalo mozzarella, room temperature

1 Tbsp. chopped fresh basil

1 Tbsp. chopped fresh oregano

1 cup ricotta cheese, room temperature

2 tsp. fresh cracked black pepper

3.2-oz. packet Rooster Street Provisions speck, room temperature

1. Cut bread on a hard bias about ¾" thick.

2. Grill or toast bread lightly.

3. Once grilled or toasted, rub surface with garlic and drizzle with 2 Tbsp. olive oil.

4. Rub flesh side of tomato into the bread until well coated but not soggy.

5. Mash buffalo mozzarella with hands in a mixing bowl. Add herbs, ricotta, 2 tsp. olive oil, and black pepper to mixture and whisk to combine.

6. To assemble sandwiches, spread each piece of bread with 1 Tbsp. cheese mixture. Top with 2-3 slices speck.

NOTE

*Enjoy with friends and a glass of white wine!*

# Crabbies

JUDY WEIDMAN, CUSTOMER OF JOHN R. STONER VEGETABLES

**Makes 48 appetizer servings, or 12 main dish servings**
*Prep. Time: 25 minutes* ❧ *Baking Time: 1 4 minutes*

½ cup (1 stick) butter

2 cups prepared cheese spread

1½ Tbsp. mayonnaise

½ tsp. garlic salt

7-oz. can crab meat *or* ½ lb. fresh or frozen crab

6 English muffins, split

1. Soften butter and cheese to room temperature.

2. Mix butter, cheese, mayonnaise, salt, and crab meat.

3. Spread on split muffins and place on baking sheet.

4. Broil until bubbly and crisp, from 1-4 minutes.

5. Cut each Crabbie into quarters to serve as an appetizer. Leave them uncut to serve as a main dish.

# Thom's Panini

THOM CAPIZZI, THOM'S BREAD

*Makes 8 sandwiches*
Prep. Time: 10-15 minutes ❦ Cooking Time: 10-15 minutes

1-lb. loaf of Thom's Bread boule of your choice: rustic Italian, rosemary, *or* kalamata olive

about 1 cup chopped spinach

olive oil

butter, softened

8 oz. fresh mozzarella cheese in ¼" slices

1 large slicing tomato, heirloom preferred

½ avocado, sliced into ⅛"-thick pieces

salt and pepper, to taste

1. Cut boule in 10 slices, then cut each slice in half.

2. Lightly sauté spinach in olive oil, adding salt and pepper to taste.

3. Spread butter lightly on outsides of bread slices.

4. Press buttered slices lightly in panini press on medium-high for 20-30 seconds.

5. Assemble each panini in this order: 1 slice of boule, cheese slice, tomato slice, avocado slice, spinach, salt and pepper, 1 slice of boule.

6. Press in panini press for 2-3 minutes. Serve hot.

NOTE

*Instead of a panini press, place the sandwich in a skillet and top with another heavy skillet to press the sandwich.*

# Molded Shrimp Spread

ETHEL STONER, JOHN R. STONER VEGETABLES

*Makes 3 cups* ❦ Prep. Time: 20 minutes ❦ Chilling Time: several hours

3-oz. pkg. lemon gelatin

1 cup boiling water

1 cup chili sauce

¼ cup horseradish

1 tsp. lemon juice

5-oz. can small shrimp, rinsed and drained

1. Add gelatin to boiling water, stirring until dissolved.

2. Chill until slightly thickened, then add all other ingredients.

3. Chill several hours in small mold until firm.

4. Unmold on serving dish and serve with crackers.

# Shrimp Cheese Spread

ETHEL STONER, JOHN R. STONER VEGETABLES

*Makes 1 pint*
*Prep. Time: 20 minutes*

½ lb. sharp cheese, grated

5-oz. can shrimp pieces, chopped

1 small onion, finely grated

1 tsp. celery salt

1 cup mayonnaise

1 Tbsp. Worcestershire sauce

1. Mix all ingredients and refrigerate.

2. Serve with an assortment of crackers.

# Spinach Squares

ETHEL STONER, JOHN R. STONER VEGETABLES

*Makes 10–12 servings*    *Prep. Time: 20 minutes*
*Baking Time: 30 minutes*    *Cooling Time: 10-15 minutes*

1 cup flour

1 tsp. salt

1 tsp. baking powder

2 eggs, beaten

1 cup milk

6 Tbsp. butter (¾ stick), softened

2 cups fresh spinach *or* 1 pkg. frozen spinach

1 lb. sharp cheddar cheese, grated

1 onion, chopped

1. Sift flour, salt, and baking powder into a large bowl. Add eggs, milk, and butter, and mix well.

2. If using fresh spinach, cook, squeeze dry, and chop. If using frozen spinach, thaw and squeeze dry.

3. Add spinach, cheese, and onion to flour and egg mixture. Spread into a greased 9"x13" pan.

4. Bake at 350° for 30 minutes. Cool 10-15 minutes, or long enough so that you can cut the mixture into squares. Serve warm.

NOTE

*This recipe disappears like magic at a party. It's become a tradition in our family.*

# Spinach Crab Cakes

DORIS SHENK, DONEGAL GARDENS

*Makes 12–15 servings*
*Prep. Time: 20 minutes*
*Cooking/Baking Time: 10-20 minutes*

1 ¼ lbs. fresh spinach
¾ cup (1 ½ sticks) butter
2 large onions, chopped
6 eggs, beaten
½ tsp. dried thyme
½ cup grated Parmesan cheese
1 Tbsp. garlic salt
1 scant Tbsp. pepper
1 lb. crab claw meat
2 cups herb bread filling, *divided*

1. Cook the spinach lightly. Chop it and squeeze dry.

2. Melt butter. Add all other ingredients except herb filling and mix well.

3. Add 1 cup herb filling and mix well.

4. Form mixture into small patties.

5. Grind 1 cup herb filling to make crumbs. Coat spinach patties with ground herb filling.

6. Deep fry or freeze for future use.

HINT

*You can serve these as a main dish, a sandwich, or an appetizer.*

# SUE GLOUNER OF THE TURKEY LADY

Sue Glouner left corporate America and opened The Turkey Lady stand with her husband, Doug, in 2001. They offer turkey in many forms—fresh, smoked, as sausage (with some 18 different varieties), in salads.

She cares as deeply about the experience of Market as she does about the food she sells. "Market is an oasis in the center of a fast-paced, high-tech world. The relationships that you develop with your customers and other standholders can't be fully described.

"There is such a passion for this Market. It's a community. It's a place for people from all walks of life to come. Standing here all day, I see everything.

"I won't soon forget the night in December when Market stayed open late for the lighting of the City's Christmas tree, just a few steps away from here on Penn Square. All the tuba players who had played outside as part of the ceremony came in here and played. It was so damp and cold out there, they were just grateful their fingers could work normally.

"I never had higher goose pimples than when the music from these dozens of tubas filled this cavernous building. I got my sister on the phone and said, 'You gotta listen to this!'"

# Turkey Sliders

SUSAN GLOUNER, THE TURKEY LADY

*Makes 12 sliders*  ❧  *Prep. Time: 20 minutes*  ❧  *Cooking Time: 20 minutes*

4 cups fresh spinach, stems removed

4 scallions, sliced thin

1 garlic clove, minced

1 lb. ground turkey

½ cup grated Locatelli Romano cheese

3 Tbsp. Worcestershire sauce

salt and pepper

3 Tbsp. olive oil

12 slider buns *or* small dinner rolls, toasted lightly

mayonnaise, sliced onions, and pickles, for serving

1. Combine spinach, scallions, garlic, turkey, Romano cheese, and Worcestershire sauce in bowl. Season with salt, and pepper.

2. Form turkey mixture into 12 patties.

3. Heat oil in large skillet over medium-high heat. Cook patties until golden brown and cooked through, about 5 minutes on each side.

4. Serve patties on buns with mayonnaise, onions, and pickles.

# Crescent-Veggie Bar

ETHEL STONER, JOHN R. STONER VEGETABLES

*Makes 10–12 servings*

*Prep. Time: 20 minutes*  ❧  *Baking Time: 8-10 minutes*  ❧  *Cooling Time: 20 minutes*

2 8-oz. pkgs. crescent rolls

2 8-oz. pkgs. cream cheese, softened

1 pkg. ranch dressing mix

¾ cup mayonnaise

raw vegetables (broccoli, cauliflower, peppers, etc.)

½-1 lb. sharp cheese, grated

1. Pat crescent roll dough into a flat layer in 9"x13" baking pan.

2. Bake at 425° until brown, about 8–10 minutes. Cool.

3. Beat cream cheese, dressing mix, and mayonnaise together until smooth. Spread over baked crescent roll dough.

4. Chop vegetables finely and spread evenly over dough.

5. Cover with grated cheese, cut into squares, and serve.

# Egg Rolls

TUYEN KIM HO, KIM'S CANDIES

*Makes 24 servings* ❦ *Prep. Time: 30 minutes* ❦ *Cooking Time: 20-30 minutes*

3 Tbsp. cooking oil, *divided*

½ lb. ground pork

½ lb. shrimp, shelled and deveined

¼ cup minced water chestnuts

1 lb. carrots, chopped

1 lb. cabbage, chopped

½ cup chopped onion

1 Tbsp. soy sauce

1 Tbsp. salt

1 Tbsp. black pepper

1 egg, beaten

24 egg roll wraps

oil for deep-frying

1. Heat 1 Tbsp. oil in frying pan and stir fry pork about 5 minutes. Set aside.

2. Heat 2 Tbsp. oil in pan. Add shrimp, water chestnuts, carrots, cabbage, and onion. Cook, stirring constantly, until shrimp turns pink.

3. Add seasonings and cooked pork. Stir until all ingredients are well mixed.

4. Spoon ingredients onto egg roll wraps. Wrap ingredients in wraps and brush edges with beaten egg to hold them together.

5. Bring oil for deep-frying to 300°. Deep-fry egg rolls for 7 minutes or until golden brown. Drain off excess oil before serving.

# Spiced Nuts

SAM NEFF, S. CLYDE WEAVER, INC.

*Makes 3-4 cups* ❦ *Prep. Time: 10 minutes* ❦ *Baking Time: 1 hour*

2 Tbsp. cold water

1 egg white

½ cup sugar

½ tsp. salt

¼ tsp. ground cinnamon

¼ tsp. ground cloves

¼ tsp. ground allspice

¾-1 lb. pecan *or* walnut halves

1. Add water to the egg white and beat lightly with a fork.

2. Add all dry ingredients and mix well.

3. Add nuts to the mixture and stir to coat.

4. Place nuts flat-side down on a greased baking sheet.

5. Bake 1 hour at 250° until brown. Cool and store in a tin.

NOTE

*My wife's great-aunt from Hagerstown, Maryland, always serves these with her Christmas cookies.*

# S'mores

JOYCE DEITER, EISENBERGER'S BAKED GOODS

*Makes 48 squares*
*Prep. Time: 15 minutes* ❧ *Cooking Time: 5-10 minutes* ❧ *Standing Time: 1 hour*

⅔ cup light corn syrup

2 Tbsp. butter

2 cups semi-sweet chocolate chips

1 tsp. vanilla

10-oz. pkg. Golden Graham cereal

3 cups mini-marshmallows, *divided*

1. Heat syrup, butter, and chocolate chips just to boiling in 3-quart saucepan, stirring constantly. Remove from heat and stir in vanilla.

2. In a large bowl pour mixture over cereal. Toss quickly until cereal is completely covered with chocolate.

3. Fold in marshmallows, 1 cup at a time.

4. Press mixture evenly into well-greased 9"x13" pan. Let stand until firm (about 1 hour).

5. Cut into 1½" squares. Store in cool place.

# High-Fiber Snack

SARAH KING, DUTCH COUNTRY DELI

*Makes 24 small bars* ❧ *Prep. Time: 10 minutes*

3 cups quick oats

1 cup grated coconut

1 cup nuts *or* raisins

½ cup wheat bran *or* oat bran

¼ tsp. salt

1 cup honey

1 cup peanut butter

1. Mix dry ingredients in a bowl.

2. In a separate bowl, mix honey and peanut butter.

3. Combine the two mixtures.

4. Pack into a 9"x13" pan or roll into balls. Refrigerate before cutting into bars.

# Concord Grape Butter

RUTH WIDDERS, IRWIN S. WIDDERS PRODUCE

*Prep. Time: 30 minutes*
*Cooking Time: 40 minutes*

4-6 cups Concord grapes
4-6 cups sugar
2 Tbsp. water

1. Mix all ingredients in a large stockpot and heat slowly until sugar dissolves.

2. When mixture comes to a full boil, boil for 20 minutes. Squeeze through a food press and put spread into canning jars. Follow manufacturer's directions for your canner to process the spread and seal the jars.

TIP

*Delicious spread for homemade bread!*


# Cool Orange

JOYCE DEITER, EISENBERGER'S BAKED GOODS

*Makes 4 servings*
*Prep. Time: 5 minutes*

½ cup frozen orange juice concentrate
¾ cup water
¾ cup milk
⅓ cup sugar
¾ tsp. vanilla
9 ice cubes, broken

Blend all ingredients in blender and serve.

TIP

*Delicious and refreshing summertime drink!*

# Milk Punch

MILDRED BLACKBILL, UTZ'S POTATO CHIPS

*Makes 24 8-oz. servings*
*Prep. Time: 5 minutes*

½ gallon milk
½ gallon orange juice
1 pint orange sherbet
½ gallon orange drink
16-oz. bottle ginger ale

Combine all ingredients and serve.

# Cranberry Frappé

ETHEL STONER, JOHN R. STONER VEGETABLES

*Makes 25 servings (5 quarts)*
*Prep. Time: 15 minutes*

12-oz. can frozen cranberry *or* red raspberry juice

water

46-oz. can unsweetened chilled pineapple juice

1 cup sugar

½ gallon red raspberry sherbet

1 quart lemon-lime soda *or* 1 quart sparkling raspberry juice, chilled

1. Mix cranberry juice with water as directed on can.

2. Add pineapple juice and sugar. Mix well.

3. Cut sherbet into pieces and place in punch bowl.

4. Add juice mixture and mix well. Immediately before serving, pour in carbonated beverage and stir well.

# Cranberry Punch

VIV HUNT, VIV'S VARIETIES

*Makes 23 8-oz. servings*
*Prep. Time: 10 minutes*

9 cups cranberry juice
9 cups unsweetened pineapple juice
4½ cups water
1 cup brown sugar
¼ tsp. salt
4½ tsp. whole cloves
4 broken cinnamon sticks

1. Mix cranberry and pineapple juices with water, brown sugar, and salt.

2. Pour into 30-cup percolator.

3. Place cloves and cinnamon sticks into the filter.

4. Turn on percolator and serve hot when it is finished.

# Party Punch

MARY ELLEN CAMPBELL, BASKETS OF CENTRAL MARKET

*Makes 1½ gallons*
*Prep. Time: 10 minutes*

1 lemon
2 limes
2 9-oz. cans frozen orange juice concentrate, thawed
3 46-oz. cans pineapple juice
6 cups cold water
42 oz. ginger ale, chilled

1. Squeeze the juice from the lemon and limes and place in punch bowl.

2. Stir in orange juice concentrate, pineapple juice, and water. Chill.

3. Before serving, add ginger ale.

TIP

*Garnish with frozen lime, lemon, or orange slices.*

# Banana Slushy Punch

SCOTT SUMMY, WILLOW VALLEY FARMS

*Makes 38–40 servings*
*Prep. Time: 15 minutes*
*Cooking Time: 10 minutes*
*Chilling Time: at least 6 hours*
*Thawing Time: approximately 1 hour*

46 oz. water
3 cups sugar
5 medium-sized ripe bananas
46-oz. can pineapple juice, *divided*
6 oz. orange juice concentrate
4 Tbsp. lemon juice
6 quarts ginger ale

1. Combine water and sugar in a saucepan. Bring to a boil, stirring until sugar is dissolved. Boil gently for 3 minutes uncovered. Cool.

2. Combine bananas and half of pineapple juice in blender.

3. Add sugar syrup and remaining pineapple juice to banana mixture.

4. Add orange and lemon juice and mix thoroughly.

5. Divide mixture into 3 containers and freeze at least 6 hours.

6. Before serving, thaw mixture to a very thick, chunky consistency, approximately 1 hour.

7. When ready to serve, slowly add 2 quarts ginger ale to each container of mixture. Stir until mixture is a slushy, pourable consistency.

TIP

*Garnish each cup with a floating orange slice or half a strawberry. Very refreshing for hot summer days.*

Apple Dumplings, page 250

Cottage Ham and String Beans, page 140

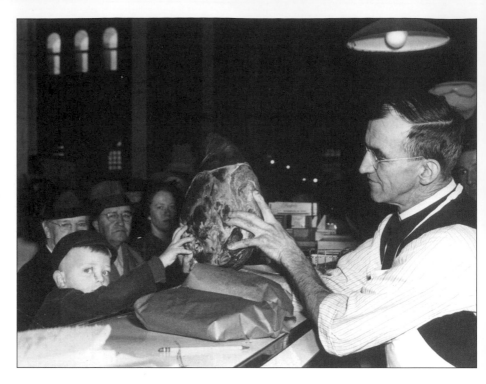

Jake Thomas selling
Easter ham to
Billy Hess in 1946

A scene from a curb market in downtown Lancaster, ca. 1925–1926

# Rhubarb Punch

RUTH ESHELMAN, GIVANT'S BAKERY

*Makes 3-4 quarts*
Prep. Time: 15 minutes    ❦    Cooking Time: 10 minutes

1 qt. 1"-thick slices rhubarb
water
2 cups sugar
2 cups water
6 lemons
1½ cups pineapple juice
1 quart ginger ale

1. Cover rhubarb pieces with water and cook about 10 minutes until soft. Drain. This makes about 3 cups juice.

2. Dissolve sugar in 2 cups water and cook about 10 minutes.

3. To sugar syrup add juice of lemons and pineapple juice.

4. Mix well and add rhubarb juice. Mix again.

5. When ready to serve, add ginger ale and ice cubes.

# Concord Grape Juice

RUTH WIDDERS, IRWIN S. WIDDERS PRODUCE

*Makes 6-8 quarts*
Prep. Time: 30 minutes    ❦    Cooking Time: about 3 minutes

8 lbs. Concord grapes
4 qts. water
¾ lb. granulated sugar

NOTE

*I serve this mixed with ginger ale after our Christmas dinner.*

1. Weigh grapes after removing stems.

2. Wash grapes and cover with water in a kettle. Let boil until shells and grapes are separated.

3. Pour mixture first through a coarse sieve and then through a fine sieve. Repeat process several times.

4. Add sugar to strained juice and boil for 5 minutes.

5. Can juice in canning jars according to manufacturer's directions.

# Lemonade

RUTH WIDDERS, IRWIN S. WIDDERS PRODUCE

*Makes 6½ quarts*
*Prep. Time: 15 minutes*
*Standing Time: 30 minutes*

6 lemons
4 cups sugar
6 cups hot water
4½ qts. cold water

1. Slice lemons into thin rounds and remove seeds.

2. Place lemon slices into a large bowl or kettle. Add sugar and pound with a wooden mallet to extract the juice.

3. Let stand for 30 minutes. Add hot water and stir until sugar is dissolved.

4. Allow to cool until you can squeeze the juice from the lemon slices. Discard the slices.

5. Stir in the cold water. Serve over ice.

NOTE

*Using the rind, pulp, and juice gives this an excellent flavor and quenches thirst.*

# BREADS AND BREAKFASTS

## Homemade Bread

MARY ELLEN SPEICHER, SALLIE Y. LAPP

*Makes 4 loaves* ❧ *Prep. Time: 30 minutes*
*Rising Time: 2½ hours* ❧ *Baking Time: 30 minutes*

½ tsp. sugar
1¼ tsp. yeast
3½ cups lukewarm water, *divided*
1½ Tbsp. salt
¼ cup vegetable oil
½ cup sugar
9-10 cups bread flour, *divided*

1. In a big bowl, add sugar and yeast to ½ cup lukewarm water. Let stand for 5 minutes.

2. Add remaining 3 cups lukewarm water, salt, oil, sugar, and 4 cups flour. Beat until thoroughly mixed.

3. Use your hands to stir in remaining 5 cups flour, adding another cup gradually if needed to get workable dough. Knead for 10 minutes.

4. Cover. Let rise until double, about an hour.

5. Knead again for 2-3 minutes. Let rise again for about an hour.

6. Knead again for 1-2 minutes. Shape into loaves. Put into greased bread pans. Let rise again until not quite doubled, about 30 minutes.

7. Bake at 350° for 30 minutes.

8. Cool slightly. Put into plastic bags while still warm for a soft crust.

# Oatmeal Bread

RUTH WIDDERS, IRWIN S. WIDDERS PRODUCE

*Makes 2 loaves or 2 dozen rolls*
*Prep. Time: 30 minutes*
*Rising Time: 2 hours*
*Baking Time: 30-40 minutes*

½ cup brown sugar
1 Tbsp. salt
1 cup dry quick oats
½ cup whole wheat flour
2 Tbsp. butter, melted
2 cups boiling water
1 Tbsp. yeast
½ cup warm water
4-5 cups white flour

1. Combine brown sugar, salt, oats, whole wheat flour, and butter in a large mixing bowl.

2. Pour boiling water over mixture and mix well.

3. Meanwhile, dissolve yeast in warm water. When batter has cooled to lukewarm, stir in yeast mixture.

4. Stir in white flour.

5. Knead for 10 minutes. Place in greased bowl, cover, and let rise until doubled.

6. Punch down and let rise again for about an hour.

7. Punch down again and shape into 2 loaves or 24 small rolls.

8. Bake at 350° for 30-40 minutes.

NOTE

*The oatmeal, whole wheat flour, and brown sugar make this bread unusually tasty.*

# Aunt Beth's Potato Buns, Timed!

EDITH R. WEAVER, FRANK WEAVER GREENHOUSES

*Makes 40 small rolls*
*Prep. Time: 25 minutes*
*Rising Time: 5 hours, then overnight, then 3 hours*
*Baking Time: 15 minutes*

1 cup mashed potatoes

½ cup lukewarm potato water from cooking potatoes

2 eggs

⅓ cup sugar

½ tsp. salt

2¼ tsp. yeast

½ cup flour

½ cup lard, softened

⅓ cup sugar

additional flour to make soft dough

1. At 5 PM, mix together mashed potatoes, ½ cup potato water, eggs, ⅓ cup sugar, salt, yeast, and ½ cup flour. Let stand.

2. At 10 PM, add ½ cup lard, ⅓ cup sugar, and enough flour to make a soft dough. Knead slightly to create a soft dough. Place in greased bowl, cover, and let rise until morning.

3. At 7 AM, punch down the dough and form into whatever size rolls you prefer. Put on baking sheets. Let rise until 10 AM.

4. Bake at 350° until slightly brown, about 15 minutes.

HINT

*Keep the dough and ingredients at room temperature at all times. Also keep the dough out of all drafts. These rolls are light and very good!*

# Dinner Rolls

PETER KOVALEC, WINDOWS ON STEINMAN PARK

*Makes 3 dozen rolls*
*Prep. Time: 30 minutes*
*Rising Time: 2 hours*
*Baking Time: 10-15 minutes*

1 cup milk
½ cup (1 stick) butter
½ cup sugar
2¼ tsp. yeast
3 eggs
4½-5 cups flour, *divided*
pinch salt

1. Scald milk. Remove from heat. Stir in butter and sugar.

2. Cool to 85°. Stir in yeast until dissolved.

3. Stir eggs into milk mixture. Then mix in 4-4½ cups flour and salt, kneading when you can no longer stir in the flour. Stop when dough is soft and not sticky or dry.

4. Let rise until doubled in size, about 45 minutes.

5. Divide into 3 balls. Roll out each into a circle. Then cut each into 12 pieces like a pizza.

6. Roll each slice up from the wide end toward the point. Place each on lightly greased baking sheet.

7. Let rise until doubled, about 30 minutes. Bake at 350° for 10–15 minutes until browned.

# Homemade Pizza

PEGGY MOYER, DONEGAL GARDENS

*Makes 6–8 servings* ❧ *Prep. Time: 25 minutes*
*Rising Time: 30 minutes* ❧ *Baking Time: 20-25 minutes*

### Crust Ingredients:

1 Tbsp. dry active yeast *or* 1 pkg.
dry active yeast

1 cup warm water

1 tsp. salt

1 tsp. sugar

2½ cups flour, *divided*

2 Tbsp. vegetable oil

### Topping Ingredients:

1-2 cups pizza sauce

1 lb. ground beef, browned

½ lb. pepperoni slices

2 green bell peppers, sliced

1 large onion, sliced

1 cup sliced olives, green or
black

1 lb. mozzarella cheese, shredded

1. Dissolve yeast in warm water. Using a fork, stir in salt and sugar.

2. Add flour ½ cup at a time, stirring with a fork until no longer sticky.

3. Add oil and stir vigorously with a fork.

4. Allow dough to rise for ½ hour.

5. Using floured hands, knead dough, then spread out on greased baking sheet with floured fingertips.

6. Spread pizza sauce over dough.

7. Add ground beef, pepperoni, peppers, onions, and olives in layers. Sprinkle cheese over top.

8. Bake at 425° for 20-25 minutes.

NOTE

*Young children like to help prepare this. Our family enjoys making different-shaped pizzas, like hearts, small fish, or other animal shapes.*

VARIATIONS

*1. Make this into a pan pizza by baking 10 minutes in a well-greased iron skillet instead of on a baking sheet.*

*2. Use a variety of other toppings that you like.*

# The New Era, Lancaster, Saturday, October 5, 1889

## THE CENTRAL MARKET, A CITY EDIFICE TO BE PROUD OF

**A fine example of the Romanesque Style of Architecture which Reflects Credit on the Architect and Contractor. Good accommodations.**

The near completion of the new Central Market House, built by the City of Lancaster to take the place of the unsightly old structures that formerly stood in the rear of the City Hall, has induced us to publish today's full description of the beautiful new structure . . .

Of the several plans presented that of Mr. James H. Warner, formerly of London, England, but now a resident of our city, was the one adopted at the meeting of City Council held March 23. He was also engaged to superintend the building operations and the result is the possession by Lancaster of one of the finest market houses in the State . . . Rains have interfered greatly with the work and prevented it being carried forward as rapidly as it would have been had the weather been more favorable, but, nevertheless, the contractors have nearly completed the building at the specified time and the work has been well done. Material and workmanship have been of the best and the structure is one that will last many years. It is a market house of which our people may well feel proud, for it combines to a marked degree the properties of architectural beauty, durability, comfort and convenience, besides being so arranged as to secure the best sanitary conditions.

The plans for securing the best light and ventilation possible are admirable . . .

The lighting of the building is partly obtained from numerous large windows on all sides, raised above the side stall, but mainly from small dormer windows on all sides scattered all about the roof, the effect of this arrangement being very pleasing. The floor, which has a general, easy slope from east to west, is of concrete and is admirably adapted to secure cleanliness, as it can easily be flushed with water from plugs placed at convenient points. This fine even floor, so easily cleaned, will leave no excuse for a dirty, ill smelling market, a subject of much universal complaint . . . The architect has confined himself principally to the south front in the design and expenditure for ornament, as most of the other parts of the building are so surrounded by buildings as not to be much seen. This elevation shows a tower upon each corner and a gable in the centre . . .

The floor plan of the building shows an admirable arrangement of stalls and aisles, with entrances on all sides of the edifice. The truckers and farmers are placed in the centre of the market, the butchers being along the walls and the fish stall at the outside of the rear of the building . . . The stalls which will be in place within two weeks will all be constructed in the most approved modern style, all being of yellow pine.

The butchers' blocks will be of oak . . . there will be 100 farmers' and truckers' stalls, 72 butchers' and 20 fish stalls, 252 altogether.

The small streets about the building will be put in good condition as soon as possible, and in a little while our people will have one of the finest market houses in the State and all at a total of $26,500 . . . the only regret is that it does not occupy a site where it could be seen to its fullest advantage . . .

# Lemon Bread

MARY ELLEN CAMPBELL, BASKETS OF CENTRAL MARKET

*Makes an 8" loaf*
*Prep. Time: 15 minutes*
*Baking Time: 1 hour*

1 cup sugar
5 Tbsp. butter, softened
2 eggs
½ cup milk
grated rind of 1 lemon
½ tsp. salt
1 tsp. baking powder
1½ cups flour
½ cup chopped walnuts, *optional*

**Glaze Ingredients:**
juice of 1 lemon
½ cup sugar

1. Cream together sugar and butter. Blend in eggs, milk, and lemon rind.

2. In a separate bowl, mix together salt, baking powder, flour, and walnuts, if you wish. Add to creamed mixture, blending well.

3. Pour into a greased 4"x8" loaf pan. Bake 1 hour at 350°.

4. Cool 5 minutes, then remove from pan.

5. Mix together glaze ingredients. Spoon over warm bread.

6. Allow to cool completely before slicing.

# Date-Nut Loaf

RUTH MARTIN, C. Z. MARTIN SONS

*Makes 10–12 servings*
*Prep. Time: 20 minutes*
*Baking Time: 1½ hours*

1 cup all-purpose flour
½ tsp. salt
2 tsp. baking powder
1 lb. dates, chopped
1 lb. English walnuts
¾ cup sugar
4 eggs, separated
1 tsp. vanilla

1. Sift flour. Measure and add salt and baking powder. Sift again.

2. Add chopped dates and whole kernels of walnuts.

3. Add sugar to mixture and stir until well blended.

4. Add well-beaten egg yolks to mixture, stirring until thoroughly mixed.

5. Fold in stiffly beaten egg whites and vanilla.

6. Pour into a well-greased loaf pan.

7. Bake at 300° for 1½ hours, or until a toothpick stuck in the center of the loaf comes out clean.

NOTE

*I remember this recipe from childhood. Mother would make it at Christmas instead of fruitcake.*

# Honey Banana Bread

ELVA E. MARTIN, RUDOLPH BREIGHNER

*Makes 1 loaf* ❧ *Prep. Time: 20 minutes* ❧ *Baking Time: 60-70 minutes*

½ cup shortening
¼ cup sugar
½ tsp. salt
½ cup honey
1 tsp. baking soda
3 large, very ripe bananas, mashed
2 eggs, beaten
2 cups flour
1 tsp. vanilla
¼ cup chopped nuts

1. Blend shortening, sugar, and salt until well mixed.

2. Add all other ingredients and mix well.

3. Pour into a well-greased loaf pan.

4. Bake at 350° for 60-70 minutes, or until a toothpick stuck in the center of the loaf comes out clean.

# Blueberry Oat Muffins

MARY CATHERINE BOWMAN, SHENK'S CHEESE CO.

*Makes 1 dozen muffins* ❧ *Prep. Time: 15 minutes* ❧ *Baking Time: 15-20 minutes*

1 cup dry rolled oats
1 cup schmierkase *or* buttermilk
1 cup flour
1 tsp. baking powder
½ tsp. baking soda
½ tsp. salt
¾ cup brown sugar, lightly packed
¼ cup corn oil *or* melted butter
1 egg, beaten
1 cup fresh *or* frozen blueberries

1. Combine oats and schmierkase in a large bowl. Let stand.

2. In another bowl combine flour, baking powder, baking soda, salt, and brown sugar. Stir and blend well.

3. Add oil and egg to the oat mixture. Mix well.

4. Add dry ingredients to oat mixture, stirring just until ingredients are moistened. Gently fold in blueberries.

5. Fill well-greased muffin tins ¾ full. Bake at 400° for 15-20 minutes.

TIP

*Make these ahead of time and freeze them. Take out of freezer and heat in microwave before serving.*

VARIATION

*Substitute chopped apples, plus 1 tsp. cinnamon, for blueberries.*

# Banana Raisin Muffins

ROSE MECK, MECK'S PRODUCE

*Makes 1 dozen muffins*
*Prep. Time: 20 minutes* ❦ *Baking Time: 25 minutes*

1 cup all-purpose flour
1 cup dry quick oats
1 Tbsp. baking powder
½ tsp. cinnamon
1 cup skim milk
½ cup mashed ripe bananas
½ cup raisins, *optional*
¼ cup vegetable oil
¼ cup brown sugar, firmly packed
1 egg white

1. Combine flour, oats, baking powder, and cinnamon in a large bowl. Set aside.

2. In another bowl, combine remaining ingredients.

3. Add to dry ingredients, mixing just until dry ingredients are moistened.

4. Line 12 medium muffin cups with paper baking cups, or grease the muffin tins themselves and fill ¾ full.

5. Bake at 375° for 25 minutes.

NOTE

*These make a quick, easy breakfast food and are a good way to use up ripe bananas.*

# Sticky Buns

THOMAS MARTIN, WILLOW VALLEY FARMS

*Makes 12 servings*
*Prep. Time: 30 minutes*
*Rising Time: 1 hour and 45 minutes*
*Baking Time: 15-20 minutes*

**Dough Ingredients:**

2¼ tsp. active dry yeast

2 Tbsp. warm water

1 cup milk

¼ cup granulated sugar

1 tsp. salt

1½ Tbsp. shortening

2 eggs

2-3 cups flour, *divided*

¼ cup (half stick) butter, melted

½ cup brown sugar

2 Tbsp. cinnamon

**Topping Ingredients:**

½ cup brown sugar

2 Tbsp. butter

1 Tbsp. corn syrup

2 Tbsp. warm water

1. Soak yeast in warm water.

2. Meanwhile, scald milk. Pour into a large bowl. Add sugar, salt, and shortening.

3. Cool mixture until lukewarm.

4. Add yeast and eggs to the milk mixture.

5. Add 2 cups flour. Add more flour as needed to make a soft dough. Knead mixture until smooth and elastic.

6. Let rise 45 minutes.

7. Meanwhile, mix all topping ingredients and heat until sugar is well dissolved. Pour topping into two greased 8" cake pans.

8. Roll out dough into a rectangle, about 12"x8". Spread melted butter, brown sugar, and cinnamon over the dough.

9. Roll up dough and cut into ¾"-1" slices.

10. Place slices of dough onto the topping and let rise for 1 hour.

11. Bake at 375° for 15-20 minutes.

---

VARIATIONS

*1. Add nuts, raisins, or coconut to the topping in Step 7.*

*2. These are excellent sliced in half horizontally and grilled for breakfast.*

# Quick Sticky Buns

JANICE KREIDER, EISENBERGER'S BAKED GOODS

*Makes 24 servings*
*Prep. Time: 20 minutes*
*Rising Time: 30 minutes*
*Baking Time: 15-18 minutes*

**Dough Ingredients:**

3¼ cups flour, *divided*

¼ cup + ½ tsp. active dry yeast

¾ cup milk

½ cup water

¼ cup (half stick) butter

¼ cup sugar

I tsp. salt

I egg

**Topping Ingredients:**

¾ cup (1½ sticks) butter

I cup brown sugar

I tsp. cinnamon

I cup chopped nuts

I Tbsp. corn syrup

I Tbsp. water

1. In a large mixing bowl combine 1½ cups flour and yeast.

2. In a saucepan heat milk, water, ¼ cup butter, sugar, and salt until warm. Do not bring to a boil.

3. Pour this mixture over yeast and flour. Add egg and beat on high speed for 3 minutes.

4. By hand stir in remaining 1¾ cups flour. Cover and let rise for 30 minutes.

5. While dough is rising, combine all topping ingredients in a saucepan and heat until melted. Pour topping into greased 9"x13" baking pan.

6. Knead dough several minutes. Drop by tablespoonfuls onto the topping. Bake at 375° for 15-18 minutes. Cool for 1 minute.

7. Cover pan with a cookie sheet and carefully invert contents of pan onto cookie sheet.

TIP

*You can let dough rise in an oven turned to the Warm setting.*

# Pfannebecker's Dewey Buns

WILLIAM L. PFANNEBECKER AND LYDIA SMITH

*Makes 6 dozen*

Prep. Time: 30 minutes ❧ Rising Time: 1½ hours ❧ Cooking Time: several minutes per bun

2 lbs. flour

½ cup sugar

½ cup shortening

2½ tsp. salt

2 cups warm water

2 oz. compressed yeast

3 tsp. malt, *optional*

2–3 cups confectioners sugar, *divided*

1. Mix flour, sugar, shortening, and salt gently to distribute salt.

2. Add water, yeast, and malt if you wish. Mix well.

3. Place on work surface and knead well into a round ball.

4. Place in greased bowl and cover with cloth. Let rise until double in size (about 30-45 minutes).

5. Divide dough into pieces and roll into long strips.

6. Cut strips into 1-oz. pieces and roll again into 5" long strips. Place strips on floured cloth or pan.

7. Cover and let rise until double in size, about 30-45 minutes.

8. Fry strips, a few at a time, in deep fat at 375° until browned.

9. Cool. Place a few strips at a time in a plastic bag with some of the confectioners sugar. Shake bag and remove buns when covered.

10. Eat immediately!

NOTE

*The Pfannebecker Stand on Central Market was well known in the local community for its Dewey Buns. Although the stand is no longer on Market, the cookbook did not seem complete without the Dewey Bun recipe. Our sincere appreciation to the Pfannebecker family for sharing this recipe with the* Lancaster Central Market Cookbook.

# Fastnachts

HILDA FUNK, GIVANT'S

*Makes 50 fastnachts* ❧ *Prep. Time: 30 minutes*
*Rising Time: overnight, then 3 hours* ❧ *Cooking Time: several minutes per fastnacht*

¼ cup warm water

2¼ tsp. active dry yeast

2 Tbsp. + 1 cup sugar, *divided*

2½ cups lukewarm milk

10 cups flour, *divided*

4 eggs, beaten

½ cup lard, melted

1 cup sugar

dash of salt

oil for deep frying

1. Dissolve yeast in warm water in a large bowl.

2. In a separate bowl mix 2 Tbsp. sugar, milk, and 4½ cups flour. Add to yeast mixture.

3. Set mixture in a warm place and let rise overnight.

4. In the morning, add eggs, lard, 1 cup sugar, dash of salt, and 4 cups flour. Add any more flour slowly—you may not need the last 1½ cups. Dough should be sticky but able to be handled.

5. Let rise until doubled, approximately 2 hours.

6. Roll out and cut with biscuit or doughnut cutter, with or without a center hole. Let rise 1 hour.

7. Deep fry in hot oil at 375° for several minutes, turning until brown on both sides.

### NOTES

*This recipe is not only a family favorite, but it also rekindles fond memories of days spent with my friend Ruth Eshelman from whom I learned the tricks of making this delicious treat!*

*Among the Pennsylvania Dutch, Shrove Tuesday is known as Fastnacht Day (the night before the fast). In a symbolic effort to rid their homes of leavening agents and to feast before Lent, many Pennsylvania Dutch cooks traditionally spent part of this day making Fastnachts.*

# Mashed Potato Doughnuts

JOANNE WARFEL, S. CLYDE WEAVER, INC.

*Makes 8 dozen doughnuts*
*Prep. Time: 30 minutes*
*Rising Time: about 3 hours*
*Cooking Time: several minutes per doughnut*

**Doughnuts:**
I cup (2 sticks) butter, softened
I cup sugar
2 cups hot mashed potatoes
I quart scalded whole milk
2 Tbsp. + I tsp. yeast
¾ cup lukewarm water
14-15 cups flour, *divided*
2 eggs
I Tbsp. salt

**Glaze:**
I lb. confectioners sugar
½ cup whole milk
2 Tbsp. butter, melted
I tsp. vanilla
¼ tsp. mace, *optional*
oil for deep-frying

1. Mix butter, sugar, and mashed potatoes together in a large bowl while the potatoes are still hot.

2. Add scalded milk to potato mixture.

3. In a separate bowl, mix yeast and lukewarm water. Add to potato mixture.

4. Add 4 cups flour and beat mixture. Let stand for 20 minutes.

5. Add eggs and salt. Mix in 10-11 cups additional flour until mixture becomes satiny. Place in a greased bowl in a warm place. Cover and let rise for 2 hours.

6. Shape dough into doughnuts and let rise about 20 minutes.

7. Meanwhile, prepare glaze by mixing sugar and milk. Add melted butter and vanilla. Add mace, if you wish.

8. Deep-fry in hot oil at 375°-400°.

9. Dip hot doughnuts into glaze.

10. Allow to cool and then serve.

# Thom's Bread French Toast

THOM CAPIZZI, THOM'S BREAD

*Makes 3–4 servings*
*Prep. Time: 10-15 minutes*
*Cooking Time: 10-15 minutes*

1-lb. loaf of Thom's Bread boule
of your choice: chocolate boule,
cranberry pecan boule, *or* rustic
Italian boule

4-5 eggs

¼ cup light cream

½ tsp. vanilla extract

1 Tbsp. raw sugar

2 Tbsp. butter

1. Cut boule in half, then slice each half into slices, about 14-16 slices total.

2. In a large mixing bowl, combine eggs, cream, vanilla, and sugar. Mix well.

3. Place bread in egg mix and soak for several minutes.

4. Melt butter in skillet over medium heat.

5. Fry slices 2-3 minutes on each side, being careful not to burn them.

6. Serve immediately with your favorite toppings, such as maple syrup, butter, bananas, and/or berries.

NOTE

*Enjoy this wonderful breakfast with your family on weekends, holidays, or whenever you can take time to focus on what's important in life.*

# Jam Granola

BRIE GARBER, AMISH FAMILY RECIPES

*Makes 10 cups*
Prep. Time: 5 minutes  ❧  Baking Time: 30 minutes

10 cups dry rolled oats
1 tsp. salt
1 tsp. vanilla
¼ cup honey
15-oz. jar Stefanie's No-Sugar-Added Strawberry Rhubarb Jam, or any other of your favorite Amish Family Recipes jams!

1. Mix all ingredients together in a large mixing bowl.

2. Spread on a large, rimmed baking sheet.

3. Bake at 350° for about half an hour, or until light brown, stirring every 5 minutes.

# Baked Oatmeal

JOANNE WARFEL, S. CLYDE WEAVER, INC.

*Makes 4–5 servings*
Prep. Time: 15 minutes  ❧  Baking Time: 30 minutes

¼ cup cooking oil
½ cup sugar
1 egg
1½ cups dry quick oats
1 tsp. baking powder
½ tsp. salt
½ cup milk

1. Mix oil, sugar, and egg together well.

2. Add all other ingredients and mix. Pour into a greased 8"-square baking pan.

3. Bake at 350° for 30 minutes. Serve warm with milk.

VARIATIONS

1. *Add ¼ cup raisins, ¼ cup nuts and ½ tsp. cinnamon to Step 2.*

2. *Line bottom of baking pan with sliced apples before adding the other ingredients.*

3. *For our family, the variations are a must. Even those who do not enjoy cooked oatmeal almost always love it this way.*

4. *Stir in ¼ cup of your choice of chopped dried fruit instead of raisins.*

# Homemade Yogurt

FANNIE S. FISHER, TOM'S FLOWER GARDEN

*Makes 1 quart*
Prep. Time: 30 minutes  ❧  Standing Time: 3 hours

I scant quart whole or reduced-fat milk

⅓ cup non-instant dry milk

I Tbsp. plain yogurt

1. Bring scant quart milk almost to the boiling point, when a thin skin forms on top.

2. Cool until comfortable to your little finger. Add dry milk and mix thoroughly.

3. Add plain yogurt and mix well again.

4. Pour mixture into a quart jar and place in a large cooking kettle with warm water (comfortable to your hand) that comes up around the sides of the jar but doesn't cover it. Cover kettle and put into unlighted oven or other warm place. Let stand for 3 hours or until yogurt has set.

5. Refrigerate until you're ready to eat

### VARIATION

*Stir in your favorite jelly or fruit after the yogurt has formed.*

# Apple Butter

RUTH WIDDERS, IRWIN S. WIDDERS PRODUCE

*Makes 5 quarts*
*Prep. Time: 20 minutes*
*Cooking/Baking Time: 3½ hours*

7 lbs. apples

3 lbs. brown sugar

1 cup apple cider vinegar *or*
apple cider

2 Tbsp. ground cinnamon

1. Cook apples until soft. Press through a food press to make a sauce. This should yield about 16 cups of sauce.

2. Add brown sugar, vinegar, and cinnamon to sauce and mix well.

3. Put into a roast pan and bake at 350° for 3 hours. Cover. Stir several times.

4. Pour into canning jars. Follow directions from the manufacturer of the canner to process and seal the jars.

HINT

*A cooking apple is best for this recipe.*

# Egg Cheese

DORIS SHENK, DONEGAL GARDENS

*Makes 6 servings*
*Prep. Time: 15 minutes*
*Cooking Time: 30 minutes*
*Chilling Time: several hours*

2 cups milk

1 Tbsp. flour

1 Tbsp. sugar

3 eggs

1 cup buttermilk

1. Heat milk almost to scalding.

2. In a separate bowl, mix together flour, sugar, eggs, and buttermilk.

3. Add to hot milk in pan. Stir until it almost reaches a boil.

4. Let boil slowly for 15 minutes until mixture separates and becomes yellow on top.

5. Drain off the liquid. Place thickened mixture into an egg cheese mold or a salad mold.

6. Chill for several hours until cheese sets.

7. Unmold onto a serving plate. Serve with King Syrup or light molasses to drizzle over slices.

NOTE

*This old-fashioned recipe was a favorite of Ted Shenk's mother. Different, but good!*

# Egg, Potato, and Cheese Casserole

JOYCE DEITER, EISENBERGER'S BAKED GOODS

*Makes 4–6 servings*
*Prep. Time: 25 minutes*
*Chilling Time: several hours* ❧ *Baking Time: 45 minutes* ❧ *Standing Time: 10 minutes*

6-8 medium potatoes
8 eggs
2 Tbsp. water
3 cups grated sharp cheese
salt and pepper to taste

1. Cook potatoes and cool in the refrigerator for several hours until chilled through. Peel, then grate.

2. Mix eggs, water, salt, and pepper together.

3. Scatter grated potatoes evenly over bottom of a greased casserole. Pour beaten egg mixture over potatoes. Spread cheese over top.

4. Bake at 350° for 45 minutes (cover with foil for the first 30 minutes). Let stand 10 minutes after baking before serving.

### NOTE

*Delicious breakfast or brunch!*

### VARIATIONS

1. *Add finely diced onion to egg mixture.*

2. *Add browned, diced ham, sausage, or bacon to egg mixture.*

# Sausage Egg Brunch

LOUELLA E. GROFF, C. Z. MARTIN SONS

*Makes 4–6 servings*
*Prep. Time: 15 minutes*
*Chilling Time: overnight*
*Baking Time: 45 minutes*
*Standing Time: 10 minutes*

2 cups unseasoned croutons

1 lb. bulk sausage, cooked and drained

1 cup grated sharp cheese

6 eggs

2 cups milk

1 Tbsp. dry mustard

1. Layer croutons, sausage, and cheese in a greased 9"x13" baking dish.

2. Beat eggs well. Add milk and mustard and mix well. Pour over sausage. Cover and refrigerate overnight.

3. Bake at 375° for 45 minutes. Let stand 10 minutes before serving.

### VARIATION

*You can use bacon, chipped ham, or chipped dried beef instead of sausage. When using bacon, fry and drain it before layering into the baking dish.*

# Aunt Vera Weaver's Baked Cheese Soufflé

SAM NEFF, S. CLYDE WEAVER, INC.

*Makes 4 servings* ❦ *Prep. Time: 20 minutes* ❦ *Baking Time: 35 minutes*

1 cup dry bread cubes (¾"-1" square)

1 cup diced medium-sharp Colby cheese

1 Tbsp. butter, melted

3 eggs, separated

½ tsp. salt

1 cup milk

1. Mix bread with cheese and butter. Add well-beaten egg yolks and salt. Mix together.

2. Heat milk to scalding. Pour over bread mixture and stir until mixed.

3. Beat egg whites until very stiff. Fold into bread and cheese mixture.

4. Pour soufflé into a small, greased casserole and bake at 350° for 35 minutes.

### NOTE

*I remember how this came out of Mother's oven "high," and by the time the family gathered around the table, the fondue, as we called it, had settled.*

# Pineapple Bread Casserole

ANNA F. KREIDER, VIV'S VARIETIES

*Makes 6–8 servings* ❦ *Prep. Time: 15 minutes* ❦ *Baking Time: 45 minutes*

½ cup (1 stick) butter, softened

1 cup granulated sugar

4 eggs

16-oz. can crushed pineapple, drained

6 slices stale bread, cubed

pinch of salt

1. Beat butter and sugar until creamy. Add eggs and beat. Add pineapple and mix thoroughly.

2. Fold in bread cubes and salt. Spoon into well-greased baking dish.

3. Bake at 375° for 45 minutes.

### NOTE

*Delicious with ham!*

# JOHN STONER OF STONER'S HOMEGROWN VEGETABLES

John Stoner's grandfather sold vegetables 1 in Lancaster's Curb Market (see page 138) before a market building was built. That makes the Stoners the family with the longest history as standholders at Lancaster Central Market.

"My dad had one six-foot-long stand, which was open one day a week. By growing everything ourselves that we sold, and by having family members selling the produce, my parents raised a family on that income," John remembers.

"I started taking major responsibility for the stand after I graduated from high school in 1958. And when Ethel and I got married in 1963, she began doing up to 40 hours a week of prep work at home—picking, washing, shelling, bunching—from our seven acres of truck farming. When our kids were in high school, Ethel began working on Market more and more." (She eventually served as President of the Standholders Association.)

Central Market is a must-stop on political candidates' campaigns. "I shook hands at our stand with three U.S. Presidents," John smiles. "Eisenhower, Kennedy, and either Ford or Carter. I can't remember which! George H.W. Bush came by the stand when we were growing vegetables hydroponically, and I handed him a cucumber!"

Today a young Amish man is handling much of the work at the Stoner stand. "Now we can sleep in on Saturday mornings til 7:00!" John says.

# Springtime Quiche

ETHEL STONER, JOHN R. STONER VEGETABLES

*Makes 12–16 servings* ❧ *Prep. Time: 25 minutes* ❧ *Cooking/Baking Time: 40 minutes*

2 unbaked 9-inch pie shells

I egg white, slightly beaten

1 ½ lbs. fresh asparagus

I tsp. salt

8 slices bacon

½ lb. Swiss cheese, grated

4 eggs

1 ½ cups half-and-half

dash nutmeg

salt and pepper to taste

10 cherry tomatoes, halved

1. Brush pie shells with egg white.

2. Wash asparagus, cut off tough ends, and set aside the 16 best spears (5 inches long). Cut remaining spears into pieces and cook in salt water 5 minutes. Drain and rinse in cold water.

3. Fry, drain, and crumble bacon. Sprinkle bottom of pie shell with bacon, cheese, and cooked asparagus pieces.

4. Mix beaten eggs, half-and-half, nutmeg, salt, and pepper together. Pour mixture into pie shell.

5. Arrange asparagus spears and cherry tomato halves spoke-fashion over pie filling.

6. Bake at 400° for 35 minutes or until firm in the center.

# Quiche Lorraine

JOYCE DEITER, EISENBERGER'S BAKED GOODS

*Makes a 9" pie* ❧ *Prep. Time: 20 minutes* ❧ *Cooking/Baking Time: 45-55 minutes*

I 9" unbaked pie shell

½ lb. bacon

I cup grated Swiss cheese

I Tbsp. grated onion

4 eggs, beaten

2 cups cream

¾ tsp. salt

¼ tsp. sugar

1. Use your favorite pie crust recipe for pastry. Place in a 9" pie pan.

2. Fry and crumble bacon. Sprinkle bacon, onion, and cheese into pastry-lined pie plate.

3. Combine eggs, cream, salt, and sugar, and mix well. Pour mixture into pie plate.

4. Bake 15 minutes at 425°. Reduce temperature to 300° and bake 30 minutes longer, or until knife inserted in center comes out clean.

# SOUPS

## Turkey Vegetable Soup

ETHEL STONER, JOHN R. STONER VEGETABLES

*Makes 8–10 servings*
*Prep. Time: 20 minutes* ❧ *Cooking Time: 1 hour 15 minutes*

1 lb. ground turkey

1 cup chopped onion

½ tsp. garlic powder

1 cup diced potatoes

1 cup grated carrots

1 cup chopped green beans

1 cup fresh corn

1 cup fresh baby limas

3 cups water

2 tsp. salt

½ tsp. pepper

1 tsp. dried basil

1 bay leaf

4 cups chopped, peeled tomatoes

1 cup peas

1. Cook ground turkey and onion together in a skillet until meat is lightly browned. Drain off excess fat. Season with garlic powder.

2. In a 6-quart kettle, combine all vegetables except tomatoes and peas. Add water. Bring to a steady simmer and cook for 10-15 minutes.

3. Add meat, seasonings, and tomatoes. Cover and simmer for 1 hour. Add peas during the last 10 minutes.

NOTE

*I like to make this soup in late summer when all vegetables are fresh except peas. I also like ground turkey because it has little fat. My family looks forward to this summer delight.*

# Ham Vegetable Chowder

LINDA KAUFFMAN, SALLIE Y. LAPP

*Makes 10–12 servings*
Prep. Time: 10 minutes
Cooking Time: about 30 minutes

2 cups cubed cooked ham
2 medium onions, chopped
5 cups cubed potatoes
1½ cups water
1 quart milk
2 Tbsp. butter
2 Tbsp. flour
¼ tsp. baking soda
6-oz. can tomato paste
1 cup corn

1. Combine ham, onions, potatoes, and water. Cook until soft, then add milk.

2. In a large, separate pan, melt butter. Stir in flour, baking soda, and tomato paste. Heat, stirring until smooth.

3. Add ham mixture and corn, and bring to a boil. Serve.

# Veal Shin Soup

ROBERTA B. PETERS, PENNSYLVANIA DUTCH GIFTS

*Serves 4*
Prep. Time: 10 minutes
Cooking Time: 1-2 hours

2–3-lb. veal shin
¼ cup diced carrots
¼ cup diced potatoes
¼ cup diced celery
2 Tbsp. parsley
2 Tbsp. flour
2 Tbsp. butter
¼ tsp. cloves
½ tsp. allspice
1 hard-boiled egg, diced

1. Cook veal in water to cover. When tender, remove meat from bone. Cook carrots, potatoes, celery, and parsley in veal broth until vegetables are soft.

2. Brown flour in butter and add to soup. Whisk to thicken. Add cloves, allspice, and diced hard-boiled egg. Stir in meat.

# Company Stew

CYNTHIA STRUBE, MARION CHEESE

*Makes 4 servings*
*Prep. Time: 20 minutes* ❦ *Cooking/Baking Time: 3 hours*

2 thick slices slab bacon
1½-lb. chuck roast
1 cup flour
1 tsp. salt
½ tsp. pepper
2 large garlic cloves
1 cup dry red wine
1 cup beef broth
1 large onion
2 large tomatoes
1 lb. miniature new potatoes
1 tsp. nutmeg
1½ tsp. thyme
1 Tbsp. parsley

1. Cut bacon into pieces and cook until crisp in small roaster or Dutch oven.

2. Cut beef into bite-size pieces. Dredge in mixture of salt, pepper, and flour.

3. Remove bacon pieces from roaster. Add beef to bacon drippings and brown.

4. Add garlic. Add wine, stirring to loosen any bits from bottom of roaster.

5. Chop onion and tomatoes.

6. Add to roaster, along with all remaining ingredients.

7. Return bacon pieces to roaster and stir mixture thoroughly.

8. Cover and bake at 325° for 2½ hours. After 1½ hours, taste. Add salt and pepper to taste if needed.

---

NOTE

*Served with crusty bread and green salad, this hearty, flavorful stew is great for cold winter evenings or tailgate parties.*

# Beef Stew

MRS. MARTHA FORRY, JOHN M. MARKLEY MEATS

*Makes 8 servings*
*Prep. Time: 15 minutes*
*Baking Time: 3 hours*

2 lbs. beef cubes
2 cups carrots, diced
2 cups potatoes, diced
2 medium onions, sliced
1 cup celery, chopped
2 tsp. quick-cooking tapioca
1 Tbsp. salt
½ tsp. pepper
1 cup tomato juice
1 cup water
1 Tbsp. brown sugar
2 cups peas

1. Place raw beef cubes in a single layer in a heavy roasting pan.

2. Add vegetables, except peas. Sprinkle tapioca, salt, and pepper over vegetables. Add tomato juice and water. Sprinkle brown sugar over everything.

3. Cover and bake at 325° for 2 hours.

4. Add peas and bake 1 more hour, or bake stew for 3 hours, microwave peas until cooked, and stir in just before serving.

NOTE

*We would put this old family recipe into the oven to bake while we went to the field to work.*

Perciatelli with Creamy Clam Sauce, page 180

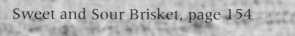
Sweet and Sour Brisket, page 154

Banana Cupcakes, page 223

# Homemade Chicken Corn Soup

BRAD LOERCHER, PARSLEY PORCH

*Makes 12–16 servings*
*Prep. Time: 20 minutes ❦ Cooking Time: 1-2 hours*

4–5-lb. roaster chicken

14 cups water, *divided*

generous pinch saffron

1 cup boiling water

3 ears fresh yellow corn, cooked
and cut off cob, *or* 15 oz. can
yellow corn, drained

3 ears fresh white corn, cooked
and cut off the cob, *or* 15-oz. can
white corn, drained

4 hard-boiled eggs, diced

1 Tbsp. dried parsley *or* 3 sprigs
fresh parsley

6 oz. medium noodles

salt and pepper to taste

1. Cook chicken in about 8 cups water. When chicken is tender, remove from broth and cool. Remove fat from chicken broth. Chop chicken.

2. Place chopped chicken, 6 cups broth, and 6 cups water in a 6-quart kettle.

3. Pour boiling water over saffron in a small bowl. Set aside. Hot water will draw out golden yellow coloring and flavoring.

4. Add drained corn, eggs, and parsley to chicken and broth. Crumble noodles into kettle and add salt and pepper to taste. Add saffron water. Stir and simmer until hot.

NOTE

*This soup is a great way to eat leftover chicken. It is so good! In fact, the soup improves as it ages, so don't eat it all at the first sitting.*

# ROGER SHENK OF SHENK'S POULTRY

Roger Shenk remembers, "When I was 10 or 12, my mom worked for Widder's [now Meck's Produce; see page 103]. I hung out. Did my homework upstairs in the Market's loft. I thought the building was huge.

"After Mom stopped working on Market, I didn't come back until 20 years later when I had the opportunity to become a standholder. Suddenly, I felt like I was 10 again—the noises, the smells.

"The best thing about Market is our regular customers. You learn their stories. You miss them when they don't come.

"People look for these kinds of relationships—and our kinds of products!—and they can't find them in many places. We add up customers' charges with pencil, paper, or in our heads, and people trust that.

"We're the polar opposite of Walmart."

# Creamy Crab Meat Soup

CHARLES FOX AND LARRY MCELHENNY, NEW HOLLAND SEAFOOD

*Makes 4–6 servings*
*Prep. Time: 20 minutes*
*Cooking Time: about 30 minutes*

1 lb. claw crab meat
2 hard-boiled eggs
grated rind of 1 lemon
1 Tbsp. butter, melted
1 Tbsp. flour
1 quart whole milk
½ cup cream
½ cup sherry

1. Pick over crab meat and remove any shell. Place in a deep mixing bowl.

2. Chop eggs finely and add to crab. Blend well and add lemon rind, butter, and flour.

3. Blend well and add milk. Pour mixture into top of double boiler. Place over boiling water. Heat thoroughly. Remove from heat.

4. Add cream. Heat and season with sherry.

5. Serve in hot bowls.

# Fish Chowder

HELEN E. BITNER, BITNERS

*Makes 6–8 servings*
Prep. Time: 20 minutes
Cooking Time: 20-30 minutes

1 lb. haddock fillet

2 cups water

2-3 large potatoes, diced

2 slices bacon

1 onion, sliced

½ cup diced celery

1 bay leaf, crumbled

2 cups milk

1 Tbsp. butter

1 tsp. salt

few grains pepper

1. Simmer haddock in water for 15 minutes. Drain, reserving broth.

2. Cook potatoes in broth until almost soft.

3. Sauté bacon until crisp. Remove from pan. In bacon drippings sauté onion and celery until golden brown.

4. Crumble fish. Add fish, onion, celery, and bay leaf to potatoes and broth.

5. Add milk and butter and simmer 5 minutes. Stir in salt and pepper.

6. Pour into serving dish and top with crumbled bacon.

# Mr. Bill's Lobster Bisque

MR. BILL'S SEAFOOD

**Makes 8 servings**
*Prep. Time: 20 minutes* ❧ *Cooking Time: 30 minutes*

1 rib celery

1 onion

1 red bell pepper

4 sticks (1 lb.) butter

½ cup flour

½ tsp. salt

½ tsp. white pepper

½ tsp. cayenne pepper

1 tsp. paprika

1 quart lobster stock (see Mr. Bill's Lobster Stock recipe on next page)

1 quart heavy cream

1 lb. steamed lobster meat

drizzle of sherry, *optional*

1. Puree celery, onion, and red pepper in food processor.

2. Sauté with butter and flour for 15 minutes to form roux.

3. Add salt, white pepper, cayenne pepper, and paprika.

4. Separately, heat lobster stock until steaming.

5. Slowly add heated lobster stock to roux in pot and whisk until smooth.

6. Turn off heat. Add cream and gently fold in lobster.

7. Garnish with a drizzle of sherry if you wish.

# Mr. Bill's Lobster Stock

MR. BILL'S SEAFOOD

*Makes 12 cups*
*Prep. Time: 5 minutes* ❧ *Cooking Time: 1 hour*

2 steamed lobster bodies
½ onion, cut up
¼ lb. carrots, cut in chunks
3 ribs celery, cut in pieces
½ lemon, cut up

1. Add ingredients to stockpot. Add water to cover.

2. Bring to a light boil.

3. Simmer 1 hour.

4. Strain through cheesecloth or fine mesh strainer.

---

**To prepare steamed lobster bodies:**

*Put 2" of water mixed with 2 Tbsp. salt in a large kettle. Place a steaming rack on the floor of the kettle. Bring the water to a rolling boil over high heat. Add the 2 lobsters. Cover the pot. For 1–2 lbs. lobster, steam 10-18 minutes; 2–3 lbs., 18-25 minutes.*

# Corn Chowder

NANCY GEIB, NANCY'S GOODIES

**Makes 6 servings**
Prep. Time: 5 minutes ❦ Cooking Time: 20-30 minutes

¼ cup chopped onion
3 Tbsp. butter
4 cups milk
2 cups chopped, cooked potatoes
2 cups creamed corn
1 ½ tsp. salt
⅛ tsp. pepper
few grains cayenne pepper
crackers, for serving

1. Sauté onion in butter until a delicate brown. Add milk, potatoes, corn, salt, pepper, and cayenne pepper.

2. Bring soup to a boil and simmer for about 5 minutes.

3. Serve a cracker or two in each portion of soup.

# Cheese and Corn Chowder

MIRIAM M. HESS, FRANK WEAVER GREENHOUSES

**Makes 6 servings**
Prep. Time: 5 minutes ❦ Cooking Time: about 20 minutes

2 cups diced potatoes
1 cup sliced carrots
1 cup chopped celery
½ cup water
1 tsp. salt
¼ tsp. pepper
2 cups creamed corn
1 ½ cups milk
⅔ cup grated cheese

1. Put potatoes, carrots, celery, and water into stockpot. Add salt and pepper and simmer for 10 minutes, covered.

2. Add creamed corn and simmer 5 more minutes.

3. Add milk and cheese. Stir over heat until cheese melts and chowder is heated through. Do not bring to a boil. Serve.

# Creamy Cheese Soup

ETHEL STONER, JOHN R. STONER VEGETABLES

*Makes 4–6 servings*  ❧  *Prep. Time: 10 minutes*  ❧  *Cooking Time: 30 minutes*

2 cups water
1 cup shredded carrots
1 medium onion, chopped
½ cup chopped celery
1 tsp. salt
2 dashes Tabasco sauce
8-oz. pkg. cream cheese, cut up
2 cups milk
2 Tbsp. butter, softened
2 Tbsp. flour
parsley

1. In 3-quart saucepan, combine water, carrots, onion, celery, salt, and Tabasco sauce. Bring to a boil, reduce heat, and cook covered for 15 minutes or until vegetables are tender.

2. Stir in cream cheese until melted. Add milk. Blend butter and flour together and add to saucepan. Cook and stir until mixture thickens and bubbles.

3. Garnish each serving with snipped parsley.

# Minestrone

THELMA THOMAS, WILLOW VALLEY FARMS

*Makes 6–8 servings*  ❧  *Prep. Time: 10 minutes*  ❧  *Cooking Time: 1½ hours*

1 cup chopped celery
1 cup chopped onion
1 clove garlic, minced
¼ cup oil
2½ tsp. salt
½ tsp. pepper
2 quarts water
2 6-oz. cans tomato paste
1 cup chopped cabbage
10-oz. pkg. peas and carrots
1 quart beef broth
2 cups cooked kidney beans
1 cup macaroni, uncooked

1. Cook celery, onion, and garlic in oil in stockpot. Add all other ingredients except kidney beans and macaroni, and simmer 1 hour.

2. Add kidney beans and macaroni, and simmer another 15 minutes.

NOTE

*Tasty and nutritious vegetable soup!*

# Simple Cassoulet

TONY PAGE, ROOSTER STREET PROVISIONS

*Makes 4–6 servings*
*Prep. Time: 15 minutes*
*Cooking Time: 30 minutes*

4 Rooster Street Provisions fresh sausage links, 1-1¼ lbs. total

2 strips Rooster Street Provisions Mustard Brown Sugar Bacon, cut into ¼" pieces

1 onion, sliced thinly

3 cloves garlic, minced

1 leek, white parts only, sliced thinly

2 cups quartered button mushrooms

½ cup white wine

3 cups chicken stock

2 cups cooked broad beans, butter beans preferred

approximately 1 quart cleaned, chopped kale

4 farm-fresh eggs

olive oil

salt and pepper to taste

1. In a 12"-14" oval or round braising pot or Dutch oven, brown the sausages on medium heat and remove.

2. Add bacon and allow to render for 5-10 minutes.

3. Add onion, garlic, leek, and mushrooms to cook in the bacon fat for 5-10 minutes.

4. Add white wine and cook until reduced by ¾. Add chicken stock and cook until reduced by ½.

5. Add beans and top with sausages.

6. Cook, covered, for an additional 10-15 minutes or until the internal temperature of the sausages is 140°.

7. At the last minute, after the heat has been turned off, mix in the kale, making sure not to overcook it.

8. In a separate nonstick saute pan, fry the eggs in a little olive oil, sunny side up.

9. Serve 1 sausage with some of the stew in a shallow bowl, topped with a sunny side up egg for each serving.

Tips for serving:

*This is really good with some warm crusty bread. We always enjoy this when the briskness of fall starts to set in.*

# Cream of Vegetable Soup

JOYCE DEITER, EISENBERGER'S BAKED GOODS

*Makes 4-6 servings*

*Prep. Time: 15 minutes* ❦ *Cooking Time: 30 minutes*

I cup diced potatoes
I cup diced carrots
¾ cup diced celery
3 cups hot water
4 Tbsp. (half stick) butter
2 Tbsp. flour
3 cups milk
2 tsp. salt

1. Cook vegetables in hot water until soft.

2. Melt butter in saucepan and add flour and blend well. Add milk and cook until thickened, stirring constantly.

3. Add vegetables with their liquid to the white sauce. Add salt and heat until mixture is hot. Serve hot.

### VARIATIONS

1. *Add ½ cup chopped onions to the vegetables and cook until soft.*

2. *Add a sprinkling of your favorite herbs, plus paprika and parsley before the final heating of the soup.*

# Cheesy Broccoli Bisque

ETHEL STONER, JOHN R. STONER VEGETABLES

*Makes 3–4 servings* ❦ *Prep. Time: 10 minutes* ❦ *Cooking Time: 40-50 minutes*

1 cup chopped onions
1 cup sliced mushrooms
3 Tbsp. butter
3 Tbsp. flour
1-2 tsp. garlic powder
3 cups chicken broth
1 cup broccoli florets
1 cup light cream *or* evaporated skim milk
1 cup Jarlsberg *or* Swiss cheese, shredded

1. In a large saucepan, sauté onions and mushrooms in butter until tender. Add flour and cook, stirring until bubbly. Add garlic powder.

2. Remove from heat and gradually add chicken broth. Return to heat. Cook, stirring until thickened and smooth.

3. Add broccoli, reduce heat, and simmer 20 minutes or until vegetables are tender.

4. Blend in cream and cheese. Simmer until heated thoroughly and cheese is melted.

# Cream of Broccoli Soup

BARBARA FINEFROCK, WILLOW VALLEY FARMS

*Makes 4 servings*
Prep. Time: 15 minutes ❦ Cooking Time: about 30 minutes

¼ cup finely chopped onions
¼ cup finely chopped celery
¼ cup (half stick) butter
3 Tbsp. flour
¼ tsp. salt
dash pepper
1½ cups chicken broth
1½ cups milk
2 cups chopped broccoli, cooked and drained
2 tsp. lemon juice
¼ tsp. garlic powder

1. In medium saucepan, sauté onion and celery in butter until tender.

2. Stir in flour, salt, and pepper. Cook 1 minute, stirring constantly until smooth and bubbly.

3. Gradually stir in chicken broth and milk. Cook until slightly thickened, stirring constantly. Do not boil.

4. Add chopped broccoli, lemon juice, and garlic powder. Heat gently, stirring frequently.

# Cream of Asparagus Soup

PAM GRIFFE, THE GOODIE SHOPPE

*Makes 4–6 servings*
*Prep. Time: 15 minutes ❦ Cooking Time: 30 minutes*

1 bunch asparagus
3 Tbsp. butter
1 small onion, diced
3 cups chicken stock
1 small potato, diced
8-oz pkg. cream cheese, softened
1 tsp. salt
1 tsp. pepper
½ cup grated Parmesan cheese
1 Tbsp. chives

1. Cut asparagus into 1″ pieces, reserving several spears for garnish.

2. Melt butter and sauté onion until tender. Add chicken stock and cook asparagus and potatoes until potatoes are fork tender.

3. Purée broth and vegetables with cream cheese in blender or food processor.

4. Return mixture to cooking pot and season. Add Parmesan cheese.

5. Serve hot and garnish with asparagus spears and chives.

# Arugula Soup

ETHEL STONER, JOHN R. STONER VEGETABLES

*Makes 4–6 servings*
Prep. Time: 15 minutes ❧ Cooking Time: 25 minutes

1 lb. potatoes, peeled and diced
1 lb. leeks, white parts only, sliced
2 quarts chicken broth
2 cups arugula leaves
1 tsp. salt
⅛ tsp. pepper
½ tsp. garlic powder
½ cup heavy cream, *optional*

1. Combine leeks and potatoes with chicken broth. Simmer 25 minutes or until tender. Add arugula and cook 10 minutes.

2. Put into blender or food processor and puree. Add seasonings. Add cream, if you wish. Serve immediately.

# Potato Leek Soup

ETHEL STONER, JOHN R. STONER VEGETABLES

*Makes 4–6 servings*
Prep. Time: 15 minutes ❧ Cooking Time: 30 minutes

3 medium-sized leeks, to make 2 cups of slices
4 medium potatoes, cubed
4 carrots, grated
water
2 cups chicken stock
2 cups skim milk
⅛ tsp. pepper
parsley, to garnish

1. Put leeks, potatoes, and carrots into a 3-quart saucepan with enough water to cover. Cook over high heat until tender.

2. Add chicken stock. When heated thoroughly, add milk and pepper. Heat to serve. Garnish with parsley before serving.

# Sauerkraut Soup

BARBARA J. WEAVER, D. M. WEAVER AND SONS, INC.

*Makes 4 servings*
Prep. Time: 15 minutes   ❦   Cooking Time: 20 minutes

1 envelope dried onion soup mix

16-oz. can stewed tomatoes

½ lb. sauerkraut

salt and pepper to taste

1 loaf French *or* German bread

1. Prepare dried onion soup as directed on the box. Add the stewed tomatoes. Add sauerkraut and season to taste. Heat until piping hot.

2. Serve with crusty French or German bread.

NOTE

*I created this recipe after tasting a similar soup at a German inn in north-central Pennsylvania on a cold, snowy night.*

# Pumpkin Cream Soup

ETHEL STONER, JOHN R. STONER VEGETABLES

*Makes 6 servings*
Prep. Time: 15 minutes   ❦   Cooking Time: 30 minutes

1½ tsp. chopped onion

3 Tbsp. butter

2½ Tbsp. flour

2¼ cups pumpkin purée

4½ cups chicken broth

1½ tsp. salt

¾ tsp. ginger

¼ tsp. nutmeg

white pepper to taste

3 egg yolks, slightly beaten

1½ cups evaporated milk, *or* skim milk

¼ cup chopped parsley

1. Sauté onion in butter until tender. Stir in flour and cook over low heat. Remove from heat.

2. Add pumpkin purée, broth, salt, ginger, nutmeg and pepper. Return to heat and stir with whisk until thick and smooth.

3. Combine egg yolks with milk and add to mixture. Bring just to boiling point, stirring constantly. Do not allow to boil.

4. Correct seasoning and add chopped parsley.

"We grow everything we sell. We're organic farmers. We start our crops from seed, growing them in the three greenhouses on our farm during the winter.

"We specialize in lettuce—we raise up to 13 varieties—and celery. I enjoy transplanting lettuce and watching it grow. And we grow seasonal vegetables, too.

"You know, it's a privilege to work with soil and plants. It isn't just work. Edith and I have so many different kinds of people as customers, it keeps us humble. It's even exciting. And it's so much fun to work with the other standholders."
—Earl Groff, Groff's Vegetables

# SALADS AND RELISHES

## Sunshine Salad

**DORIS SHENK, DONEGAL GARDENS**

*Makes 8–10 servings* ❧ *Prep. Time: 15 minutes* ❧ *Chilling Time: overnight*

**Salad Ingredients:**

1 bunch romaine lettuce

2 bunches red leaf lettuce

½ red onion

2 avocados

16-20 cherry tomatoes, whole or halved

**Dressing Ingredients:**

1 cup cider vinegar

1 cup vegetable oil

½ cup honey

2 tsp. poppy seeds

salt and pepper to taste

1. Wash lettuce and shake off excess water. Tear into bite-size pieces and place in a plastic bag with paper towel. Refrigerate overnight to crisp.

2. Put lettuce into a large bowl. Slice onion into thin pieces and add to salad. Peel and slice avocados and add to salad.

3. Add cherry tomatoes.

4. To prepare dressing, mix all ingredients in a small bowl or jar and stir or shake until well blended.

5. Pour dressing over salad and toss well. Season with salt and pepper.

**TIPS**

*Good any time of year!*

**VARIATION**

*Substitute mandarin oranges for cherry tomatoes.*

# Seven-Layer Salad

MARILYN DENLINGER, IRWIN S. WIDDERS PRODUCE

*Makes 8–10 servings*
*Prep. Time: 20 minutes* ❧ *Chilling Time: overnight*

1 large head lettuce

1 cup chopped celery

¼ cup chopped onion

½ lb. bacon, cooked and crumbled

1-1½ cups frozen peas, thawed

6 hard-boiled eggs, sliced

1 cup light mayonnaise

8 oz. cheese, shredded

1. Layer lettuce, celery, onion, bacon, peas, and eggs in a glass bowl.

2. Spread mayonnaise over salad. Sprinkle cheese on top.

3. Cover and refrigerate overnight.

4. When it's time to eat, serve layered, or toss everything together.

# Gourmet Tossed Salad

ETHEL STONER, JOHN R. STONER VEGETABLES

*Makes 6–8 servings* ❦ *Prep. Time: 15 minutes*

**Salad Ingredients:**
radicchio leaves
arugula
red leaf lettuce
watercress
romaine lettuce

**Dressing Ingredients:**
2-3 tsp. shallots *or* scallions
½ tsp. dry mustard
¼ tsp. salt
⅛ tsp. freshly ground pepper
1 Tbsp. lemon juice
½ cup good quality olive oil
1 tsp. fresh parsley *or* dill

1. On individual plates, or in a salad bowl, arrange all the greens, which have been washed and drained.

2. Prepare a basic vinaigrette by combining all dressing ingredients. Shake together in a jar, or whisk together. Pour over greens just before serving.

### NOTE

*One of many unique things about Central Market is the availability of home-grown arugula and radicchio. My husband, John, grows all of these greens on our farm. Our customers especially enjoy arugula and have nicknamed John, "Captain Arugula." Another standholder, Regine Ibold, gave me this recipe, and she should have the credit for it.*

# Spinach Salad

RUTH GERLACH, IRWIN. S WIDDERS PRODUCE

*Makes 6 servings*  ❧  *Prep. Time: 15 minutes*

8 cups fresh spinach

¼ cup bacon bits

1 hard-boiled egg, chopped

**Dressing:**

½ cup sugar

1 cup vegetable oil

⅓ cup ketchup

½ cup vinegar

1 medium onion, minced

2 Tbsp. Worcestershire sauce

1. Combine all dressing ingredients and chill.

2. Just before serving, tear spinach into small pieces. Toss with as much of the dressing as you wish. Top with bacon bits and chopped egg.

# Spinach Salad With Hot Bacon Dressing

MARILYN WIDDERS DENLINGER, IRWIN S. WIDDERS PRODUCE

*Makes 6 servings*  ❧  *Prep. Time: 15 minutes*  ❧  *Cooking Time: 5-10 minutes*

1 cup sugar

1 tsp. salt

1 tsp. cornstarch *or* flour

1 tsp. prepared mustard

2 eggs, beaten

½ cup milk

½ cup vinegar

½ lb. bacon

1 tsp. bacon drippings

1 lb. spinach, washed and chopped

½ lb. mushrooms, sliced

8 hard-boiled eggs, sliced

1. Put sugar, salt, cornstarch or flour, and mustard in a blender. Mix.

2. Add beaten eggs and mix again.

3. Blend in milk and vinegar.

4. Pour mixture into a saucepan and cook uncovered until thickened.

5. Fry bacon and add crumbled pieces to dressing. To enhance taste, add bacon drippings.

6. Wash spinach in water to remove all sand. Garnish spinach with mushrooms and sliced eggs. Serve with hot dressing.

**From the other side of the Market stand . . .**

# EARL GROFF OF GROFF'S VEGETABLES

Earl Groff's family has been selling vegetables on Central Market since 1946. (If you like genealogy, Earl's grandmother, Edna Meck Groff, was a cousin to Rose Meck's [see page 103] grandmother and John Stoner's [see page 55] mother, who were sisters. Standing market gets in your blood!)

"We grow everything we sell. We're organic farmers. We start our crops from seed, growing them in the three greenhouses on our farm during the winter. We specialize in lettuce—we raise up to 13 varieties—and celery. I enjoy transplanting lettuce and watching it grow. And we grow seasonal vegetables, too.

"You know, it's a privilege to work with soil and plants. It isn't just work.

"A couple years back, some F&M students [Franklin and Marshall College is on the west side of Lancaster City] were doing a study on Central Market. They asked if they could come out to our farm and see how we get ready for Market. We cut spinach out in the field. We washed and bagged it so they would see the whole process. They were so interested in learning.

"Edith and I have so many different kinds of people as customers, it keeps us humble. It's even exciting. And it's so much fun to work with the other standholders. We were on a hike hours away from home, and we came upon a couple. The woman said, 'You look familiar. Oh, I buy lettuce from you!'"

# Warm Raspberry Salad

CINDY COVER, MARION CHEESE

*Makes 6–8 servings*
*Prep. Time: 15 minutes* ❧ *Cooking Time: 5 minutes*

1 medium head romaine lettuce, *or* equivalent amount of mixed salad greens

8-oz. can water chestnuts, drained and sliced

½ tsp. cracked black pepper

3 Tbsp. walnut oil

½ cup slivered almonds

¾ lb. mushrooms, cleaned and sliced

¼ cup raspberry vinegar

1. Wash and tear salad greens. Combine with water chestnuts and season with pepper. Chill.

2. Heat walnut oil in large skillet. Add almonds and sauté over high heat for 1–2 minutes. Add sliced mushrooms and sauté another 2 minutes. Add raspberry vinegar and stir briefly.

3. Pour dressing over chilled greens and toss. Serve immediately.

### NOTE

*This dish allows salad to be a more substantial part of a meal. It is tart and full of textures.*

# Blue Cheese Potato Salad

KATHLEEN PIANKA, MARION CHEESE

*Serves 4–6*
*Prep. Time: 15 minutes* ❧ *Cooking Time: 20 minutes*

2 lbs. new red potatoes, cut into quarters

boiling water

2 celery ribs, chopped

3 scallions, chopped

½ cup sour cream

½ cup mayonnaise

¼ cup crumbled Stilton *or* your favorite blue cheese

¼ cup chopped fresh parsley

salt and pepper to taste

1. Put potatoes into boiling water. Cook for 15 minutes. Drain well. Salt potatoes while hot.

2. Combine all ingredients and serve.

### NOTE

*A good quality blue cheese is essential.*

# Irish Tomato Salad

GRACE KAUFFMAN, FUNK BROTHERS, INC.

*Makes 4–8 servings* ❧ *Prep. Time: 15 minutes* ❧ *Standing Time: 1-2 hours*

I small cucumber, chopped

I small green bell pepper, chopped

6 scallions with their tops

6 Tbsp. fresh parsley

½ cup fresh mint

3 Tbsp.-½ cup vegetable oil

¼ cup lemon juice

I tsp. salt, *optional*

4 large tomatoes, thinly sliced

red leaf lettuce

1. Mix together cucumber, green pepper, scallions, parsley, and mint in blender for several seconds.

2. Add vegetable oil, beginning with a few tablespoons and using up to ½ cup, as you wish.

3. Add lemon juice and salt. Blend for several seconds. Pour mixture over tomato slices and let stand for 1-2 hours.

4. Arrange over red leaf lettuce and serve.

NOTE

*Beautiful, bright salad with a delicious taste! Goes especially well with pork, lamb, or veal.*

# Fresh Broccoli Salad

RUTH THOMAS, THOMAS PRODUCE

*Makes 8 servings* ❧ *Prep. Time: 15 minutes* ❧ *Standing Time: 1 hour* ❧ *Cooking Time: 10-15 minutes*

I cup mayonnaise

½ cup granulated sugar *or* honey

2 Tbsp. vinegar

3 strips bacon

I large head broccoli

I Tbsp. minced onion

I medium carrot, peeled and grated

¾ cup raisins

½ cup cashews, *optional*

1. Mix mayonnaise, sugar, and vinegar to make dressing. Set aside for 1 hour.

2. Fry bacon strips, then crumble and set aside.

3. Prepare vegetables, cutting broccoli into bite-size pieces.

4. Toss bacon, vegetables, raisins, and cashews together. Pour dressing over salad and serve immediately.

NOTE

*I like when my family eats foods with bulk and fiber. This salad is one way to get these foods into their diet, and they like it.*

# Cauliflower Salad

EDITH R. WEAVER, FRANK WEAVER GREENHOUSES

*Makes 6–8 servings* ❧ *Prep. Time: 15 minutes* ❧ *Chilling Time: several hours or overnight*

I head cauliflower

½ lb. bacon

I small onion, diced

8 oz. cheese, grated

green lettuce *or* spinach

I cup salad dressing

½ cup sugar

2 Tbsp. vinegar

green lettuce *or* spinach leaves, for serving

1. Clean cauliflower and cut into small florets.

2. Fry bacon until it is crisp. Crumble it.

3. Mix cauliflower, bacon, onion, and cheese together.

4. Blend salad dressing, sugar, and vinegar, then pour over salad and toss lightly. Refrigerate several hours or overnight.

5. Serve on green lettuce or baby spinach leaves.

NOTE

*Refreshing salad for any time of year!*

# Pepper Cabbage

ANNA F. KREIDER, VIV'S VARIETIES

*Makes 10–12 servings* ❧ *Prep. Time: 15 minutes* ❧ *Cooking Time: 5 minutes*

8 cups shredded cabbage

I large red *or* green bell pepper, diced

I cup diced celery

I carrot, shredded

I small onion, shredded

salt to taste

**Dressing:**

2 cups sugar

I cup vinegar

½ cup water

I tsp. celery seed

I tsp. mustard seed

1. In a large bowl, mix cabbage, pepper, celery, carrot, and onion. Sprinkle with salt and toss.

2. Mix all dressing ingredients and bring to a boil. Boil for 1 minute. Cool until lukewarm.

3. Pour dressing over salad and mix thoroughly. This will keep well for a long time in the refrigerator.

# Green Bean Salad

RUTH HARNISH, SPRING GLEN FARM KITCHENS, INC.

*Makes 6–8 servings* ❦ *Prep. Time: 15 minutes*

3 cups green beans, cooked
4 hard-boiled eggs
I medium onion
I large dill pickle
2 Tbsp. vinegar
I tsp. salt
⅔ cup mayonnaise

1. Chop green beans, eggs, onion, and dill pickle. Combine.

2. Mix together vinegar, salt, and mayonnaise.

3. Pour over bean mixture. Stir gently.

4. Chill and serve.

# Marinated Mushrooms

ROSE MECK, MECK'S PRODUCE

*Makes 4–6 servings*
*Prep. Time: 15 minutes* ❦ *Cooking Time: 10 minutes* ❦ *Chilling Time: several hours or overnight*

I ½ lbs. fresh mushrooms
⅓ cup vinegar
⅓ cup salad oil
I Tbsp. brown sugar
I tsp. prepared mustard
2 tsp. parsley flakes
I tsp. salt
I small onion, thinly sliced

1. Boil mushrooms 5 minutes in water. Drain them.

2. Combine all other ingredients. Pour over mushrooms.

3. Chill in a covered dish overnight or at least for several hours.

# Carrot Salad

ROBERTA B. PETERS, PENNSYLVANIA DUTCH GIFTS

*Makes 3–4 servings*
Prep. Time: 15 minutes ❧ Chilling Time: overnight ❧ Cooking Time: 15 minutes

6-8 carrots
water
1 green bell pepper
1 medium onion
15-oz. can tomato soup
½ cup vinegar
½ cup oil
¾ cup sugar

1. Slice carrots and cook in water until soft.

2. Dice pepper and onion. Mix with soup, vinegar, oil, and sugar.

3. Drain water off carrots and add to mixture.

4. Refrigerate overnight and then serve.

# Black Bean Salad with Roasted Red Peppers

REGINE IBOLD, THE SPICE STAND

*Makes 4–6 servings*
*Prep. Time: 20 minutes  ❧  Cooking Time: 5 minutes*

2 15-oz. cans black beans, drained and rinsed

3-4 scallions, sliced

2-3 plum tomatoes, diced

6 Tbsp. olive oil

5 Tbsp. fresh cilantro, chopped

salt to taste

3-4 red bell peppers

3 Tbsp. lemon juice

1 tsp. coarse black pepper

1. Combine all ingredients, except red peppers, lemon juice, and black pepper, and toss in a glass bowl.

2. To prepare peppers, hold them, one at a time, with tongs over a gas flame until skin is bubbled and getting dark.

3. Place peppers in a paper bag and let them steam.

4. Peel, de-seed, and slice into quarters.

5. Sprinkle peppers with lemon juice and freshly ground pepper.

6. Garnish bean salad with pepper wedges and serve.

NOTE

*Beautiful, easy, and nutritious!*

# Hummus Salad or Chickpea Salad

GARY ALHUSSEINI, HABIBI'S

*Makes 4–6 servings*
*Prep. Time: 10 minutes* ❧ *Cooking Time: 5 minutes*

10-oz. can chickpeas

¼ cup flat-leaf parsley, chopped

1 medium tomato, diced

1 clove garlic, chopped *or* pressed

pinch of salt and pepper

3 Tbsp. fresh lemon juice

4 Tbsp. olive oil

1. Boil chickpeas 3-5 minutes. Drain.

2. Combine chickpeas with parsley, tomato, garlic, salt, and pepper. Add lemon juice and olive oil.

3. Serve hot or cold.

NOTE

*Very filling, especially on cold days. Nutritious and economical.*

VARIATION

*For another dish, called* Foul M'dammas, *substitute broad beans for chickpeas.*

# Rhubarb Salad

JOYCE FAIR, UTZ'S POTATO CHIPS

*Makes 8 servings*
*Prep. Time: 15 minutes* ❧ *Cooking Time: about 10 minutes* ❧ *Chilling Time: several hours*

3 cups rhubarb, finely cut

⅔ cup sugar

¼ tsp. salt

⅓ cup water

6-oz. pkg. strawberry gelatin

1 cup finely chopped celery

2½ cups water

1 Tbsp. lemon juice

½ cup chopped nuts

1. Cook together rhubarb, sugar, salt, and ⅓ cup water.

2. Add gelatin, celery, 2½ cups water, lemon juice, and nuts. Mix well.

3. Chill until firm.

# Cranberry Relish

ANNA MARY NEFF, S. CLYDE WEAVER, INC.

*Makes 8–10 servings* ❦ *Prep. Time: 15 minutes*

1 lb. frozen cranberries
1 orange, peeled
6-8 red apples, cored
8-oz. can crushed pineapple
1 cup sugar

1. Grind cranberries, orange, and apples together.

2. Add pineapples and sugar. Mix well.

3. Keeps well in the fridge. Or freeze leftovers.

# Cranberry Orange Salad

JOYCE DEITER, EISENBERGER'S BAKED GOODS

*Makes 8 servings*
*Prep. Time: 15 minutes* ❦ *Chilling Time: 4 hours or overnight*

6-oz. pkg. strawberry gelatin
1½ cups boiling water
16-oz. can jellied cranberry sauce
1 Tbsp. grated orange rind
2 oranges, finely diced
⅔ cup chopped pecans
lettuce, for serving

1. Dissolve gelatin in boiling water.

2. Stir cranberry sauce with fork, or whisk until smooth. Add to gelatin. Add orange rind, blending well.

3. Chill until slightly thickened. Stir in oranges and pecans. Mix well.

4. Pour into 5-cup mold. Chill until firm, about 4 hours or overnight. Unmold onto a bed of lettuce.

NOTE

*A family favorite over the holidays.*

# Apple Salad

MRS. AARON KING, KAUFFMAN'S FRUIT FARM

*Makes 4–5 servings* ❦ *Prep. Time: 15 minutes*

4-5 apples, cored but unpeeled

½-¾ cup raisins

½ cup nuts

½ cup celery, diced

¾ cup mayonnaise *or* salad dressing

¼ cup milk

¼ cup sugar

sweetened vinegar, *optional*

lettuce leaves, for serving

1. Dice apples. Add raisins, nuts, and celery and mix gently but well.

2. Combine mayonnaise, milk, and sugar and blend well. Add a little sweetened vinegar if you wish.

3. Pour this combination over apple mixture and mix well.

4. Serve on lettuce leaves.

### VARIATIONS

1. *Use a combination of Red and Golden Delicious apples to add color and flavor.*

2. *Use lemon juice instead of vinegar.*

# Raspberry Jello Salad

JANE BRENNEMAN, BRENNEMAN FARM

*Makes 6–8 servings*
*Prep. Time: 15 minutes* ❦ *Cooking Time: 15 minutes* ❦ *Chilling Time: about 1 hour*

6 tart apples, peeled and diced

6 heaping tsp. sugar

pinch of salt

2 cups water, *divided*

6-oz. pkg. raspberry gelatin

**Dressing:**

½ cup mayonnaise

1 Tbsp. milk

2-3 tsp. sugar

1. Add 6 heaping tsp. sugar, salt, and 1¼ cups water to apples in large saucepan. Boil until apples are soft.

2. Add remaining ¾ cup water to mixture. Stir in gelatin while mixture is still hot. Chill until set.

3. Serve with dressing on the side.

# Spiced Cantaloupe

ARLENE LEAMAN, S. CLYDE WEAVER, INC.

*Makes 8–10 servings*
*Prep. Time: 15 minutes* ❧ *Cooking Time: 10 minutes*

2-3 cups firm cantaloupe chunks
1 cup sugar
½ cup water, *or more*
4 Tbsp. vinegar
½ tsp. salt
1 drop oil of cloves
1 drop oil of cinnamon

1. Pack cantaloupe into quart jar.

2. Mix all other ingredients and bring to a boil. Pour hot syrup over cantaloupe in jar. Can according to your canner's instructions.

3. I enjoyed spiced cantaloupe as a girl when my mother made it. Today I make it for my own family.

VARIATIONS

1. *Multiply this recipe and do more than one jar at a time.*

2. *Eliminate oil of cloves and oil of cinnamon and have pickled cantaloupe instead of spiced cantaloupe.*

# Grace's Chow Chow

GRACE KAUFFMAN, FUNK BROTHERS, INC.

*Makes 6–8 quarts*
*Prep. Time: 30 minutes*
*Cooking Time: 3-10 minutes for each vegetable, plus 20 minutes for mixture of vegetables*

I quart diced cucumbers

I quart string beans, green *or* yellow

I quart corn

I quart chopped celery

I quart fresh lima beans

I pint chopped green bell peppers

I pint chopped red bell peppers

I cup small onions, *optional*

I quart vinegar

3 cups sugar

I cup water

½ tsp. turmeric

I Tbsp. salt

1. Chop all vegetables to desired size. Cook each one separately until tender but not soft. Drain vegetables and mix together.

2. In a large kettle, combine vinegar, sugar, and water. Bring to a boil. Add turmeric and salt.

3. Add all vegetables to hot liquid and bring to boiling point.

4. Pack into hot jars and seal according to your canner's instructions.

NOTE

*Typically Pennsylvania Dutch! Looks like a quilt in a jar.*

VARIATION

*Use dried lima beans that have been soaked and cooked until they are just tender.*

# The North American, Philadelphia, Sunday, July 5, 1908

## HOW IS THIS FOR A HOUSEWIFE'S PARADISE?

*If there is a paradise for the market goer, it should be Lancaster. The fame of the fair city and its wonderful markets has spread beyond the borders of the state. Many Philadelphians go there to purchase supplies for their tables.*

*Fresh and delicious from the surrounding country, these supplies come every market day, and the prices prevailing are astonishingly cheap, when compared with those of larger cities. Market Day in Lancaster is an institution, and one of which the pretty city is justly proud. And its busy scenes are full of interest for the chance visitor.*

Beginning about 1 o'clock every market morning, miscellaneous processions of vehicles from various directions clatter and rumble into Lancaster.

Entering the city, the wagons pass down tree embowered streets, glimmering with the fitful blue luster of electric lamps. Closed shutters frown down upon the picturesque drivers of the wagons—men with patriarchal beards and broad-brimmed hats and women huddled up on the seats wearing plain dresses with peaked capes and plain bonnets.

To various hotels in the city they drive the wagons. They go into the rear sheds of the Farmer's Hotel, the Franklin House, the Sorrel Horse, the Lincoln and the Leopard. While a man climbs out and ties the horse a woman jumps from the wagon, several young girls, even children, appear mysteriously, rubbing their eyes. A lantern is lit and they begin unloading the wagon—a wagon bursting with fatness—of baskets of vegetables, eggs, butter, meat, chickens and a plethora of things good to eat.

By the time the sun rises, more than 1500 farmers will have arrived, and by 10 o'clock possibly from 10,000 to 12,000 people will have purchased their eatables. Considering the size of the city, it is possibly the biggest market in the United States, and, many claim, the cheapest.

At 2 o'clock Saturday morning the doors of the Central Market House are opened; at 3 the buyers began to arrive. At the other markets people go still earlier. By 9 or 10 the markets are over.

"The people who don't want to get up in the morning," declared a citizen, "go to the afternoon market." This market, however, is largely attended by the families of working men who get paid Saturday morning.

Saturday is the big market day. From outlying towns, people come on trolley cars with great big baskets. From towns five, 10 and 15 miles away, thrifty housewives come; even from Philadelphia many come on Saturdays with great hampers, to [gather] in the week's supply of vegetables. Scores of families of railroad employees living in Philadelphia who enjoy annual passes do their marketing in Lancaster.

From 4 o'clock in the morning—before the sun illumines the narrow streets about it—until after 9 o'clock, crowds throng the market house. From 500 to 1000 persons flow in a steady stream along the aisles between the stalls at times.

Most of them are women, with big baskets holding a bushel of stuff. Some evidently are poor, with cheap dresses; others very elegantly attired.

Mayor J. P. McCaskey naturally regards Lancaster with pride.

"There is no doubt the markets are about the finest and cheapest in the country," he declared. "The people of the country get their wealth from the soil—they don't depend upon Wall Street."

# Ten-Day Pickles

ETHEL STONER, JOHN R. STONER VEGETABLES

*Makes 12 pints*
*Prep. Time: about 15 minutes a day for 10 days*
*Cooking Time: 2½ hours total*

7 lbs. of 6"-7" long, 1"-thick cucumbers
½ cup salt
2 quarts water, *divided*
4 cups water
1 Tbsp. alum
5 cups vinegar, *divided*
4 lbs. sugar
3 cinnamon sticks, ¾-oz. total
2 Tbsp. celery seed
2 Tbsp. whole allspice

1. Slice cucumbers into ¾"-thick slices and place into large crock. Cover with a mixture of ½ cup salt dissolved in 4 cups water. Double liquid, if necessary, to cover slices.

2. Allow cucumbers to soak in this mixture for three days.

3. After third day, drain and cover completely with cold water. Do this each day for days 4, 5, and 6.

4. On day 7, drain again and cook pickles in a solution of 4 cups water, alum, and 1 cup vinegar. Bring to a boil, and boil over low heat for 2 hours, covered.

5. After cooking, drain and pour liquid away. Return pickles to crock.

6. Mix sugar, 4 cups vinegar, cinnamon sticks, celery seed, and allspice, and bring to a boil. Boil for 3 minutes. Pour hot liquid over pickles in crock.

7. On days 8 and 9, drain liquid and save it. Reheat liquid to boiling point and pour over pickles again.

8. On day 10 heat pickles and liquid to boiling. Place in jars and seal according to your canner's instructions.

# Zucchini Pepper Relish

### REBECCA KING, JOHN R. STONER VEGETABLES

*Makes 5–6 pints*
*Prep. Time: 20 minutes* ❧ *Chilling Time: overnight* ❧ *Cooking Time: 40 minutes*

10 cups chopped zucchini

4 sweet bell peppers, chopped

4 cups chopped onions

⅓ cup salt

3½ cups sugar

2½ cups vinegar

1 tsp. turmeric

½ tsp. celery seed

½ tsp. black pepper

1. Put zucchini, peppers, and onions into a bowl. Stir in salt and refrigerate overnight.

2. Drain and rinse in cold water.

3. Add all other ingredients to mixture and bring to a boil.

4. Boil for 30 minutes and put into jars to seal. Follow your canner's directions to can.

# Barbecue Relish

### RUTH WIDDERS, IRWIN S. WIDDERS PRODUCE

*Makes about 11–13 pints* ❧ *Standing Time: 12 hours* ❧ *Cooking Time: 1 hour or longer*

10 cucumbers

15 green tomatoes

½ cup salt

2 green sweet bell peppers

4 red sweet bell peppers

8 large onions

1 stalk celery, about 8 ribs

4 cups cider vinegar

2 Tbsp. flour

1 tsp. turmeric

1 Tbsp. celery seed

1 tsp. mustard seed

1 tsp. dry mustard powder

6 cups granulated sugar

1. Take center seeds out of cucumbers. Grind cucumbers and tomatoes (not too fine). Add ½ cup salt and let stand covered for ½ day. Strain off juice.

2. Meanwhile, put sweet peppers, onions, and celery through a grinder.

3. Pour into large kettle and cover with cider vinegar. Add flour, turmeric, celery seed, mustard seed, mustard powderd, and sugar.

4. Stir in tomato-cucumber mixture.

5. Boil uncovered for 1 hour or longer until it thickens.

6. Can in pint jars according to the instructions with your canner.

# Stuffed Eggs

HELEN THOMAS, HELEN THOMAS PRODUCE

*Makes 12 halves*
*Prep. Time: 15 minutes*

6 hard-boiled eggs
2 Tbsp. mayonnaise
1 tsp. vinegar
¼ tsp. salt
dash of pepper
¼ tsp. paprika
½ tsp. prepared mustard

1. Cut eggs in half and remove yolks. Set aside white parts of eggs.

2. Mash yolks and blend with all remaining ingredients. Fill the whites of the eggs with this mixture. Serve.

# Red Beet Eggs

JOYCE DEITER, EISENBERGER'S BAKED GOODS

*Makes 1 dozen eggs*
*Prep. Time: 20 minutes*  ❧  *Cooking Time: 15 minutes*  ❧  *Chilling Time: 12 hours*

12 eggs
½ cup brown sugar
½ cup granulated sugar
½ tsp. salt
¼ cup water
¾ cup vinegar
1 quart canned red beets and juice

1. Cover eggs with lukewarm water in a saucepan. Heat until water comes to a full boil. Remove from heat and let stand in water for 20 minutes. Run cold water over eggs to cool them quickly. Peel eggs.

2. Mix brown sugar, granulated sugar, salt, water, and vinegar in a saucepan. Heat until sugar is dissolved, stirring occasionally.

3. Add red beets and juice to this mixture and pour over the peeled eggs.

4. Refrigerate at least 12 hours.

5. Serve eggs sliced in half.

"Dandelion greens are a scavenger's delight (or you can buy them at Central Market). They must be gathered before flowering, or the end result is too bitter and tough. Look along fence rows or at the edges of wooded areas. The large single clumps are easiest to clean. Cut the dandelion out of the ground with a knife. Cut at the root which is below the heart. This will keep the plant together when you wash the greens."

—Sam Neff, S. Clyde Weaver

# VEGETABLES AND PASTAS

## Potato Filling

ANNA MARY NEFF, S. CLYDE WEAVER, INC.

*Makes 10–12 servings*
*Prep. Time: 20 minutes* ❧ *Cooking/Baking Time: 1 hour*

6 cups boiled potatoes

3 eggs

1 ½ cups milk

2-3 cups dry bread crumbs *or* cubes

½ cup (1 stick) butter

½ cup chopped onions

1 cup chopped celery

½ cup chopped parsley

salt and pepper to taste

small amount crushed saffron, *optional*

¼ cup water, *optional*

1. Mash potatoes and add eggs, milk, and bread crumbs. Mix well.

2. Sauté onions and celery lightly in butter.

3. Add to potato mixture.

4. Add parsley and salt and pepper to taste.

5. If you want to add saffron, soak it in ¼ cup water. Add to potato mixture.

6. Mix well and pour into a greased casserole. Bake at 350° for 45 minutes to 1 hour until golden brown.

NOTE

*Saffron is a seasoning used in Lancaster County to flavor chicken and other recipes made with chicken. It is the stamen of the saffron crocus flower. The best comes from Spain. I always use only a small amount.*

# Bread Filling

MRS. ROBERT FUNK, FUNK BROTHERS, INC.

*Makes 4 servings* ❧ *Prep. Time: 15 minutes* ❧ *Cooking/Baking Time: 1½ hours*

½ cup (1 stick) butter
¼ cup chopped onion
¼ cup chopped celery
2 eggs
½ tsp. poultry seasoning
1 tsp. parsley flakes
salt and pepper to taste
pinch saffron
2 cups milk
12-oz. pkg. bread cubes

1. Melt butter in large stockpot. Add celery and onion, and cook until tender.

2. In blender, mix eggs, seasonings, and milk.

3. Pour egg mixture over bread cubes.

4. Fold into butter mixture on stove. Cook over low heat about 20 minutes, stirring occasionally.

5. Put in greased baking dish and bake at 250° for 1 hour.

# Gourmet Potatoes

ROSE MECK, MECK'S PRODUCE
MRS. ROBERT FUNK, FUNK BROTHERS, INC.

*Makes 8 servings* ❧ *Prep. Time: 20 minutes* ❧ *Cooking/Baking Time: 1 hour*

6 large potatoes
¼ cup (half stick) butter, melted
⅓ cup chopped onion
1-2 cups shredded cheddar cheese
1 cup sour cream
1 tsp. salt
¼ tsp. pepper
paprika

1. Cook potatoes in skins. Refrigerate until chilled through.

2. Peel and shred coarsely.

3. In a saucepan, sauté onion in butter. Do not brown.

4. Fold potatoes, onion, cheese, and sour cream together. Add salt and pepper. Sprinkle with paprika.

5. Place in a greased baking dish and bake at 350° for 25 minutes or until potatoes are bubbling hot.

HINT

*You can make these ahead of time and freeze them until you're ready to serve them.*

# Scalloped Potatoes

RUTH THOMAS, THOMAS PRODUCE

*Makes 8 servings*
*Prep. Time: 20 minutes  ❧  Baking Time: 1 hour*

8 medium potatoes
1 medium onion, diced
8 slices bacon, diced
½ cup flour
1 tsp. salt
¼ tsp. pepper
1 cup milk, *or* less

1. Wash potatoes. Peel them if you wish. Cut into thin slices.

2. In a greased casserole dish layer potatoes, onion, bacon, flour, salt, and pepper. Repeat layers.

3. Make sure there is a 2-inch space between top layer and top of casserole dish.

4. Pour enough milk over potatoes to almost cover potatoes.

5. Bake at 350° for 1 hour or until done. Stir once while baking.

TIP

*To prevent casserole from cooking over, always use raw bacon and an uncovered dish. Fat from the bacon keeps the milk from boiling over.*

*The Pennsylvania Dutch like their meat and potato meals! "We grow potatoes, so we often serve them."*

# Sweet Potato Croquettes

RUTH WIDDERS, IRWIN S. WIDDERS PRODUCE

*Makes 40 large croquettes*
*Prep. Time: 30 minutes*
*Cooking/Baking Time: 1 hour*
*Chilling Time: overnight*

12 lbs. sweet potatoes
¾ cup (1½ sticks) butter, melted
3 tsp. salt
½ cup brown sugar
½ tsp. black pepper
5 eggs, beaten
2-3 cups bread crumbs
1 cup vegetable oil

1. Cook sweet potatoes until soft. Drain and peel them. Mash either by hand or with an electric mixer.

2. Add butter, salt, sugar, and pepper. Mix well and refrigerate overnight.

3. Form mixture into croquettes, each in the shape of a small egg. Dip each croquette in beaten egg and then into the crumbs.

4. Fry in the oil, turning until evenly browned. Do not let them get too dark.

5. Lay on baking sheets lined with waxed paper and freeze.

6. After croquettes are frozen, package and store in freezer.

7. To serve, heat in 325° oven for 20 minutes.

NOTE

*Easy last-minute meal to pull from the freezer.*

**From the other side of the Market stand . . .**

# Rose Meck of Meck's Produce

Rose Meck's grandfather, Frank Hess, sold fresh produce at Central Market. Today, Rose and Bob's two adult sons run the family's good-sized stand.

"My parents, Irwin and Ruth Widders, took over the stand from my grandpa when I was eight or nine, so Market has just always been part of my life. And we raised our kids here," Rose reflects.

"We have 65 acres in southern Lancaster County, and our sons rent another 20 acres. That's where we grow most of our in-season produce, especially sweet corn, tomatoes, peppers—and sunflowers!

"In 1975, my parents were voted 'the favorite stand on Central Market.' Part of the reward was having the Mayor of Lancaster work at our stand. I remember him selling strawberries. Today's Mayor and his wife are also our regular customers.

"Whenever someone at our stand has a birthday, the Hole in the Wall Puppet Theatre owner and puppeteer always stands in the aisle and announces it to everyone—then leads 'Happy Birthday' for all to join in who are nearby!"

# Sweet Potato and Apple Casserole

ROSE MECK, MECK'S PRODUCE

*Makes 6 servings*
*Prep. Time: 15 minutes    ❦    Baking Time: about 1 hour*

6 sweet potatoes

2 cups apple slices, peeled

½ cup brown sugar, firmly packed

½ tsp. salt

2 Tbsp. butter

1. Cook sweet potatoes until tender. Chill.

2. Peel and cut into slices.

3. Grease a 2-quart casserole dish. In it, arrange alternating layers of sweet potatoes and apple slices.

4. Sprinkle brown sugar and salt over top. Dot with 2 Tbsp. butter.

5. Bake uncovered at 350° for 50 minutes.

NOTE

*Great potato dish for Thanksgiving!*

# Sweet Potato Pudding

RUTH WIDDERS, IRWIN S. WIDDERS PRODUCE

*Makes 6 servings*
Prep. Time: 20 minutes ❦ Cooking/Baking Time: about 1 hour

3 or 4 good-sized sweet
potatoes; enough to make 2-3
cups mashed sweet potatoes

6 Tbsp. brown sugar

1 tsp. salt

2 tsp. butter, melted

1 cup milk

2 eggs

1 cup miniature marshmallows

1. Cook sweet potatoes in skins until soft. Peel and mash.

2. Add sugar, salt, melted butter, and milk. (It is best to add ingredients while potatoes are still hot.)

3. Add eggs and beat well with mixer.

4. Pour into a greased baking dish. Top casserole with marshmallows.

5. Bake at 350° for 45 minutes, or until center is completely set.

HINT

*This dish may be prepared in advance. Great for Thanksgiving and Christmas dinner.*

# Sweet Potato Casserole

PATRICIA A. CARTER, MCCOMSEY FAMILY

*Makes 6 servings*
*Prep. Time: 20 minutes* ❧ *Baking Time: 30 minutes*

4-5 good-sized sweet potatoes;
enough to make 3-4 cups
mashed potatoes

⅓ cup sugar

2 eggs

1 tsp. vanilla

½ cup milk

½ cup (1 stick) butter, melted

*Topping Ingredients:*

1 cup brown sugar

⅓ cup flour

⅓ cup butter, softened

1 cup chopped pecans

1. Cook sweet potatoes in skins until soft. Peel and mash.

2. Add sugar, eggs, vanilla, milk, and melted butter to mashed potatoes. Mix well.

3. In a separate bowl, cut topping ingredients together with pastry cutter until crumbly.

4. Place sweet potato mixture in a greased baking dish. Sprinkle with topping mixture.

5. Bake at 350° for 30 minutes.

# Baked Corn

LOUELLA E. GROFF, C. Z. MARTIN SONS
REBECCA KING, JOHN R. STONER VEGETABLES

*Makes 4 servings*
*Prep. Time: 10 minutes*
*Baking Time: 40 minutes*

2 cups corn, cooked

1 cup milk

⅔ cup cracker *or* bread crumbs

3 Tbsp. butter, melted

½ tsp. salt

⅛ tsp. pepper

1 Tbsp. sugar

2 eggs

1 tsp. minced onion

1. Combine all ingredients in a blender and mix lightly.

2. Pour into a greased 1-quart baking dish and bake at 350° for 40 minutes.

### NOTE

*Grandma used to make this for us when we went to her place.*

### VARIATIONS

1. *Use 2½ cups cream-style corn plus 1 Tbsp. flour instead of whole-kernel corn. To bake, place baking dish in a large pan with 1" of water.*

2. *Use 2½ cups frozen corn. Thaw, and add 2 Tbsp. flour to thicken corn.*

 *This is a real comfort food. My two grown sons always want me to make corn pudding when they come home for a meal.*

GRACE KAUFFMAN, Funk Brothers, Inc.

# Corn Fritters

RUTH WIDDERS, IRWIN S. WIDDERS PRODUCE

*Makes 4 servings*
Prep. Time: 20 minutes ❦ Cooking Time: 10-15 minutes

2 eggs

½ cup milk

1 pint corn, drained

1 cup flour, sifted

1 tsp. baking powder

1 tsp. salt

1 tsp. sugar

1 tsp. oil

½ cup cooking oil

1. Beat eggs and stir in milk.

2. Add corn and beat in flour, baking powder, salt, sugar, and 1 tsp. oil.

3. Heat cooking oil by tablespoonfuls as needed in a saucepan. Drop corn mixture by tablespoonfuls into hot oil. Turn to brown. Drain and serve hot.

### VARIATION

*Serve with maple syrup or powdered sugar.*

# Corn Pie

CYNTHIA STRUBE, MARION CHEESE

*Makes 1 9" pie*
*Prep. Time: 30 minutes  ❦  Baking Time: 1 hour*

2 cups fresh corn
½ cup milk
1 Tbsp. butter
1 tsp. salt
1 tsp. sugar
1 Tbsp. parsley, chopped
2 hard-boiled eggs, diced
1 9" double unbaked pie crust

1. Heat corn with milk and butter.

2. Remove from heat and carefully stir in remaining ingredients.

3. Place corn mixture in bottom crust in pie pan.

4. Cover top with pastry. Pinch or flute edges together. Prick top with fork.

5. Bake at 400° for 10 minutes. Reduce oven temperature to 325° and bake an additional 35 minutes. Serve hot.

# Broccoli Rice Dish

SARA JANE WENGER, TOM'S FLOWER GARDEN

*Makes 6 servings*

Prep. Time: 15 minutes ❧ Cooking/Baking Time: 50 minutes

½ cup rice

4 Tbsp. (half stick) butter

1 cup chopped celery

1 small onion, chopped

2 cups chopped fresh broccoli

10-oz. can cream of mushroom soup

1 cup grated sharp cheese

1 cup buttered bread crumbs *or* crushed corn flakes

1. Cook rice according to directions on package.

2. Sauté celery and onion in butter until tender.

3. Thoroughly mix all ingredients together except bread crumbs or corn flakes.

4. Pour into greased baking dish and top with bread crumbs or crushed corn flakes.

5. Bake at 350° for 30 minutes.

# Cauliflower Casserole

RUTH THOMAS, THOMAS PRODUCE

*Serves 4-6*

*Prep. Time: 20 minutes* ✿ *Cooking/Baking Time: 35 minutes*

4 Tbsp. (half stick) butter
4 Tbsp. flour
1 ½ tsp. salt, *divided*
2 cups milk
1 large head fresh cauliflower
2 hard-boiled eggs
¼ tsp. pepper
¼ cup creamy mild cheese cubes
½ cup buttered bread crumbs

1. Prepare white sauce by melting butter in heavy saucepan. Add flour and 1 tsp. salt and stir until well blended.

2. Slowly add milk, stirring constantly until smooth and bubbly.

3. Cut head of cauliflower into florets and cook until soft. Drain.

4. Mix eggs, ½ tsp. salt, pepper, cheese cubes, and cooked cauliflower together in a large bowl.

5. Add white sauce to mixture and stir well. Pour into greased 1½-quart baking dish.

6. Place bread crumbs on top.

7. Bake at 375° for 25 minutes.

VARIATION

*Substitute broccoli for cauliflower.*

# Gnocchi with Roasted Cauliflower

DELGIORNO'S ITALIAN SPECIALTIES

*Makes 4 servings*
*Prep. Time: 15 minutes ❧ Baking/Cooking Time: 30 minutes*

I small head fresh cauliflower, cut into small florets

12 fresh sage leaves

3 Tbsp. olive oil

½ tsp. kosher salt

¼ tsp. black pepper

I lb. frozen gnocchi

¼ cup grated Parmigiano Reggiano cheese

1. On a rimmed baking sheet, toss cauliflower, sage, oil, salt, and pepper. Place in oven and roast at 400° for 25–30 minutes, or until the cauliflower is golden brown and tender. Toss once during roasting.

2. While the cauliflower is roasting, cook the gnocchi according to the package directions.

3. Dip out 1 cup of the pasta water and set aside.

4. Drain the remaining water off gnocchi and place gnocchi in a large serving dish.

5. Toss gnocchi with roasted cauliflower and Parmigiano Reggiano cheese.

6. Add a bit of the reserved pasta cooking water if the pasta seems dry after it's been tossed with the roasted cauliflower and cheese.

# Spicy Green Beans

SARA JANE WENGER, TOM'S FLOWER GARDEN

*Makes 6 servings* ❦ *Prep. Time: 20 minutes* ❦ *Cooking/Baking Time: 1 hour 20 minutes*

3 cups chopped tomatoes
2 Tbsp. minced onion
2 Tbsp. diced celery
1 Tbsp. sugar
½ tsp. oregano
1 bay leaf
½ tsp. chili powder
dash of red pepper
½ tsp. garlic salt
⅛ tsp. cloves
⅛ tsp. pepper
2 Tbsp. flour
½ cup water
1 quart canned green beans
½ cup buttered bread crumbs
¼ cup cheese, grated

1. Mix tomatoes, onions, celery, sugar, and all seasonings and spices together. Simmer 15 minutes.

2. Mix flour with water to form a paste. Add to tomato mixture and cook until thickened.

3. Pour green beans into a casserole dish. Pour tomato mixture over beans. Top with bread crumbs and grated cheese.

4. Bake at 350° for 1 hour.

# Barbecued Lima Beans

ETHEL STONER, JOHN R. STONER VEGETABLES

*Makes 6–8 servings* ❦ *Prep. Time: 10 minutes* ❦ *Baking Time: 1 hour*

¾ cup chopped onion
½–1 cup brown sugar
1 cup ketchup
⅔ cup dark corn syrup
29-oz. can dried white lima beans
1 tsp. salt
1 Tbsp. liquid smoke
9 drops Tabasco sauce
½ lb. bacon slices, browned

1. Combine onion, sugar, ketchup, and syrup in a large bowl.

2. Drain lima beans and stir into mixture. Add seasonings.

3. Brown bacon and crumble it. Add bacon to bean mixture.

4. Pour into baking dish and bake uncovered at 400° for 1 hour or until beans are bubbly hot.

# Scalloped Carrots

MARY ELLEN SPEICHER, SALLIE Y. LAPP

*Makes 8–10 servings*
*Prep. Time: 20 minutes   ❧   Cooking/Baking Time: 1 hour*

12 medium carrots
4 Tbsp. (half stick) butter
4 Tbsp. flour
1½ cups milk
¼ cup chopped onions
¾ tsp. celery salt
½ cup diced cheese
1 tsp. prepared mustard
⅛ tsp. pepper
½ cup crushed potato chips

1. Dice carrots and cook until tender, but not too soft.

2. Make a white sauce by melting butter over medium heat. Add flour and stir until well mixed. Slowly add milk, stirring constantly.

3. Add onions, celery salt, cheese, mustard, and pepper.

4. Pour carrots into greased baking dish. Top with white sauce.

5. Top with crushed potato chips.

6. Bake at 350° for 45 minutes.

# Ginger Lime Carrots

SAM NEFF, S. CLYDE WAVER, INC.

*Makes 8–10 servings*
*Prep. Time: 10 minutes   ❧   Cooking Time: 15 minutes*

3 lbs. carrots, peeled and sliced
3 cups water
1½ tsp. salt
2 Tbsp. butter
2 Tbsp. honey
2 Tbsp. fresh lime juice
1 Tbsp. grated lime peel
1 Tbsp. grated fresh ginger root
lime slices, for garnish

1. Cook carrots for 10 minutes in 3 cups salt water. Drain water from carrots.

2. Heat butter, honey, lime juice, lime peel, and ginger in a saucepan for 5 minutes.

3. Pour glaze over carrots and stir until well glazed.

4. Put carrots in serving dish and garnish with lime slices.

# Cheese and Honey-Glazed Carrots

### DEB MARTIN, MARTIN'S HOME-BAKED GOODS

*Makes 4–6 servings* ❧ *Prep. Time: 15 minutes* ❧ *Cooking/Baking Time: 25 minutes*

6 large carrots, peeled and halved lengthwise

salt, to taste

¼ cup honey

1 cup shredded cheese

1. Cook carrots in a small amount of boiling salt water until carrots are just tender, about 10 minutes. Do not overcook.

2. Drain and place carrots in a greased baking dish. Drizzle with honey. Sprinkle shredded cheese over carrots.

3. Bake at 400° for 10 minutes, or broil until cheese melts.

# Asparagus Mushroom Casserole

### HELEN E. BITNER, BITNERS

*Makes 6 servings* ❧ *Prep. Time: 20 minutes* ❧ *Cooking/Baking Time: 40 minutes*

2 lbs. fresh asparagus

½ lb. mushrooms, cleaned and sliced

½ cup (1 stick) butter, *divided*

6 Tbsp. flour

3 cups milk

1 tsp. salt

1 tsp. chives

2 tsp. finely chopped pimento

3 hard-boiled eggs, sliced

1 cup buttered bread crumbs

1. Cut asparagus in pieces and cook until just tender. Set aside.

2. Sauté mushrooms in 2 Tbsp. butter. Set aside.

3. Melt 6 Tbsp. butter in heavy saucepan. Blend in flour, cooking and stirring until mixture is bubbly. Slowly add milk, stirring constantly. Heat until white sauce is thickened and smooth.

4. Remove from heat and add salt, chives, and pimento.

5. Stir mushrooms and eggs into white sauce.

6. Place drained asparagus in greased 2-quart baking dish. Cover with mushroom and white sauce mixture.

7. Sprinkle bread crumbs over top and bake at 325° for 20 minutes.

 *Drop mushrooms. Reduce salt to ½ tsp. Add ¾ grated sharp cheese in Step 5.*

– RUTH WIDDERS, Irwin S. Widders Produce

# Spinach Casserole

ETHEL STONER, JOHN R. STONER VEGETABLES

*Makes 6 servings* ❧ *Prep. Time: 20 minutes* ❧ *Cooking/Baking Time: 30-40 minutes*

2 lbs. fresh spinach, *or* 4 10-oz. pkgs. frozen spinach

3 Tbsp. butter

½ cup chopped onion

1 cup buttered bread crumbs

2 Tbsp. flour

1 cup milk

1 cup grated cheddar cheese

1. Steam spinach until wilted, or thaw and squeeze dry. Drain.

2. Heat butter and sauté onion until tender but not brown.

3. Add flour. Blend gradually.

4. Add milk, stirring constantly.

5. When thickened, add cheese and heat until melted.

6. Place steamed spinach in a greased baking dish. Pour cheese sauce over spinach and top with bread crumbs.

7. Bake at 400° for 20-30 minutes.

# Dandelion Greens With Hot Bacon Dressing

SAM NEFF, S. CLYDE WEAVER, INC.

*Makes 6–8 servings* ❧ *Prep. Time: 20 minutes* ❧ *Cooking Time: about 15 minutes*

5 strips lean bacon

3 Tbsp. flour

½ cup brown sugar

⅔ cup water

⅓ cup vinegar

4-6 quarts dandelion greens

1. Fry bacon and remove from pan.

2. Brown flour in drippings in saucepan. Add brown sugar, water, and vinegar. Heat until mixture thickens, stirring constantly.

3. Remove from heat and add crumbled bacon to mixture.

4. Fill a 6-quart kettle with cleaned dandelion greens and steam until tender. Drain.

5. Toss dressing and dandelion greens together and serve.

VARIATION

*Garnish with hard-boiled eggs.*

# GATHERING DANDELION GREENS

Dandelion is one of those special vegetables that brings back many memories of growing up in Lancaster County. Hot Bacon Dressing is a traditional sweet and sour. The proportions of sugar and vinegar may be adjusted to the individual's preference. Generally, we in Lancaster enjoy more sour. The above recipe is medium.

Dandelion greens are a scavenger's delight (or you can buy them at Central Market). They must be gathered before flowering or the end result is too bitter and tough. Look along fence rows or at the edges of wooded areas. The large single clumps are easiest to clean. Cut the dandelion out of the ground with a knife. Cut at the root which is below the heart. This will keep the plant together when you wash the greens.

After gathering a nice shopping bag full, clean each plant under running water and remove dead leaves around the exterior. Rinse thoroughly. Before putting the greens into a kettle for steaming, cut off the root and a bit of the heart so the leaves separate. The heart buds are also edible if not too large.

The season for dandelion greens is short, but I look forward to it every year. I make mental notes of where I see the flowers blooming in the spring and return to those spots the following March. I now live in the city of Lancaster and find that the cemeteries are great dandelion beds. This is especially true if they are fenced and have little pet traffic!

—SAM NEFF, S. Clyde Weaver, Inc.

# Brussels Sprouts Sauté

FUNK BROTHERS, INC.

*Makes 4 servings* ❧ *Prep. Time: 10 minutes* ❧ *Cooking Time: 6-8 minutes*

3 Tbsp. butter

2 large carrots, sliced

2 cups Brussels sprouts, halved

1 medium leek, sliced

1 Tbsp. water

¼ tsp. caraway seeds

¼ tsp. salt

⅛ tsp. pepper

sour cream, *optional*

1. Melt butter in a large skillet over medium heat. Sauté carrots for 3 minutes.

2. Stir in Brussels sprouts and leeks, and sauté 2 more minutes.

3. Add water. Cover and steam for 5 minutes or until Brussels sprouts are crispy tender. Add additional water, if necessary.

4. Sprinkle with caraway seeds, salt, and pepper. Serve with a dollop of sour cream, if you wish.

NOTE

*This vegetable combination has a wonderful flavor!*

# Eggplant Creole

ETHEL STONER, JOHN R. STONER VEGETABLES

*Makes 4–6 servings* ❧ *Prep. Time: 20 minutes* ❧ *Cooking/Baking Time: 45 minutes*

1 medium eggplant, peeled and diced

salt water

3 Tbsp. butter

3 Tbsp. flour

3 large tomatoes, peeled and chopped, *or* 2 cups canned tomatoes

1 small green bell pepper, chopped

1 small onion, chopped

1 tsp. salt

1 Tbsp. brown sugar

1 bay leaf

2 whole cloves

½-¾ cup bread crumbs

butter

1. Boil eggplant cubes in salt water for 12 minutes. Drain and place into greased baking dish.

2. In heavy saucepan, melt butter. Add flour and stir until well blended.

3. Add tomatoes, pepper, and onion to butter and flour mixture.

4. Add salt, brown sugar, bay leaf, and cloves. Cook 5-10 minutes.

5. Remove bay leaf and cloves. Pour mixture over eggplant in baking dish.

6. Cover with bread crumbs and dot with butter.

7. Bake at 350° for 30 minutes.

# Baked Eggplant Casserole

MILDRED BRACKBILL, UTZ'S POTATO CHIPS

*Makes 6–8 servings* ❦ *Prep. Time: 10 minutes* ❦ *Baking Time: 30 minutes*

2 cups cubed eggplant
2 eggs, beaten
2 Tbsp. flour
2 Tbsp. butter
1 cup milk
1 small onion, finely chopped
2 slices bread, torn into cubes
1 tsp. salt
1 Tbsp. ketchup
¼ tsp. pepper
1 cup shredded sharp cheese

1. Mix all ingredients together thoroughly except cheese.

2. Pour into greased baking dish. Top with cheese.

3. Bake at 350° for 30 minutes.

# Eggplant Parmesan

ROSE MECK, MECK'S PRODUCE

*Makes 6 servings* ❦ *Prep. Time: 20 minutes* ❦ *Cooking/Baking Time: 30 minutes*

1 medium eggplant
1 Tbsp. cooking oil
1 cup bread crumbs
½ cup grated Parmesan cheese
2 Tbsp. parsley flakes
1 tsp. salt
1 tsp. dried oregano
6 small tomatoes, chopped
2 medium onions, chopped
1 green *or* red bell pepper, chopped
2 dashes garlic salt
2 Tbsp. oil
½ cup tomato sauce
1 cup cheddar cheese, grated

1. Peel eggplant. Cut into ½"-thick slices and brown lightly on both sides in cooking oil. Place into a 9"x13" greased baking dish.

2. Mix bread crumbs, Parmesan cheese, parsley flakes, salt, and oregano together. Cover each eggplant slice with this mixture.

3. In a saucepan combine tomatoes, onions, peppers, garlic salt, oil, and tomato sauce. Simmer 15 minutes.

4. Spread on top of eggplant in baking dish.

5. Top with grated cheddar cheese.

6. Bake at 375° for 15 minutes.

# Easy Eggplant Bake

ETHEL STONER, JOHN R. STONER VEGETABLES

*Makes 8 servings* ❦ *Prep. Time: 20 minutes* ❦ *Cooking/Baking Time: 45 minutes*

1 medium eggplant

salt and pepper to taste

1 medium onion, chopped

1 cup sliced fresh mushrooms

1-2 Tbsp. butter

10-oz. can cream of mushroom soup

1 cup buttered bread crumbs

¼ tsp. garlic salt

¼ tsp. paprika

1½ cups grated cheese

1. Pare, dice, and cook eggplant until soft. Salt and pepper to taste. Drain.

2. Place in greased 7"x11" baking dish.

3. Sauté onion and mushrooms in butter.

4. Add mushroom soup and pour over eggplant.

5. Season bread crumbs with garlic salt and paprika.

6. Cover ingredients in baking dish with a layer of cheese and then a layer of buttered bread crumbs.

7. Bake at 350° for 30 minutes.

# Butternut Squash Tart

WENDY HESS, WENDY JO'S HOMEMADE

*Makes 4–6 servings*
*Prep. Time: 20 minutes* ❦ *Baking Time: 40 minutes*

2 9" unbaked Wendy Jo's pie crusts

1 medium butternut squash, seeded, roasted, and cubed in ½" pieces

1 pint cherry tomatoes, halved

8 large eggs, beaten

2 Tbsp. nutritional yeast *or* Parmesan cheese

salt and pepper to taste

fresh oregano sprigs, for garnish

1. Bake pie crusts at 350° for 10 minutes.

2. Remove crusts from oven. Distribute vegetables and eggs between the two pie shells.

3. Sprinkle with nutritional yeast or cheese, salt, and pepper.

4. Bake until filling is firm, about 30 minutes.

5. Garnish with oregano.

# Baked Squash

SARA JANE WENGER, TOM'S FLOWER GARDEN

*Makes 4 servings*
*Prep. Time: 10 minutes ❧ Baking Time: 1 hour*

2 cups summer squash, cubed
6 Tbsp. butter, melted
1 cup chopped onion
1 cup grated cheese
½ cup milk
½ cup cream
2 cups bread cubes

1. Mix all ingredients together except bread cubes.

2. Pour into greased baking dish. Top with bread cubes.

3. Bake at 350° for 50 minutes.

4. Reduce oven temperature to 300° and bake another 10 minutes.

# Baked Zucchini Almondine

ETHEL STONER, JOHN R. STONER VEGETABLES

*Makes 6 servings*
*Prep. Time: 20 minutes ❧ Cooking/Baking Time: 35 minutes*

4 cups grated zucchini
1¼ cups grated cheese, *divided*
1 cup bread crumbs
¾ cup chopped onion
¼ tsp. garlic powder
3 Tbsp. butter
1 tsp. salt
¼ tsp. pepper
½ cup milk
2 eggs
½ cup slivered almonds

1. Combine zucchini, 1 cup cheese, and bread crumbs. Turn into greased 1½-quart casserole dish and set aside.

2. Sauté onion and garlic powder in butter. Add salt and pepper and blend into zucchini.

3. Combine milk and eggs and pour over zucchini mixture, stirring to moisten.

4. Top with remaining ¼ cup cheese and almonds. Bake at 350° for 30 minutes.

NOTE

*Of all the ways to prepare zucchini, this is the best!*

**Vegetables and Pastas** ❧ **121**

# Baked Zucchini

MRS. ADA ROHRER, JOHN M. MARKLEY MEATS

*Makes 4–6 servings*  ❧  *Prep. Time: 5 minutes*  ❧  *Baking Time: 45-55 minutes*

3 cups sliced zucchini

1½ cups cracker crumbs

3 eggs, beaten

½ tsp. salt

½ cup (1 stick) butter, melted

2 cups shredded cheddar cheese

1 cup milk

1. Mix all ingredients together and place in greased, uncovered baking dish.

2. Bake at 350° for 45-55 minutes or until set.

# Sage Butter Sauce for Pumpkin Ravioli

DELGIORNO'S ITALIAN SPECIALTIES

*Makes 2 servings*  ❧  *Prep. Time: 15 minutes*  ❧  *Cooking Time: 10-15 minutes*

1 cup olive oil

4 large shallots, cut crosswise into thin rounds, separated into rings

6 Tbsp. (¾ stick) butter

8 large fresh sage leaves, thinly sliced

½ tsp. dried crushed red pepper flakes

⅓ cup pine nuts, toasted

1 dozen pumpkin ravioli

1. Heat olive oil in heavy small saucepan over medium-high heat.

2. Working in 2 batches, fry shallots until crisp and dark brown, about 2 minutes.

3. Using slotted spoon, transfer shallots to paper-towel-lined plate to drain.

4. Cook butter in large pot over medium heat until beginning to brown, about 3 minutes.

5. Remove from heat.

6. Add sage and red pepper flakes to butter.

7. Meanwhile, cook pumpkin ravioli according to directions. Drain well.

8. Add ravioli to pot with butter sauce. Toss gently to coat.

9. Transfer to plates, drizzling any sauce left in pot over ravioli.

10. Top with fried shallots and pine nuts. Serve immediately.

# Hot Herbed Tomatoes

SAM NEFF, S. CLYDE WEAVER, INC.

*Makes 6 servings*
*Prep. Time: 10 minutes* ❧ *Baking Time: 16-18 minutes*

2 pints cherry tomatoes
¾ cup bread crumbs
⅓ cup minced onion
I clove garlic, minced
¼ cup minced fresh parsley
¼-½ tsp. dried thyme
¾ tsp. salt
¼ tsp. pepper
¼ cup olive oil

1. Line baking dish with tomatoes in a single layer. Bake at 375° for 10 minutes.

2. Mix bread crumbs, onion, garlic, parsley, thyme, salt, and pepper together. Spread over tomatoes. Drizzle olive oil over top. Broil for 6-8 minutes until browned and heated through. Serve.

# Tomato Pie

SARAH KING, DUTCH COUNTRY DELI

*Makes 6 servings*
*Prep. Time: 20 minutes* ❧ *Baking Time: 30 minutes*

2 cups buttermilk baking mix
⅔ cup milk
4 *or* 5 medium tomatoes, sliced
½ tsp. dried oregano
½ tsp. dried basil
½ tsp. dried parsley
½ tsp. salt
½ tsp. pepper
½ tsp. garlic powder
I cup mayonnaise
8 oz. shredded mozzarella cheese

1. Mix the buttermilk baking mix and milk.

2. Pat into 10" pie plate.

3. Place sliced tomatoes on crust.

4. Sprinkle oregano, basil, parsley, salt, pepper, and garlic powder on tomatoes.

5. Mix mayonnaise and cheese and spread on top.

6. Bake at 350° for 30 minutes or until pie is set.

# Orange Beets

ETHEL STONER, JOHN R. STONER VEGETABLES

*Makes 4 servings*
Prep. Time: 10 minutes
Cooking Time: 10-15 minutes

2-3 medium beets, peeled and grated
½ cup chopped onion
2 Tbsp. butter, melted
1 Tbsp. flour
3 Tbsp. orange juice
1 Tbsp. vinegar
3 Tbsp. brown sugar
¼ tsp. nutmeg

1. Cook beets in small amount of salt water until crisp tender (about 10-12 minutes).

2. Sauté onion in butter. Stir in flour, orange juice, vinegar, and sugar. Cook, stirring constantly, until well blended.

3. Pour sauce over cooked beets. Season with nutmeg and serve.

# Harvard Beets

MARY K. BREIGHNER, RUDOLPH BREIGHNER

*Makes 4-6 servings*
Prep. Time: 5 minutes
Standing Time: 30 minutes
Cooking Time: 10 minutes

½ cup sugar
1½ tsp. cornstarch
¼ cup mild vinegar
¼ cup water
12 small cooked beets, sliced
2 Tbsp. butter

1. In a saucepan, mix sugar and cornstarch. Add vinegar and water and bring to a boil. Boil 5 minutes, stirring frequently.

2. Add sliced beets to mixture and turn off heat. Let stand for 30 minutes or longer. Just before serving, bring to a boil. Add butter and serve.

# Cheese Scalloped Onions

MRS. ADA ROHRER, JOHN M. MARKLEY MEATS

*Makes 8 servings*
*Prep. Time: 20 minutes*
*Cooking/Baking Time: 50 minutes*

3 large onions, halved
1 cup cubed cheese
4 slices buttered toast, torn up
½ cup (1 stick) butter
½ cup flour
2 cups milk
½ tsp. salt
¼ tsp. pepper
2 eggs, beaten
½ cup bread crumbs

1. Cook onions in boiling water about 10-15 minutes. Stir to separate into rings. Drain well and place half of onions into a greased 2-quart baking dish.

2. Add half of cheese and 2 pieces toast. Repeat the layers.

3. Melt butter in saucepan, blend in flour, and stir in milk gradually. Cook, stirring constantly, until thick. Add salt and pepper.

4. Add a little white sauce to the beaten eggs. Gradually add this mixture to rest of white sauce. Pour sauce over layered onions. Top with bread crumbs.

5. Bake at 350° for 30 minutes.

# Roasted Summer Vegetables

JANELLE AND KENDAL YODER, LETTUCE TOSS SALAD

*Makes 6 servings*
*Prep. Time: 15 minutes*
*Cooking Time: 20 minutes*

10-12 cups chopped vegetables such as zucchini, yellow squash, bell peppers, onions, baby carrots, broccoli. Chopping vegetables that take longer to soften into smaller pieces helps mixture to cook evenly.

⅓ cup olive oil

⅓ cup balsamic or red wine vinegar

2 tsp. dried basil or ¼ chopped fresh basil

1. Whisk together olive oil, vinegar, and basil in roomy bowl.

2. Add chopped vegetables. Toss to coat.

3. Let marinate at room temperature for 15 minutes.

4. While vegetables marinate, preheat grill on high heat or oven to 400°.

5. Place marinated vegetables into a grill basket or spread out on a rimmed baking sheet.

6. For grilling: Place grill basket onto the grill. Turn heat down to medium low. Cover and grill for 15-20 minutes, stirring every 5 minutes.

7. For oven: Place baking sheet into oven and roast at 400° for 20 minutes, stirring every 5 minutes.

NOTES

*Whole baby carrots can be cooked in the microwave for a few minutes until slightly softened before adding to the other chopped vegetables.*

*This recipe pairs excellently with my Macaroni and Cheese recipe on page 130. This is a good vegetable dish for a family with picky eaters: just pick out the stuff you like!*

# Egg and Vegetable Casserole

ALICE SHENK, SHENK CHEESE CO.

*Makes 6–8 servings* ❦ *Prep. Time: 20 minutes* ❦ *Cooking/Baking Time: 30 minutes*

I cup diced potatoes
I cup diced celery
I cup diced carrots
I small onion, minced
4 Tbsp. (half stick) butter
4 Tbsp. flour
I tsp. salt
⅛ tsp. pepper
2 cups milk
4 hard-boiled eggs, sliced
½ cup grated cheese
¼ cup buttered bread crumbs

1. Cook and drain potatoes, celery, and carrots until as soft as you like them.

2. Sauté onion in butter until tender but not brown. Blend in flour, seasonings, and milk, stirring constantly.

3. Add drained vegetables and mix thoroughly.

4. Pour half of creamed vegetables into greased baking dish. Top with half of sliced eggs. Repeat layers.

5. Sprinkle top with cheese and bread crumbs.

6. Bake at 400° for 15-20 minutes or until slightly browned.

NOTE

*My mother made this dish over 50 years ago and served it as a one-dish meal along with home-canned fruit. I still enjoy it.*

# Vegetable Lasagna

ETHEL STONER, JOHN R. STONER VEGETABLES

*Makes 4–6 servings* ❦ *Prep. Time: 25 minutes* ❦ *Cooking Time: 55 minutes*

6 lasagna noodles

2 Tbsp. vegetable oil

1½ cups chopped onion

1 clove garlic, minced

1 green bell pepper, sliced

15-oz. can tomato sauce

15-oz. can tomato paste

1 large tomato, chopped

½ tsp. dried basil

1 tsp. dried oregano

1 lb. cottage cheese, small curd

1 cup grated Parmesan cheese, *divided*

1 egg, slightly beaten

2 10-oz. pkgs. chopped spinach, thawed, *or* 2 lbs. fresh spinach, chopped

2-3 Tbsp. butter

2½ cups zucchini, thinly sliced

2½ cups fresh mushrooms, sliced

6 oz. mozzarella cheese, sliced

1. Cook lasagna noodles until tender (about 5 minutes). Drain and rinse in cold water.

2. Mix together oil, onion, garlic, and green pepper. Cook on high in microwave uncovered for 2½ minutes.

3. Stir in tomato sauce, tomato paste, tomatoes, basil, and oregano. Mix well. Cook covered in microwave for 15 minutes (power 5).

4. Make a cheese mixture by mixing cottage cheese, ¼ cup Parmesan cheese, and beaten egg.

5. Make a spinach cheese mixture by squeezing moisture out of frozen spinach and folding in the remaining Parmesan cheese. Or mix chopped fresh spinach with cheese.

6. Sauté zucchini in 2-3 Tbsp. butter until tender.

TO ASSEMBLE LASAGNA:

1. Spread layer of tomato sauce in bottom of a greased glass baking dish.

2. Cover with three noodles.

3. Layer on ½ of zucchini, ½ of mushrooms, ½ of spinach cheese mixture, and ½ of cottage cheese mixture.

4. Repeat all of the above steps, beginning and ending with the sauce.

5. Microwave on high (power 10) for 10 minutes covered. Reduce to medium (power 5) and cook covered for 18 more minutes.

6. Top with mozzarella cheese. Cover and let stand for 5 minutes before serving.

### VARIATIONS

1. *Sauté onion, garlic, and green pepper on top of stove for 5 minutes or until tender. Add tomato sauce, tomato paste, tomato, basil, and oregano and mix well. Simmer for 20 minutes, covered.*

2. *After lasagna is assembled, bake in conventional oven for 45 minutes at 350°. Top with mozzarella cheese and return to oven for 5 more minutes.*

# My Homemade Noodles

MRS. WILLIAM MELLINGER, SHUTT'S CANDIES

*Makes about 4 cups noodles*
*Prep. Time: 30 minutes*

**4 medium eggs**
**3 cups all-purpose flour**

1. Beat eggs well. Add flour and mix.

2. Roll out dough as thinly as possible and cut into narrow strips.

3. When dough has partially dried, stack the strips and cut cross-wise into thin noodles. Allow to dry thoroughly before storing.

4. Prepare noodles for serving by adding to boiling water.

# Macaroni and Cheese

JANELLE AND KENDAL YODER, LETTUCE TOSS SALAD

*Makes 8 servings*
*Prep. Time: 20 minutes*
*Baking Time: 20 minutes*

8 oz. whole wheat pasta, uncooked

2 Tbsp. (¼ stick) butter

1 Tbsp. flour

¼ tsp. ground mustard

½ tsp. salt

⅛ tsp. freshly ground black pepper

1½ cups milk

8 oz. shredded cheddar cheese

***Optional Topping:***

2 Tbsp. (¼ stick) butter

¾ cup bread crumbs

1. Cook pasta according to package directions. Drain cooked pasta. Return to cooking pot on hot burner for a minute or two to dry cooked pasta. Pour pasta into greased 2-quart. baking dish.

2. While pasta cooks, make a white sauce by melting butter in saucepan over medium heat. Whisk in flour, mustard, salt, and pepper. Stir for 1 minute.

3. Slowly add milk, stirring constantly. Continue to cook, stirring constantly, until mixture thickens slightly. Do not boil.

4. Remove from heat. Stir in cheese until melted.

5. Pour cheese sauce over cooked pasta in baking dish.

6. For optional topping, melt butter in small saucepan. Stir in bread crumbs until well-coated. Sprinkle over pasta and cheese.

7. Bake in 350° oven for 20 minutes or until bubbly.

# MEAT, POULTRY, AND SEAFOOD

## Baked Ham Slice

DAVID AND LINDA LAPP, COUNTRY MEADOWS FARMS

*Makes 6–8 servings*
*Prep. Time: 10 minutes*
*Baking Time: 75 minutes*

I cup brown sugar
2 tsp. flour
I tsp. dry mustard
2 lb. center-cut ham slice, uncooked
a few drops of vinegar
¼ cup water

1. Combine sugar, flour, and dry mustard.

2. Spread half of mixture on one side of ham slice and sprinkle with vinegar.

3. Place ham in greased baking dish and let stand 5 minutes.

4. Turn ham over and spread with remaining mixture and sprinkle with vinegar.

5. Add water around the edges.

6. Bake at 425° uncovered for 15 minutes. Then turn oven to 325° and continue baking for 1 hour, uncovered. Serve with sauerkraut if you wish.

# Glazed Ham Balls

ARLENE LEAMAN, S. CLYDE WEAVER, INC.
*Makes 8–10 servings*
*Prep. Time: 20 minutes*
*Cooking/Baking Time: 1 hour 15 minutes*

2½ lbs. cooked ground ham

1¼ cups dry quick oats

1 cup milk

3 eggs, slightly beaten

**Sauce:**

1 cup, plus 2 Tbsp., light brown sugar, firmly packed

3 Tbsp. cornstarch

1½ Tbsp. prepared mustard

1¾ cups pineapple juice

½ cup light corn syrup

3 Tbsp. cider vinegar

½ tsp. cloves

1. Combine ground ham, oats, milk, and eggs. Shape into 1½ inch balls (makes about 40-45 balls). Place in a lightly greased baking dish. Bake at 350° for 1 hour.

2. Combine all ingredients for the sauce. Bring to a boil, stirring constantly. Reduce heat and simmer for 3 minutes. Pour sauce over ham balls and serve.

NOTE

*Sometimes I serve these for Sunday dinner when we are the host family for church.*

**From the other side of the Market stand . . .**

# CARL CHARLES OF S. CLYDE WEAVER

Carl Charles manages this smoked meats/cheeses/salads/olives stand—an icon with deep roots in Lancaster's Central Market.

"We have our regular customers, and most of them live nearby. But one family from Maryland also comes weekly. At Christmas and Easter, they bring their extended family, stand in the aisle, and sing a carol for us.

"Then there's the family who lives near the Pennsylvania-Maryland border. They have nine kids, ages 2 to 23, and they all come once a year. They buy a lot!

"Central Market has its occasional singing flash mob. The first time it happened, the group sang 'The Hallelujah Chorus.' When they first started, we didn't know what was going on, but it was very cool!"

# Weaver's Ham Loaf

ARLENE LEAMAN, S. CLYDE WEAVER, INC.

*Makes 4–6 servings* ❦ *Prep. Time: 25 minutes* ❦ *Baking Time: 1½ hours*

**Ham loaf:**
1 lb. Weaver's fresh, bulk sausage
1 lb. ground ham
2 eggs
1 cup bread crumbs
1 cup milk
1 tsp. prepared mustard

**Syrup:**
½ cup water
½ cup cider vinegar
½ cup brown sugar
1 tsp. dry mustard

1. Mix thoroughly all ingredients for ham loaf and form into 4 or 6 small individual loaves.

2. Bake at 350° for 45 minutes.

3. While ham loaf bakes, prepare syrup by mixing all ingredients together in a saucepan. Bring to a boil, stirring constantly.

4. Baste ham loaves with syrup and continue baking for another 30 minutes.

TIP
_____

*This recipe was developed by my mother. She often served ham loaf to company.*

# Pineapple Glaze

FRANCES KIEFER, KIEFER'S MEATS AND CHEESE

*Makes 1½ cups* ❦ *Prep. Time: 5 minutes* ❦ *Cooking Time: 15 minutes*

1 cup pineapple juice
1 Tbsp. cornstarch
⅓ cup light corn syrup
¼ cup light brown sugar, firmly packed

1. In a saucepan, mix pineapple juice and cornstarch. Stir until smooth.

2. Add all remaining ingredients and bring to a boil over medium heat, stirring constantly.

TIP
_____

*Delicious over ham! Leftover glaze tastes wonderful over ice cream.*

# Apricot Glazed Ham with Mustard Sauce

SAM AND NANCY NEFF, S. CLYDE WEAVER, INC.

*Makes 12–16 servings* ❧ *Prep. Time: 20 minutes* ❧ *Baking Time: 3 hours*

8-10 lb. ham

½ cup apricot jam

2 Tbsp. cider vinegar

2 Tbsp., plus ½ cup, Dijon mustard, *divided*

whole cloves

6-8 Tbsp. maple syrup

1. Score ham. Dot with cloves.

2. Mix jam, vinegar, and 2 Tbsp. mustard together.

3. With the fattier side up, spread ½ of jam mixture over top of ham. Bake at 325° for 1½ hours.

4. Re-glaze and bake an additional 1 hour.

5. Re-glaze and bake an additional ½ hour.

6. To prepare mustard sauce, mix maple syrup with remaining ½ cup mustard. Serve with baked ham.

### VARIATION

*Use peach jam instead of apricot jam.*

# Best Baby Back Ribs

SUZANNE STOLTZFUS, STOLTZFUS FRESH MEATS LLC

*Makes 3-4 servings* ❧ *Prep. Time: 10 minutes* ❧ *Baking Time: 2½-3 hours*

2½-3 lbs. baby back ribs

1 tsp. garlic powder

1 tsp. pepper

1 tsp. seasoned salt

1 medium onion, sliced

1 cup Stoltzfus Delicious Rib Sauce

1. Place ribs bone-side down in a large roasting pan.

2. Combine garlic powder, pepper, and seasoned salt. Sprinkle over ribs.

3. Top with sliced onions.

4. Cover lightly and bake at 350° for 2½-3 hours, putting the rib sauce on the ribs for the last ½ hour of baking.

# Elegant Creamed Ham

RUTH S. LANDIS, KIEFER'S MEATS AND CHEESE

*Makes 4–6 servings*
*Prep. Time: 20 minutes*
*Cooking Time: about 20 minutes*

½ cup (1 stick) butter

½ cup diced onion

1 cup diced celery

1 cup diced red *or* green bell pepper

½ cup, plus 2 Tbsp., flour

½ tsp. dry mustard

1 tsp. Worcestershire sauce

½ tsp. Tabasco sauce

5 cups milk

1 cup grated cheddar cheese

1 lb. cooked ham, cubed

1. Melt butter in large pan. Add onion, celery, and peppers. Cook until onion is yellow.

2. Over low heat blend flour and seasonings into mixture. Gradually stir in milk. Cook until thickened, stirring constantly.

3. Add cheese and ham and heat thoroughly.

4. Serve over biscuits, toasted English muffins, waffles, or toast.

NOTE

*Easy to prepare. Great for a quick meal or even a midnight treat.*

# Savory Sausage and Potato Pie

JUDITH E. MARTIN, PAUL L. SENSENIG AND SONS

*Makes 6–8 servings*
*Prep. Time: 20 minutes*
*Cooking/Baking Time: 45 minutes*

5 medium potatoes

1 tsp. salt

1 egg, beaten

½ cup finely chopped onion

½ cup crushed corn flakes

2 tsp. dried parsley

1. Cook potatoes in salt water. Peel and mash.

2. Add egg and blend. Add onion, corn flakes, and parsley.

3. Spread mixture evenly into bottom and up the side of a greased 10" pie plate or baking dish.

4. Brown sausage in skillet. Remove and drain all but 1 Tbsp. drippings.

1 lb. bulk sausage

½ cup chopped green bell
peppers

2 tsp. cornstarch *or* flour

10-oz. can cream of mushroom
soup

2 cups cooked corn, drained

1 cup shredded cheese

5. Sauté green peppers in drippings. Stir in sausage and cornstarch *or* flour. Add soup and corn.

6. Blend well and heat thoroughly.

7. Turn mixture into potato crust and sprinkle with cheese.

8. Bake at 400° for 25 minutes.

# Sausage Casserole

DORIS REINHART, D.M. WEAVER AND SONS, INC.

*Makes 6–8 servings*
*Prep. Time: 15 minutes*
*Cooking/Baking Time: about 1 hour*

4 eggs

2 cups milk

2 quarts soft bread cubes

4 Tbsp. (half stick) butter, melted

1 Tbsp. parsley, chopped

1 tsp. onion, minced

1 tsp. salt

1 tsp. sage *or* poultry seasoning

1 lb. bulk sausage

1½ cups frozen peas

2 small potatoes, chopped and
cooked until softened

1. Beat eggs. Add milk. Pour over bread cubes in large bowl.

2. Combine butter and seasonings. Add to bread cubes and mix well.

3. Brown sausage in a skillet. Drain off drippings.

4. Mix bread filling with sausage, peas, and potatoes.

5. Place in greased baking dish and bake at 350° for 45 minutes.

# THE CURB MARKET

Early in the history of Lancaster, the space allotted for the town market became insufficient. In the 1820s, in order to relieve the situation, farmers were permitted to back their wagons up to the curbs along the streets and sell their wares directly from their vehicles or temporary stands. This assemblage of sellers became known as the curb market.

The curb market was not a random arrangement. City ordinances specified which areas of which streets could be used for marketing. The places were neither occupied by market wagons on a first-come first-served basis, nor were they free for the taking.

In 1818 the curb market occupied West King Street as far as Prince Street and the whole of Center Square. By 1845 it extended a block in each direction from the Center Square on King and Queen Streets. In 1898 the curb market changed its dimensions again. There were 57 spaces on East King Street, 35 on Duke Street, and 9 in Center Square. These spaces were auctioned off, the same as those in the market house.

During its final period, the curb market extended from Center Square on East King Street to Duke, down Duke to Vine, and west on Vine to Prince where it reached almost to Orange Street. In the same areas, stores and businesses also rented space along the fronts of their buildings to the operators of smaller businesses and their "basket stands."

The rows of wagons with upturned shafts and the sumptuous displays of farm produce were somewhat of an early-day tourist attraction in Lancaster.

After the First World War, motor vehicles began replacing horse-drawn wagons at the curb market. Eventually it was the increased auto traffic in town that caused the curb market to be impractical and unsafe. On January 1, 1927, the city decreed that this colorful institution come to an end. The standholders were offered space in the Southern Market.

# Choucroute Garnie

CHRISTINE WEISS, GERMAN DELI

*Makes 4–6 servings*
*Prep. Time: 20 minutes*
*Cooking Time: 1 hour 15 minutes*

3 Tbsp. lard *or* vegetable oil

½ lb. thickly sliced double smoked bacon, cut into 1" squares

2 medium onions, halved and sliced crosswise

2 cloves garlic, minced

2 lbs. sauerkraut, rinsed

2 medium apples, peeled, cored, and grated

1 potato, peeled and grated

1 cup dry white wine

½ cup apple cider *or* juice

⅓ cup chicken broth *or* water

½ tsp. dried thyme, crumbled

1 bay leaf

8 bruised juniper berries *or* 1 Tbsp. gin

3 cloves

pinch of salt

4-6 (about 1½ lbs.) knockwurst, *or* good quality frankfurters

4-6 (about ¾ to 1¼ lbs.) weisswurst

1. Heat lard in large Dutch oven over medium heat. Add bacon and sauté until browned (about 8 minutes). Remove bacon and reserve.

2. Add onion and more lard to Dutch oven if necessary. Lower heat. Sauté onions until soft, not browned.

3. Add garlic and toss until fragrant. Add sauerkraut, apples, and potato. Toss for 2 minutes.

4. Add wine, apple cider, broth, thyme, bay leaf, juniper berries or gin, cloves, and salt to taste. Cover and simmer 30-35 minutes.

5. Prick sausages all over with fork. Tuck sausages into sauerkraut. Add reserved bacon. Cover and simmer another 30 minutes or until sausages are heated through.

6. Correct seasonings.

TIP

*Serve with an assortment of mustards, pickles, boiled potatoes, dark bread, beer or light wine. Follow with a salad. Excellent for New Year's Day or Super Bowl meal!*

# Cottage Ham and String Beans

REGINE IBOLD, THE SPICE STAND

*Makes 6–8 servings*
Prep. Time: 15 minutes ❦ Standing Time: 1 hour ❦ Cooking Time: 1 hour

1½ lbs. yellow string beans

1½ lbs. green string beans, *or use all green beans*

1 red onion, chopped

1 carrot, chopped

3 cloves garlic, peeled but left whole

¼ cup olive oil

2-3-lb. boneless pork shoulder butt

2 lbs. fresh plum tomatoes, *or use canned and drain them*

2 tsp. dried basil leaves, *or use fresh basil leaves, sliced*

salt and pepper to taste

1. Snap ends of beans and soak in cold water for 1 hour.

2. In Dutch oven sauté onion, carrot, and garlic in olive oil until soft. Add string beans and nestle ham in middle.

3. Top with plum tomatoes and basil leaves. Do not add water; beans shed their own liquid.

4. Cook covered 1 hour or until ham is cooked through.

# Ham Zucchini Potato Dish

MARILYN DENLINGER, IRWIN. S. WIDDERS PRODUCE

*Makes 6 servings*
Prep. Time: 15 minutes ❦ Cooking Time: 25 minutes

2 lbs. ham, cubed

1½ cups water, *divided*

5 medium potatoes, sliced thin

3 medium zucchini, sliced thin

8 oz. cheese, grated

pepper to taste

1. Brown ham in skillet in ½ cup water. After browning, add 1 more cup water to make a tasty broth.

2. Add potatoes and cook about 15 minutes or until nearly tender.

3. Stir in zucchini and cook until crisp tender.

4. Sprinkle with cheese and pepper and serve.

# Asparagus Ham Bake

*Makes 6–8 servings*  ❧  *Prep. Time. 15 minutes*  ❧  *Baking Time: 45 minutes*

¾ cup milk

I cup cream of mushroom soup

2 cups ham cubes, cooked

3 Tbsp. chopped onion

I cup cooked rice

3 cups diced fresh asparagus

½ cup shredded sharp cheese

I½ cups bread crumbs, buttered

1. Combine milk, soup, ham, onion, and rice.

2. Spoon half of this mixture into a greased baking dish. Top with half of asparagus. Repeat.

3. Top with cheese and bread crumbs.

4. Bake at 375° for 45 minutes or until asparagus is done to your liking.

*Notes*

*Wonderful asparagus taste!*

# Dutch Noodles Florentine

MARY ELLEN CAMPBELL, BASKETS OF CENTRAL MARKET

*Makes 6 servings*  ❧  *Prep. Time: 15 minutes*  ❧  *Cooking Time: about 30 minutes*

I lb. bacon

I lb. uncooked noodles

10-oz. pkg. frozen spinach *or* I lb. fresh spinach

½ cup (I stick) butter

I egg, lightly beaten

I½ cups heavy cream

2 cups freshly grated Parmesan cheese

salt and pepper to taste

1. Cook bacon and drain it. Crumble and set aside.

2. Cook noodles according to directions.

3. If using frozen spinach, thaw and drain. If using fresh spinach, wash well and drain.

4. Melt butter in large, heavy saucepan. Add spinach and heat through. Add drained noodles and toss lightly.

5. In another pan combine egg, cream, cheese, salt, and pepper. Heat over very low heat for 5 minutes.

6. Pour over noodle mixture and gently toss.

7. Serve in a heated dish.

# Snitz and Knepp

PAUL B. MARTIN, SPRING GLEN FARM KITCHEN, INC.

*Makes 8 servings*

*Prep. Time: 25 minutes* ❦ *Standing Time: overnight* ❦ *Cooking Time: 4 hours 15 minutes*

**Snitz:**

2 cups dried tart apples

water

1½ lbs. cured ham *or* 1 ham hock

2 Tbsp. brown sugar

**Knepp:**

2 cups flour

3½ tsp. baking powder

½ tsp. salt

1 egg, beaten

2 Tbsp. (¼ stick) butter, melted

⅓-½ cup milk

1. Cover dried apples with water and soak overnight.

2. In the morning cover ham with cold water in a large stockpot and cook slowly for 3 hours.

3. Stir in brown sugar and cook 1 hour longer.

4. Sift together all dry ingredients. Stir in beaten egg and melted butter. Add milk to make a batter stiff enough to drop from a spoon.

5. Add apples to boiling ham.

6. Drop batter (knepp) by spoonfuls into boiling ham and apples.

7. Cover pan tightly and cook snitz and knepp 10-12 more minutes. Do not lift cover until ready to serve.

# Roasted Pig Stomach

ARLENE LEAMAN, S. CLYDE WEAVER, INC.

*Makes 8–10 servings*
*Prep. Time: 20 minutes ❦ Cooking/Baking Time: 3½ hours*

1 small onion, chopped
½ cup chopped celery
2 Tbsp. (¼ stick) butter
2 eggs
4-6 cups cubed bread
1 quart diced potatoes
1½ lbs. bulk sausage
milk *or* water to moisten bread
salt and pepper to taste
1 pig stomach
½ cup water

1. Sauté onion and celery in butter.

2. In a large bowl, mix eggs and bread cubes. Add onions and celery.

3. Add potatoes and sausage. Add enough liquid (milk or water) to moisten the mixture. Mix thoroughly. Season to taste.

4. Stuff the pig stomach with sausage filling, being careful not fill too tightly since the stomach shrinks while baking. Close opening of stomach with thread and skewers.

5. Place stuffed stomach in a roasting pan with ½ cup water and bake covered at 350° for 2 hours.

6. Uncover and bake another hour or until skin is brown and tender.

TIP

*If you have more sausage filling than fits in the stomach, bake the rest of it in a greased baking dish for 1 hour or until heated through.*

NOTE

*The Leaman family has warm memories of the days when Grandma would have the whole family (about 30 people) over for a Sunday dinner of roasted pig stomach!*

# Stuffed Acorn Squash

ETHEL STONER, JOHN R. STONER VEGETABLES

*Makes 4 servings*
*Prep. Time: 20 minutes*
*Cooking/Baking Time: about 1 hour*

2 acorn squash, halved and seeded

1 lb. ground beef *or* ground turkey

½ cup chopped apple

1 tsp. curry powder

½ lb. cheese, cubed

2 Tbsp. marmalade *or* apricot preserves

½-¾ tsp. salt

1 cup thinly sliced apples

1 Tbsp. butter

¼ tsp. cinnamon

¼ tsp. nutmeg

1. Place squash in lightly greased baking dish with cut side down. Bake at 400° for 35-40 minutes or until tender.

2. Brown meat and drain off excess fat.

3. Add chopped apples and curry powder. Cook until tender.

4. Add cheese, preserves, and salt, stirring occasionally until cheese is melted.

5. Sauté thin apple slices in butter until tender. Season lightly with cinnamon and nutmeg.

6. Remove squash from oven. Place on serving plates and fill cavity with meat mixture.

7. Top with sautéed apples.

NOTE

*My family thinks this combination is out of this world!*

# Filled Noodles

CYNTHIA STRUBE, MARION CHEESE

*Makes 4 servings*
*Prep. Time: 30 minutes*
*Cooking Time: 30 minutes*

**Filling Ingredients:**
1 lb. ground beef
1 medium onion, finely chopped
¾ cup bread crumbs
1 egg, lightly beaten
salt and pepper to taste

**Dough Ingredients:**
2 cups flour
½ tsp. salt
2 eggs, lightly beaten
¼ cup cold water
3—4 quarts water
4 beef bouillon cubes
parsley
1 Tbsp. butter

1. Thoroughly mix all filling ingredients. Divide into 4-6 patties.

2. To make noodle dough, mix flour, salt, eggs, and cold water. Knead with fingers until well mixed. Divide dough into 4-6 equal pieces.

3. On floured surface roll out dough until each piece is large and flat enough to hold and cover a meat patty. Place meat patty in center of each dough piece. Bring opposite ends of dough together and press firmly. Moisten finger with water and rub over dough to seal.

4. Bring 3-4 quarts water to a boil. Add bouillon cubes and parsley. Drop filled noodles into boiling water and cook for 30 minutes at a low boil.

5. Brown butter by heating slowly until it's turning brown.

6. Remove noodles from pot to dinner plate and pour browned butter over noodles.

NOTE

*I grew up with this special treat.*

# Beef Casserole

RUTH MELLINGER, C. H. THOMAS AND SON

*Makes 6 servings*
*Prep. Time: 25 minutes*
*Cooking/Baking Time: 1½ hours*

2½ lbs. ground beef
salt and pepper to taste
1 quart Thomas's beef broth
2½ cups diced potatoes
1½ cups diced celery
1 small onion, chopped
2 cups peas
3 Tbsp. flour
½ cup water

**Pastry Ingredients:**
1½ cups flour
⅔ cup shortening
1 tsp. salt
4 Tbsp. milk

1. Brown ground beef in skillet. Salt and pepper to taste.

2. Cook potatoes, celery, and onion in beef broth until almost tender. Stir in peas.

3. Drain and save broth.

4. Mix 3 Tbsp. flour with water to make a paste. Add paste to beef broth and bring to a boil. Boil until broth is slightly thickened, stirring constantly.

5. Combine meat, cooked vegetables, and thickened broth in a large greased baking dish.

6. To prepare pastry, cut shortening into flour.

7. Add salt and milk and mix by hand until pastry is pliable.

8. Roll out and layer over meat and vegetables in baking dish.

9. Cut slits in pastry for steam to escape. Flute the edges.

10. Bake at 350° about 45 minutes or until crust is golden brown.

TIP

*This freezes well before or after baking.*

# Roast Cabbage and Beef

### HELEN THOMAS, HELEN THOMAS PRODUCE

*Makes 6–8 servings* ❧ *Prep. Time: 25 minutes* ❧ *Cooking/Baking Time: 2½ hours*

½ lb. beef cubes

I small head cabbage

salt and pepper to taste

saffron, *optional*

4 medium potatoes

4 medium apples

I green bell pepper, chopped

**Bread Stuffing:**

6-8 slices bread, cubed

2 eggs, beaten

I cup milk

I tsp. parsley

I tsp. onion

I tsp. poultry seasoning

1. Put ½ head of cabbage, leaves separated, in bottom of roast pan. Sprinkle with salt, pepper, and saffron.
2. Layer beef cubes over cabbage.
3. Mix all ingredients for bread dressing, and layer over beef cubes in roast pan.
4. Repeat cabbage layer.
5. Put apple slices around edge of pan and raw, cubed potatoes in center.
6. Layer peppers over potatoes.
7. Pour ½ cup water over layers.
8. Bake covered at 300° for 2 hours.

NOTE

*I received this recipe from Mary Lauver after enjoying it at her house.*

# Cabbage Bundles

### DORIS SHENK, DONEGAL GARDENS

*Makes 6–8 servings* ❧ *Prep. Time: 30 minutes* ❧ *Cooking/Baking Time: 1½ hours*

I medium head cabbage

1½ lbs. ground beef

2 cups cooked rice

salt and pepper to taste

garlic salt

2-3 cups tomato juice *or* spaghetti sauce

1. Boil whole head of cabbage for 10-12 minutes. Separate leaves and set aside to drain.
2. Brown ground beef. Blend rice and beef together and season to taste.
3. Spoon about 2 Tbsp. mixture into each cabbage leaf. Roll up leaves and hold with toothpicks.
4. Place in greased baking dish.
5. Cover with tomato juice or spaghetti sauce.
6. Bake at 350° for 1 hour.

# Porcupine Balls

WILLOW VALLEY FARMS

*Makes 4–6 servings*
*Prep. Time: 25 minutes* ❦ *Baking Time: 1½ hours*

1 cup bread crumbs
1 cup milk
2 eggs, beaten
1 lb. ground beef
1 medium onion, chopped
½ cup chopped celery, *optional*
¼ cup rice, uncooked
2 cups tomato juice

1. In a good-sized bowl, soak bread crumbs in milk.

2. Add beaten eggs. Add all other ingredients except tomato juice and mix well.

3. Shape into balls.

4. Place balls into baking dish. Pour tomato juice over balls.

5. Bake at 350° for 1½ hours.

# Meat Loaf

ESTHER EISENBERGER, EISENBERGER'S BAKED GOODS

*Makes 6–8 servings*
*Prep. Time: 20 minutes* ❦ *Baking Time: 1 hour*

2 lbs. ground beef
2 eggs
1½ cups bread crumbs
1 envelope onion soup mix
¾ cup ketchup
8-oz. can tomato sauce

1. Mix all ingredients together except tomato sauce.

2. Shape into loaf and put into loaf pan. Pour tomato sauce over top.

3. Bake at 375° for 1 hour.

# Koenigsberger Klopse (delicate croquettes in sauce)

CHRISTINE WEISS, GERMAN DELI

*Makes 4–5 servings*
*Prep. Time: 30 minutes*
*Cooking Time: about an hour*

### Klopse:

9 slices stale white bread, crusts removed

water

5 anchovy fillets

1¾ lbs. ground meat, mixture of beef and pork

2 cups grated, cooked potatoes

2 eggs

1 Tbsp. flour, plus more for coating

⅛ tsp. salt

dash of pepper

2 Tbsp. capers

### Sauce:

4 Tbsp. (½ stick) butter

3 Tbsp. flour

3 Tbsp. capers

1½ tsp. lemon juice

½ tsp. salt

pepper

4 cups beef or vegetable stock

1. Soak bread in water about 2 minutes. Squeeze water out of bread.

2. Mince anchovies as fine as possible.

3. Blend bread, anchovies, ground meat, potatoes, eggs, 1 Tbsp. flour, salt, pepper, and capers together well.

4. Form mixture into 18 balls about the size of small eggs.

5. Roll balls in flour and drop into a large, deep pot of boiling salted water.

6. Cook for 12 minutes.

7. Remove from water and keep klopse warm.

8. To prepare sauce, melt butter in a large kettle with a lid. Add flour and blend well with a fork. Do not brown. Add capers, lemon juice, salt, and pepper.

9. Bring stock to a boil in a separate pan.

10. Add boiling stock to sauce. Stir well until smooth with a fork or egg whisk to prevent lumps.

11. Cover and simmer slowly for 15 minutes, stirring frequently to prevent burning.

12. Add klopse to sauce and simmer for 3 minutes.

TIP

*We like this served with mashed potatoes and asparagus.*

**Meat, Poultry, & Seafood**   149

# Barbecued Meatballs

JUDITH E. MARTIN, PAUL L. SENSENIG AND SONS

*Makes about 8 meatballs* ❧ *Prep. Time: 25 minutes* ❧ *Baking Time: 1 hour*

**Meatballs:**
1 lb. ground beef
1 cup bread crumbs
½ cup milk
2 eggs
1 tsp. salt
⅛ tsp. pepper

**Sauce:**
1½ Tbsp. Worcestershire sauce
3 Tbsp. brown sugar
¼ cup vinegar
½ cup ketchup
½ cup water
½ cup chopped onions

1. Mix all meat ingredients together well.

2. Shape into balls. Place into a rectangular greased baking dish.

3. Mix all sauce ingredients well. Pour sauce over balls.

4. Bake uncovered at 350° for 45-60 minutes or just until balls are done to your liking.

# Tangy Fruity Meatballs

VIV HUNT, VIV'S VARIETIES

*Makes 6–8 servings* ❧ *Prep. Time: 30 minutes* ❧ *Cooking Time: about 40 minutes*

2 lbs. ground beef
1 egg, slightly beaten
1 large onion, grated
salt and pepper to taste
12-oz. bottle chili sauce
10-oz. jar grape jelly
juice of 1 lemon

1. Thoroughly mix ground beef, egg, and onion. Salt and pepper to taste.

2. Shape into small balls.

3. Mix chili sauce, grape jelly, and lemon juice to make sauce.

4. Drop meatballs into sauce in a pan. Simmer until meatballs are cooked through.

NOTE

*Prepare this recipe ahead of time, freeze it, and you've got a dish that's ready to go anytime.*

# Italian Steak Sandwiches

JOYCE DEITER, EISENBERGER'S BAKED GOODS

*Makes 8 servings* ❧ *Prep. Time: 20 minutes* ❧ *Cooking Time: 1 hour*

2 cups tomato juice

6-oz. can tomato paste

2 Tbsp. spaghetti sauce

⅓ cup sugar *or* less, to taste

2 lbs. chipped steak or ground beef

½ cup chopped onion

salt and pepper to taste

16 slices cheese

8 steak rolls

1. Mix together tomato juice, tomato paste, spaghetti sauce, and sugar. Simmer over low heat for 1 hour.

2. Fry chipped steak or ground beef. When browned, add onion, salt, and pepper.

3. Add the sauce and mix well, simmering for 20 minutes.

4. Put mixture into steak rolls and top each roll with two slices of cheese.

5. Place sandwiches in oven and heat until cheese melts. Serve immediately.

HINT

*Freeze any leftover sauce to use later.*

VARIATION

*Serve the meat and cheese in pita bread for easier handling, especially for young children.*

# Salisbury Steak

JANICE KREIDER, EISENBERGER'S BAKED GOODS

*Makes 6 servings* ❧ *Prep. Time: 25 minutes* ❧ *Cooking/Baking Time: 1 hour*

**Burgers:**

6 crackers, broken

½ cup milk

2 lbs. ground beef

2 tsp. salt

⅛ tsp. pepper

1 egg, well beaten

¼ cup chopped onion

1 tsp. dried parsley

⅛ tsp. dried oregano

⅛ tsp. dried basil

**Gravy:**

3 cups water

2 Tbsp. flour

1 cup water

salt and pepper to taste

1. Soak crackers in milk until softened.

2. Mix together all ingredients for burgers, including the crackers and milk.

3. Shape mixture into 6 oblong burgers.

4. Brown slightly on each side. Save the drippings. Place burgers into greased baking dish.

5. Prepare a gravy by adding 3 cups water to the beef drippings. Bring to a boil.

6. Make a smooth paste with flour and 1 cup water. Add paste to boiling drippings in a thin stream. Stir quickly and constantly to prevent lumps.

7. Add seasonings. Heat until thickened.

8. Pour gravy over beef patties.

9. Bake at 300° for 45 minutes.

# No-Peek Casserole

MRS. ADA ROHRER, JOHN M. MARKLEY MEATS

*Makes 6 servings* ❧ *Prep. Time: 10 minutes* ❧ *Baking Time: 3 hours*

½ lb. fresh mushrooms, sliced

2 Tbsp. (¼ stick) butter

2 lbs. bite-size beef cubes

10¾-oz. can cream of mushroom soup

1 envelope dry onion soup mix

1. Sauté mushrooms in 2 Tbsp. butter.

2. Mix all ingredients in a greased 2-quart baking dish and cover tightly.

3. Bake at 300° for 3 hours. Do not peek!

4. Serve over noodles or rice.

# Creamed Dried Beef

RUTH MARTIN, C. Z. MARTIN SONS

*Makes 3–4 servings* ❦ *Prep. Time: 10 minutes* ❦ *Cooking Time: 15-20 minutes*

1-2 Tbsp. butter
¼ lb. chipped dried beef
4 Tbsp. flour
3 cups milk

1. Melt butter in skillet over low heat. Add dried beef and stir occasionally until lightly browned.

2. Add flour. Stir until dried beef is well coated with flour.

3. Slowly add milk, stirring constantly until thickened.

4. Serve over toast or baked potatoes.

### VARIATION

*Use chipped turkey ham instead of dried beef.*

# Beef-Macaroni Skillet

ALICE SHENK, SHENK CHEESE CO.

*Makes 6 servings* ❦ *Prep. Time: 10 minutes* ❦ *Cooking Time: 25-35 minutes*

1 lb. ground beef
1 medium onion, chopped
3 cups tomato juice
1 Tbsp. Worcestershire sauce
1 Tbsp. vinegar
1 tsp. salt
⅛ tsp. pepper
1 tsp. dry mustard
1 cup elbow macaroni, uncooked

1. Brown beef and onion in large skillet. (You may begin with frozen ground beef and thaw in skillet.)

2. Add all remaining ingredients and simmer about 20 minutes or until macaroni is done. Stir occasionally to prevent sticking.

3. An easy dish for unexpected company!

### VARIATIONS

1. *For a lower fat diet, use ground turkey.*

2. *Add ¼ lb. sliced fresh mushrooms.*

3. *Use a different kind of pasta if you wish.*

**Meat, Poultry, & Seafood** ❦ **153**

# Savory Sweet Pot Roast

MILDRED BRACKBILL, UTZ'S POTATO CHIPS

*Makes 6–8 servings*
*Prep. Time: 15 minutes*
*Cooking Time: 3 hours*

3-4 lb. boneless beef roast

1 medium onion, sliced

10-oz. can cream of mushroom soup

½ cup water

¾ cup brown sugar

¼ cup vinegar

2 tsp. salt

1 tsp. prepared mustard

1 tsp. Worcestershire sauce

1. Brown meat on top and bottom in Dutch oven.

2. Add onions and brown them, too.

3. Blend together all other ingredients and pour over meat.

4. Cover and bake for 2½ to 3 hours at 300°.

# Sweet and Sour Brisket

RUTH ESHLEMAN, GIVANT'S BAKERY

*Makes 10 servings*
*Prep. Time: 15 minutes*
*Baking Time: 3 hours*

6 lb. beef brisket

2 onions, sliced

¾ cup brown sugar

½ cup vinegar

1 cup ketchup

1 cup water

1 Tbsp. salt

pepper

1. Place brisket in a Dutch oven. Brown on all sides.

2. Add onions and brown them.

3. Blend all other ingredients and pour over meat.

4. Cover and bake for 3 hours at 325°.

NOTE

*This recipe was given to me by a favorite cousin. I enjoy serving it to guests.*

# Grilled Leg of Lamb

SAM NEFF, S. CLYDE WAVER, INC.

*Makes 8 servings*
*Prep. Time: 15 minutes*
*Marinating Time: 2 hours*
*Grilling Time: about 30 minutes, depending on grill temperature*

**5-6 lb. leg of lamb, boned and butterflied**

*Marinade:*
¼ cup olive oil
1 Tbsp. dried oregano
1 tsp. dried rosemary
1 tsp. dried thyme
¼ tsp. black pepper

**Final Basting Ingredients:**
¼ cup lemon juice
½ tsp. dried oregano
1 tsp. salt

1. Mix all ingredients for marinade. Place butterflied leg in baking dish and pour marinade over top. Marinate 2 hours, turning occasionally.

2. Place leg on charcoal grill (gas grill tends to flame and needs water to control).

3. Use marinade oil to baste leg as it cooks, turning occasionally. Salt as you prefer.

4. Grill until thermometer registers 140° in thickest part of meat.

5. Mix final basting ingredients and use to baste leg.

6. Continue grilling until thermometer registers 160° for pink and 175° for well done.

7. Serve with lemon wedges.

TIP

*The lemon is used to cut the fat of the lamb. If you have ever been offended by the "wooliness" of lamb/mutton, this recipe is worth a try. The lemon makes a lot of difference, but do not use the lemon baste too early in the grilling process or it will dry out the meat.*

# Lamb Stew

SAM NEFF, S. CLYDE WEAVER. INC.

*Makes 8 servings*
*Prep. Time: 15 minutes*
*Cooking/Baking Time: 2 hours*

1 Tbsp. olive oil

3 cups roasted* lamb cubes

½ cup brandy *or* cognac

¼ cup wine vinegar

1 cup dry red wine

2 cups beef stock

12 pearl onions

4 carrots, chopped

2-3 potatoes, chopped

2 Tbsp. cornstarch *or* potato starch

2 Tbsp. fruit jelly

2 Tbsp. tomato paste *or* 4-6 Tbsp. tomato sauce

1 tsp. dried rosemary

1 tsp. dried thyme

1 tsp. black pepper

2 bay leaves

¼ cup chopped parsley

½-1 tsp. salt

1. Heat olive oil in skillet and brown lamb cubes. Don't crowd the skillet or the meat will steam and not brown. Transfer to greased baking dish.

2. Heat brandy or cognac in skillet and ignite.

3. Add vinegar, wine, and beef stock. Bring to a boil.

4. Add all remaining ingredients and cook 5-10 minutes. Pour mixture into baking dish with lamb cubes and stir gently.

5. Cover and bake at 350° for 1 hour. Uncover and bake another 30 minutes. Serve.

TIP

*This is an excellent way to use leftover roasted lamb. I have tried it with fresh lamb and find it is just not the same.*

Cajun Shrimp, page 181

Brussels Sprouts Sauté, page 118

Simple Cassoulet, page 69

# Lamb Balls With Sour Cream and Capers

SAM NEFF, S. CLYDE WEAVER, INC.

*Makes 4–6 servings*
*Prep. Time: 20 minutes*
*Cooking Time: about 30 minutes*

**Meatballs:**

1½ lbs. ground lamb
½ cup chopped onion
1 clove garlic, minced
½ cup bread crumbs
1 egg, beaten
2 Tbsp. chopped fresh parsley
2 Tbsp. chopped fresh dill
¼ tsp. dried thyme
½ tsp. lemon juice
oil

**Sauce:**

1½ Tbsp. butter
½ cup chopped onion
1 Tbsp. paprika
½ tsp. dried thyme
½ cup white wine
1 cup chicken broth
2 Tbsp. cornstarch dissolved in 2 Tbsp. water
3 Tbsp. capers, drained
1 cup sour cream
2 Tbsp. chopped fresh dill
salt and pepper to taste

1. Mix all meat ingredients and roll into balls.

2. Sauté meatballs in oil until lightly browned. Remove from pan. Pour off excess fat.

3. To prepare sauce, sauté onion in 1½ Tbsp. butter. Stir in paprika, thyme, and wine.

4. Bring mixture to a boil and add chicken broth.

5. Bring to a boil again and stir in the cornstarch and water mixture. Cook until slightly thickened.

6. Add meatballs, capers, sour cream, dill, salt, and pepper. Heat but do not bring to a boil.

7. Serve over hot rice or barley.

NOTE

*Before returning to the family business, Nancy and I lived in Crete for two years. This is an adaptation of a recipe from that area. It tastes great and does not have any of the gaminess some people associate with lamb.*

# Chicken Provencal with Pesto

REGINE IBOLD, THE SPICE STAND

*Makes 6–8 servings*
*Prep. Time: 25 minutes*
*Baking Time: 1 hour 35 minutes*

**Pesto:**

2 cups fresh basil *or* 2 Tbsp. dried basil

½ cup olive oil

2 Tbsp. pine nuts

2 cloves garlic crushed

1 tsp. salt

½ cup freshly grated Parmesan cheese

2 Tbsp. grated Romano cheese

3 Tbsp. butter, softened

**Chicken:**

6 medium onions, coarsely chopped

½ cup olive oil

2 28-oz. cans plum tomatoes

1 Tbsp. fresh thyme *or* 1 tsp. dried thyme

1 Tbsp. fresh tarragon *or* 1 tsp. dried tarragon

1 Tbsp. fresh rosemary *or* 1 tsp. dried rosemary

4 cloves fresh garlic, minced

2-3 lb. chicken, cut up

2 cups chicken broth

4 cups dry white wine

1½-2 lbs. small new potatoes in skins

2 loaves French bread

1. To prepare pesto blend all ingredients except cheeses and softened butter in a blender or food processor. Pour into a bowl and add cheeses and butter, mixing by hand.

2. In a large skillet or Dutch oven, sauté onions in olive oil until transparent.

3. Add tomatoes with their juice. Add all herbs, garlic, chicken, chicken broth, wine, and half of pesto.

4. Cover and bake at 350° for 35 minutes.

5. Add potatoes and bake 1 hour or until potatoes are tender when pierced with fork.

6. Serve in deep soup plates with plenty of hot French bread to mop up juices. Serve remaining pesto at table.

NOTE

*This is a peasant dish from Provence where cooking aromas fill the house like perfume. This is our all-time favorite pesto, which is great year-round on pasta or in soups.*

# Chicken with 40 Cloves Garlic

REGINE IBOLD, THE SPICE STAND

*Makes 8 servings*
*Prep. Time: 20 minutes*
*Baking Time: 1½ hours*

⅔ cup olive oil

8 chicken legs, 8 chicken thighs, skin removed if you wish

4 ribs celery, chopped

2 medium onions, chopped

4 Tbsp. fresh chopped flat-leaf parsley

1 Tbsp. fresh tarragon *or* 1 tsp. dried

½ cup dry vermouth

salt and pepper to taste

nutmeg

40 cloves garlic, unpeeled

2 loaves French bread

1. Put olive oil in shallow dish and coat chicken pieces with it.

2. Cover bottom of a heavy 6-quart casserole with mixture of celery and onion. Add parsley and tarragon. Lay oiled chicken pieces on top.

3. Pour vermouth over them. Sprinkle with salt, pepper, and a little nutmeg. Intersperse garlic cloves with chicken pieces.

4. Cover tightly with foil and lid. Bake at 375° for 1½ hours without peeking.

5. Serve chicken pieces, pan juices, and garlic cloves with thin slices of hot French bread. Garlic may be squeezed from its husk and spread on bread like butter.

NOTE

*I first prepared this Provencal dish 18 years ago, the night before my youngest son, Hans, was born. The next morning the nursery at St. Joseph's Hospital reeked of garlic! My doctor and pediatrician came to the room and said, "So this is the mother of the garlic baby!" They still call Hans "the garlic baby." He is now 6' 3" and loves garlic.*

# Hungarian Chicken Livers

CINDY COVER, MARION CHEESE

*Makes 4–6 servings* ❦ *Prep. Time: 25 minutes* ❦ *Cooking Time: about 30 minutes*

5 slices bacon

1 large green bell pepper, chopped

1 large onion, chopped

¾ lb. fresh mushrooms, cleaned and sliced

2 Tbsp. hot Hungarian paprika

1½ lbs. chicken livers, rinsed and patted dry

1 cup sour cream

cooked rice *or* noodles

1. Fry bacon in large skillet. Remove, crumble, and set aside.
2. Keep ¼ cup bacon drippings in the pan. Add peppers and onions and sauté until golden.
3. Add mushrooms and paprika and sauté a few minutes longer.
4. Add chicken livers to skillet and sauté over high heat just until cooked through.
5. Remove from heat. Add reserved bacon and sour cream.
6. Return to burner and heat gently. Do not boil.
7. Serve over rice or noodles.

# Sour Cream Chicken

DARLA LAMOUREUX, WILLOW VALLEY FARMS

*Makes 8 servings* ❦ *Prep. Time: 25 minutes* ❦ *Chilling Time: overnight* ❦ *Baking Time: 55 minutes*

1 cup sour cream

2 Tbsp. lemon juice

2 tsp. Worcestershire sauce

1 tsp. paprika

1½ tsp. salt

¼ tsp. pepper

1 cup fine bread crumbs

½ cup (1 stick) butter, melted, *divided*

4 whole chicken breasts, split, boned, and skinned

1. Combine sour cream, lemon juice, Worcestershire sauce, paprika, salt, and pepper. Mix well.
2. Coat chicken breasts with this mixture and refrigerate overnight, covered.
3. Roll chicken in bread crumbs. Place chicken pieces in a greased baking dish.
4. Spoon ¼ cup melted butter over chicken.
5. Bake uncovered at 325° for 40 minutes.
6. Spoon remaining butter over chicken and bake 15 minutes longer.

TIP

*Easy to prepare the day before an elegant dinner party!*

# Pineapple Salsa Chicken

### BRIE GARBER, AMISH FAMILY RECIPES

*Makes 6 servings* ❧ *Prep. Time: 10 minutes* ❧ *Cooking Time: 30 minutes*

2 Tbsp. (¼ stick) butter

6 boneless skinless chicken breast halves

¼ tsp. salt

16-oz. jar Lynn's Pineapple Salsa from Amish Family Recipes (*or* use Rodney's Mango Salsa *or* Shea Peach Salsa)

2 cups hot, cooked rice

1. In a skillet, melt butter over medium heat. Add chicken in 2 batches and sprinkle with salt.

2. Sauté each batch until browned, turning occasionally.

3. Return all chicken to skillet. Reduce heat to low and cover, cooking just until a fork can be inserted easily, about 15-20 minutes.

4. Pour in Lynn's Pineapple Salsa and simmer until warm, 5-10 more minutes.

5. Arrange chicken on a platter of cooked rice, spooning salsa over chicken and rice.

# One-Dish Chicken and Gravy

### HELEN HARNISH, WILLOW VALLEY FARMS

*Makes 4–6 servings* ❧ *Prep. Time: 15 minutes* ❧ *Baking Time: 1 hour 5 minutes*

1 frying chicken, cut up

¼ cup flour

¼ cup (half stick) butter, melted

1 tsp. chopped onion

1 cup evaporated milk

10-oz. can cream of mushroom soup

1 cup grated mild cheddar cheese

¾ tsp. salt

⅛ tsp. pepper

paprika

1. Roll chicken pieces in flour. Place skin down in melted butter in a greased 9"x13" baking dish.

2. Bake uncovered at 425° for 30 minutes.

3. Turn chicken and bake 10-15 minutes longer. Pour off excess fat.

4. In a separate bowl mix onion, milk, soup, cheese, salt, and pepper. Pour over chicken and sprinkle with paprika.

5. Cover with foil and bake at 325° for 20 minutes.

6. Serve with rice.

# Chicken Crackers

MRS. S. CLYDE WEAVER, S. CLYDE WEAVER, INC.

*Makes 8–10 servings* ❦ *Prep. Time: 30 minutes* ❦ *Cooking/Baking Time: 1 hour 20 minutes*

5-6 lb. whole chicken

chopped parsley

1½ quarts water

½ cup, plus 2 Tbsp., flour

1 cup cold water

**Crackers:**

2 cups flour

¾ cup (1½ sticks) butter, softened

½ tsp. salt

3 Tbsp. milk *or* cream

fresh parsley

1. Cook chicken and parsley in water for about 1 hour until tender.

2. Cool. Then remove meat from bones and cut into pieces. Save 1½ quarts chicken stock.

3. Prepare a gravy with chicken stock. Bring stock to a boil. Meanwhile, dissolve ½ cup plus 2 Tbsp. flour in cold water. Pour into boiling broth in a thin stream, stirring continually until stock thickens into gravy. Add chicken pieces and heat thoroughly.

4. To prepare crackers, cut butter into flour until small pea-size pieces form. Add salt. Stir in milk, 1 Tbsp. at a time, until the dough forms a ball as you mix it together.

5. Roll out thin.

6. Cut into ¾" squares and place on a greased cookie sheet.

7. Bake at 425° for 10 minutes until golden brown.

8. Put crackers into one or two serving dishes and pour gravy over top. Garnish with parsley and serve.

TIP

*Grandmother Weaver served these along with ham, fish, and oyster crackers at a traditional Lancaster County family dinner.*

# Chicken Pot Pie With Puff Pastry

KATHLEEN PIANKA, MARION CHEESE

*Makes 4–6 servings*

*Prep. Time: 20 minutes  ❦  Cooking/Baking Time: about 1 hour*

I large white cooking onion

2 ribs celery, chopped

4 Tbsp. (half stick) butter

3 large carrots, cut on bias into chunks

2 cups peas

I cup green beans

I quart chicken stock

1 ½ lbs. chicken tenderloin

4 Tbsp. flour

½ cup cold water

I-lb. piece puff pastry

1. Sauté onion and celery in butter. Set aside.

2. Blanch carrots, peas, and green beans for 4 minutes. Set aside.

3. Bring chicken stock to a boil.

4. Poach chicken in stock until just done, about 5 minutes. Remove chicken. Cut into bite-sized pieces.

5. In separate bowl whisk flour and water until smooth. Add slowly to boiling chicken stock, whisking until smooth.

6. Add all vegetables and chicken to stock.

7. Spoon into a 9"x12" greased baking dish.

8. Top with a piece of puff pastry. Trim so pastry just covers the edge. Bake at 350° for 40 minutes. When finished, pastry will be golden brown.

NOTE

*Country favorite with an elegant touch!*

# Granny's Chicken Pot Pie

SUSIE BARR, BARR FARMS

*Makes 6-8 Servings*
*Prep. Time: 45 minutes ❧ Cooking Time: 1¼ hours*

3½- or 4-lb. stewing chicken
1 tsp. salt
1 tsp. pepper
1 pinch saffron, *optional*
6 *or* 7 potatoes, peeled and cut in quarters
¼ cup (half stick) butter
¼ cup finely chopped onion
¼ cup finely chopped celery
1 carrot, finely chopped
3 eggs
3 tsp. oil
3 cups flour
6-8 Tbsp. water

1. Cut chicken in pieces. Place in stockpot and cover with water.

2. Add salt, pepper, and a pinch of saffron.

3. Cook until soft, 25-35 minutes.

4. Cool. Remove chicken from bones and set aside.

5. Add potatoes, butter, onion, celery, and carrot to stock. Bring to a hard boil, cooking until vegetables soften.

6. Meanwhile, in a bowl, mix eggs, oil, and flour together, adding water a spoonful at a time until dough holds together when stirred with a fork.

7. Roll dough about ¼" thick in a large square.

8. Cut into 2" squares. Drop one at a time into boiling broth.

9. Cook about 30-40 minutes. When the pot pie noodles are nearly done cooking, stir cooked chicken into pot until heated through.

# Plantain and Chicken Curry

BETTY LICHTY, HORN OF PLENTY

*Makes 4 servings*
*Prep. Time: 20 minutes* ❦ *Cooking Time: 40 minutes or so*

4 chicken breast halves

4 cups water

1 onion, sliced

1 medium apple, peeled and cut in cubes

4 Tbsp. (half stick) butter

1 bay leaf

2 Tbsp. flaked coconut, plus more for garnish

3 tsp. curry powder

3 Tbsp. flour

salt and pepper to taste

1 cup heavy cream

1 ripe plantain (yellow skin with black spots), cubed

1. Boil chicken breasts until tender in about 4 cups water. Remove chicken from broth. Reserve 1½ cups broth.

2. Cut chicken in bite-size cubes.

3. In a saucepan, sauté onion and apple in butter.

4. Add bay leaf, coconut flakes, and curry powder. Sprinkle with flour and sauté for 3 minutes. While stirring, add reserved broth.

5. When sauce is smooth, add salt and pepper to taste. Add cream, plantain, and chicken. Simmer for 10 minutes.

6. Serve over bed of rice and garnish with coconut flakes.

# Lattice-Top Chicken Bake

LOUELLA E. GROFF, C. Z. MARTIN SONS

*Makes 4–6 servings*
*Prep. Time: 25 minutes*
*Baking Time: 13-20 minutes*

1 lb. fresh *or* frozen broccoli, broken into florets

1 lb. fresh *or* frozen cauliflower, broken into florets

1 lb. fresh *or* frozen carrots, sliced

10-oz. can cream of chicken soup

¾ cup milk

¼ tsp. seasoned salt

2 cups cooked, chopped chicken

1 cup shredded cheddar cheese, *divided*

1 onion, chopped, *divided*

1 cup biscuit mix

1 egg, lightly beaten

¼ cup milk

1. Parboil fresh vegetable or thaw and drain vegetables if frozen.

2. Combine soup, milk, salt, chicken, vegetables, ½ cup cheese, and half of onions.

3. Spread mixture into a greased 8"x12" baking dish.

4. Combine biscuit mix, egg, and milk to form a soft dough.

5. Spoon over hot chicken mixture to form a checkerboard design.

6. Bake uncovered at 350° for 10-15 minutes.

7. Top with remaining cheese and onions and bake 3-5 minutes more until cheese melts and onions are lightly browned.

NOTE

*Good for Sunday dinner!*

# Chicken Filling Bake

REUBEN AND MARY LAPP, COUNTRY MEADOWS FARMS

*Makes 10–12 servings*
*Prep. Time: 15 minutes*
*Baking Time: 1¼ hours*

9 slices bread

2-4 cups cooked, chopped chicken

½ cup (1 stick) butter, melted

1½ cups chicken broth

4 eggs, beaten

1 cup milk

1 tsp. salt

9 slices cheese

2 10¾-oz. cans cream of mushroom soup

2 cups crushed buttery crackers *or* corn flakes

1. Place bread slices in bottom of greased 9"x13" baking pan.

2. Top with chopped chicken.

3. Melt butter in a saucepan.

4. Add chicken broth, eggs, milk, and salt. Whisk.

5. Pour mixture over bread and chicken.

6. Top with cheese slices and spread soup on top.

7. Cover with crushed buttery crackers or corn flakes.

8. Bake uncovered at 350° for 1¼ hours.

TIP

*I got this recipe from my mother-in-law. She served it at a family gathering, and we all wanted to try it for our own families. This is our family favorite! I almost always bake two chickens, serve baked chicken one day, then use the leftovers to prepare this recipe. Delicious served with mashed potatoes and peas.*

# Hot Chicken Salad

VIV HUNT, VIV'S VARIETIES

*Makes 12 servings* ❧ *Prep. Time: 20 minutes* ❧ *Cooking Time: about 1 hour*

3-lb. chicken
1 cup uncooked rice
1 cup diced celery
¾ cup mayonnaise
½ cup chopped onions, lightly sautéed
10¾-oz. can cream of chicken soup
3 hard-boiled eggs, chopped
2-oz. jar pimentos
2 Tbsp. chopped green bell peppers
1 Tbsp. chopped onion
1 Tbsp. lemon juice
¼ tsp. salt
8-oz. can sliced water chestnuts
½-1 cup buttered bread crumbs

1. Cook chicken. Cool and remove from bones. Chop into small pieces.

2. Cook rice according to package directions.

3. Mix all ingredients except bread crumbs and spoon into a greased casserole. Top with bread crumbs.

4. Bake at 350° for 45 minutes.

NOTE

*My daughter-in-law, who is a wonderful cook, made this for our first meal together.*

# Turkey Filling

MARY W. HESS, FUNK BROTHERS, INC.

*Makes 10–12 servings* ❧ *Prep. Time: 20 minutes* ❧ *Baking Time: about 2 hours*

1 small turkey *or* 1 large roasting chicken
¾ cup water
4 cups soft bread crumbs
2 eggs
2 tsp. salt
1 cup finely chopped celery
1 cup finely chopped carrots
10¾-oz. can cream of mushroom soup
1 cup milk

1. Roast turkey or chicken in oven in ¾ cup water until very soft. Reserve the breast for cold sandwiches.

2. Remove all meat from bones.

3. Put all ingredients into large mixing bowl, including broth from baking fowl. Mix well, adding milk as needed. This mixture should be very moist.

4. Put into roaster and bake at 350° for 30 minutes to 1 hour.

# Turkey Loaf

RUTH L. MELLINGER, C. H. THOMAS AND SON

*Makes 8 servings*
*Prep. Time: 20 minutes*
*Baking Time: 1-1¼ hours*

3 eggs
1½ cups tomato juice
1 cup dry quick oats
1 tsp. Worcestershire sauce
1 tsp. poultry seasoning
1 tsp. salt
pepper to taste
3 lbs. ground turkey
2-3 Tbsp. ketchup

1. Beat eggs. Add tomato juice, oats, Worcestershire sauce, poultry seasoning, salt, and pepper. Blend well. Add ground turkey and mix well.

2. Form into a loaf and place in a greased 9"x13" baking pan. Brush top with ketchup.

3. Bake at 350° for 1-1¼ hours.

# Shepherd's Pie

DENISE TORBERT, THE GOODIE SHOPPE

*Makes 4 servings*
*Prep. Time: 20 minutes*
*Baking Time: 30-40 minutes*

2 cups mashed potatoes, *divided*
2 cups cooked vegetables
1 cup diced, cooked turkey
3 slices bread, cubed
1 cup gravy
¼ tsp. pepper
¼ tsp. dried oregano
¼ tsp. dried basil
dash of seasoning salt

1. Line a greased baking dish with 1 cup mashed potatoes.

2. Fill with vegetables, turkey (or any leftover meat), bread cubes, gravy, and seasonings. Cover with 1 cup mashed potatoes.

3. Bake at 350° for 30-40 minutes.

TIP
_____

*Great way to use leftovers!*

# Turkey Sausage with Fettuccine

SUSAN GLOUNER, THE TURKEY LADY

*Makes 4 servings*
*Prep. Time: 15 minutes*
*Cooking Time: 15 minutes*

¾ lb. fettucine

2 Tbsp. butter, *divided*

¼ cup olive oil

8 cloves garlic, peeled, sliced

2 Tbsp. finely chopped fresh sage

1 lb. sweet Italian turkey sausage,
casing removed

¼ tsp. dried red pepper

salt and pepper, to taste

1 cup (about 3 oz.) grated
Asiago cheese

1. Cook pasta according to directions on package.

2. Meanwhile, melt 1 Tbsp. butter and olive oil in heavy skillet over medium heat.

3. Add garlic slices and saute until golden. Remove garlic from skillet.

4. Increase heat to medium high and saute sage until it starts to crisp.

5. Add sausage and saute until browned, breaking it up with a fork.

6. Drain pasta. Add pasta and remaining 1 Tbsp. butter to skillet.

7. Toss pasta with sausage mixture. Add red pepper. Season with salt and pepper to taste.

8. Transfer pasta and sausage to a large bowl. Top with Asiago cheese and crispy garlic.

**From the other side of the Market stand . . .**

# JIM ZINK OF THE HERB SHOP

Jim Zink opened The Herb Shop on Central Market in 1994. For 20 years he weighed out orders for his customers from his more than 250 sparkling glass jars, filled with herbs and spices, 60 kinds of loose and bagged teas, and plain and flavored pastas.

In the time-honored tradition of Central Market, Jim just passed the stand to his granddaughter, Corrie Breen.

"Every day I came to Market was a good day," Jim smiles. "It wasn't like a job. I looked forward to coming.

"The customers want us to be here. They're thankful for what we all sell.

"It's casual, and you make friends here. Pretty soon you know who's sick, who's getting married. ... "

# Herbed Fish en Papillote

CORRIE BREEN, LANCASTER, PA

*Makes 2 servings*
*Prep Time: 5 minutes*
*Baking Time: 12 minutes*

2 4-oz. fish fillets
1½ tsp. lemon juice
1 Tbsp. butter, softened
2 tsp. Fish Herbs blend from The Herb Shop
parchment paper

1. Combine lemon juice, butter, and Fish Herbs in a small bowl.

2. Cut two pieces of parchment paper, approximately 12″ square.

3. Rub each fillet of fish with the herb mixture and place just off-center in each piece of parchment paper. Fold the paper over the fish until the edges meet. Tightly crimp the edges and fold them inward until you have a tight packet that steam cannot escape.

4. Place the packets on a baking sheet and place in oven. Bake at 375° until the packets are fully puffed up and the fish is cooked through, about 12 minutes.

NOTES

1. *Almost any fish will work for this recipe. Simply reduce the cooking time for a more delicate fish and increase the time for a firmer fish.*

2. *My grandmother founded The Herb Shop in 1980. One of her favorite foods was fish, and she created our blend of Fish Herbs specifically to enhance her fish entrees. I believe this simple recipe really showcases the herb blend she created. While she never got to try this specific preparation, I think she would have loved it.*

# Stuffed Flounder in Basil Cream Sauce

ETHEL STONER, JOHN R. STONER VEGETABLES

*Makes 6–8 servings*
*Prep. Time: 20 minutes*
*Cooking/Baking Time: 45 minutes*

¼ cup chopped onion

4 Tbsp. (half stick) butter, *divided*

½ lb. fresh crab meat *or* 7½-oz. can crab meat

½ cup fresh mushrooms *or* 3-oz. can mushrooms, drained but juice reserved

½ cup cracker crumbs

2 Tbsp. parsley

2 Tbsp. mayonnaise

8 flounder fillets, about 2 lbs. total

3 Tbsp. flour

1 cup milk

3-oz. pkg. cream cheese, softened

1 Tbsp. dried basil

garlic powder

1 Tbsp. Worcestershire sauce

4 oz. Swiss cheese, grated

paprika

1. Sauté onion in 1 Tbsp. butter until onion is transparent. Stir in crab meat, mushrooms, cracker crumbs, parsley, and mayonnaise. Spread over fillets.

2. Roll up fillets and place seam-side down in greased baking dish.

3. Melt remaining 3 Tbsp. butter in saucepan. Blend in flour and add milk, cream cheese, and mushroom liquid, if you wish.

4. Cook mixture until it thickens.

5. Add basil, garlic powder, and Worcestershire sauce.

6. Pour mixture over fillets in baking dish.

7. Bake at 400° for 25 minutes.

8. Remove from oven and sprinkle with Swiss cheese and paprika.

9. Return to oven and bake 10 minutes longer.

# Haddock Flake Pie

CHARLES FOX AND LARRY MCELHENNY, NEW HOLLAND SEAFOOD

*Makes 6 servings*
*Prep. Time: 25 minutes*
*Cooking/Baking Time: 45 minutes*

3 Tbsp. butter

1 onion, sliced

3 Tbsp. flour

1 tsp. salt

⅛ tsp. pepper

⅛ tsp. dried thyme

½ cup whole milk

1½ cups fish stock

2 small carrots, cooked and diced

1 small potato, cooked and diced

1 tsp. Worcestershire sauce

1 lb. haddock, flaked

pie dough, enough to cover top of casserole, approximately the same amount needed to top an 8" pie

1. Melt butter and brown onion lightly. Stir in flour, salt, pepper, and thyme.

2. When well blended, add milk and fish stock, stirring constantly.

3. Continue stirring and add carrots and potatoes. Stir until sauce thickens.

4. Add Worcestershire sauce and flaked fish.

5. Pour into a greased baking dish and cover with pastry crust.

6. Bake at 450° for 20-25 minutes or until top is golden brown.

# Tuna Spinach Casserole

CYNTHIA STRUBE, MARION CHEESE

*Makes 4 servings* ❧ *Prep. Time: 20 minutes* ❧ *Cooking/Baking Time: 30 minutes*

2 10-oz. pkgs. frozen chopped spinach *or* 1 lb. fresh spinach

2 7-oz. cans tuna, drained

2 Tbsp. lemon juice

6 Tbsp. grated cheese, *divided*

⅔ cup bread crumbs

½ tsp. salt

1 tsp. nutmeg

dash of pepper

1 cup mayonnaise

1 large tomato

1. Thaw frozen spinach. Squeeze dry. Or chop fresh spinach. Steam just until it wilts, and squeeze dry.

2. Combine tuna, lemon juice, 4 Tbsp. cheese, bread crumbs, salt, nutmeg, and pepper.

3. Add spinach and mix well. Fold in mayonnaise.

4. Place mixture in 1-quart, greased baking dish. Cover with thinly sliced tomato.

5. Sprinkle remaining cheese over tomatoes.

6. Bake at 350° for 20 minutes.

# Deviled Crab Meat

RUTH ESHLEMAN, GIVANT'S BAKERY

*Makes 6 servings* ❧ *Prep. Time: 20 minutes* ❧ *Cooking/Baking Time: 45 minutes*

2 Tbsp. (¼ stick) butter

2½ Tbsp. flour

1½ cups milk

2 cups crab meat

1 tsp. salt

¼ tsp. paprika

2 Tbsp. lemon juice

1 cup buttered bread crumbs

1. Melt butter and add flour. Slowly stir in milk to make a thickened white sauce.

2. In a separate bowl, mix crab meat, salt, paprika, and lemon juice. Add to white sauce, stirring constantly.

3. Pour mixture into a buttered baking dish. Put bread crumbs on top.

4. Bake at 400° for 25 minutes.

# Crab Casserole

SARA JANE WENGER, TOM'S FLOWER GARDEN

*Makes 4-6 servings*  ❦  *Prep. Time: 20 minutes*  ❦  *Baking Time: 1 hour 20 minutes*

½ cup (I stick) butter
½ lb. cheese, grated
I cup milk, *divided*
I Tbsp. flour
I lb. crab meat
pepper and paprika to taste
cracker crumbs

1. Melt butter. Add cheese and melt, stirring constantly.

2. Stir in ¾ cup milk. Thicken mixture with flour that has been mixed with ¼ cup milk.

3. Add crab meat and seasonings to mixture. Place in greased baking dish.

4. Top with cracker crumbs and bake at 325° for 1 hour.

# Cheesy Crab Pie

ETHEL STONER, JOHN R. STONER VEGETABLES

*Makes a 9" pie*  ❦  *Prep. Time: 15 minutes*  ❦  *Baking Time: 40-45 minutes*

½ cup mayonnaise
2 Tbsp. flour
2 eggs, beaten
I cup evaporated milk
6½-oz. can flaked crab meat
8 oz. Swiss cheese, grated
¼ cup chopped onion
I 9" unbaked pie shell

1. Combine mayonnaise, flour, eggs, and milk. Mix until well blended.

2. Drain crab meat and grate cheese.

3. Add crab meat, cheese, and onion to mayonnaise mixture.

4. Place into unbaked pie shell and bake at 350° for 40-45 minutes.

VARIATIONS

1. *Add ¼ cup chopped green bell peppers to Step 3.*

2. *Use Italian Fontina cheese instead of Swiss. It does not become rubbery when cooked and allows the crab to show well.*

# Crab Cakes

RUTH WIDDERS, IRWIN S. WIDDERS PRODUCE

*Makes 8 servings*
*Prep. Time: 20 minutes*
*Chilling Time: several hours*
*Cooking Time: about 20 minutes*

1 lb. crab meat
2 Tbsp. lemon juice
1 Tbsp. butter
1 Tbsp. all-purpose flour
½ cup milk
salt to taste
2 eggs
2 Tbsp. mayonnaise
1 cup bread crumbs
⅛ tsp. pepper
1 tsp. dry mustard
1 tsp. Worcestershire sauce

**Breading:**
3 Tbsp. flour
½ cup bread crumbs
2-3 Tbsp. shortening

1. Pick over crab meat and discard any bits of shell or cartilage. Sprinkle lemon juice over crab meat.

2. Make a medium white sauce by melting butter. Stir in flour, milk, and salt to taste. Stir constantly until mixture is smooth and thickened.

3. Beat eggs. Then mix them with the white sauce.

4. Add mayonnaise, bread crumbs, pepper, dry mustard, and Worcestershire sauce. Stir well.

5. Gently combine crab meat with mixture.

6. Chill until firm enough to shape into cakes.

7. Prepare crumbs for breading cakes by mixing 3 Tbsp. flour and ½ cup bread crumbs.

8. Dredge crab cakes in flavored bread crumbs. Fry in shortening, turning a few times, until both sides are browned.

NOTE

*This is my favorite seafood recipe. The crab cakes are delicious with a baked potato and salad.*

# Shrimp or Roast Pork Fried Rice

TUYEN KIM HO, KIM'S CANDIES

*Makes 4 servings*
*Prep. Time: 15 minutes*
*Cooking Time: 15-20 minutes*

2 eggs

pinch of salt

4 Tbsp. oil, *divided*

1 clove garlic, minced

4 cups cooked rice

¼ tsp. sugar

2 Tbsp. soy sauce

1 cup diced roast pork *or* cooked shrimp

½ cup sliced carrots, cooked

½ cup peas, cooked

1. Beat eggs lightly and add a pinch of salt.

2. Heat 1 Tbsp. oil in a frying pan. Scramble eggs until they are cooked through but still moist and fluffy.

3. Remove from pan and cut into small pieces.

4. Scrape pan and heat the remaining 3 Tbsp. oil. Add minced garlic and rice and stir-fry 3-4 minutes until coated with oil.

5. Dissolve sugar in soy sauce and sprinkle mixture over rice. Add the eggs and roast pork or shrimp. Stir until well mixed.

6. Add carrots and peas and heat through before serving.

# Scallops and Pasta Romano

CYNTHIA STRUBE, MARION CHEESE

*Makes 6 servings*
*Prep. Time: 15 minutes*
*Baking Time: about 30 minutes*

1 lb. bay scallops

2 cloves garlic, minced

½ cup (1 stick) butter at room temperature, *divided*

2 Tbsp. dried parsley flakes

1 tsp. dried basil

¼ tsp. pepper

8-oz. pkg. cream cheese, softened

⅔ cup boiling water

8 ozs. fettucini, linguine, *or* spaghetti

¾ cup grated Romano *or* Parmesan cheese, *divided*

1. Cook scallops and garlic in ¼ cup butter just until scallops are done. Keep warm.

2. Combine remaining ¼ cup butter, parsley, and basil in a double boiler. Blend in pepper and cream cheese.

3. Stir in boiling water and mix well. Keep warm over pan of hot water.

4. Cook pasta according to package directions and drain.

5. Toss scallop mixture into pasta.

6. Sprinkle with ½ cup grated cheese and toss.

7. Pour cream cheese mixture over pasta and toss until well coated.

8. Place pasta into serving dish and sprinkle with remaining ¼ cup grated cheese.

---

NOTE

*A wonderful combination of seafood, pasta, and herbs!*

# Perciatelli with Creamy Clam Sauce

CORRIE BREEN, THE HERB SHOP

*Makes 4 servings*
*Prep. Time: 15 minutes*
*Cooking Time: 20 minutes*

8 oz. perciatelli pasta

1 Tbsp. olive oil

¼ cup finely diced onion

2 cloves garlic, minced

½ tsp. dried oregano

½ tsp. dried thyme

¼ tsp. crushed red pepper flakes

¼ tsp. white pepper

pinch salt

½ cup dry white wine

¼ cup clam juice

1 lb. clams, steamed and picked from shells

½ cup heavy cream

grated Parmesan, to taste

1. Cook perciatelli al dente, according to package directions. Drain and set aside.

2. While the pasta is cooking, heat the oil over medium heat in a large saute pan.

3. Add the onions and cook until soft, about 3 minutes.

4. Add the garlic, oregano, thyme, red pepper flakes, salt, and pepper and, stirring often, cook until fragrant, about 1 minute.

5. Add the wine and clam juice and cook for 5 minutes.

6. Add the clams and cook until heated through, about 2 minutes.

7. Add the cream and simmer for 5 minutes, or until sauce starts to thicken.

8. Toss sauce with the pasta until well coated. Divide into four portions and top each with desired amount of Parmesan cheese.

NOTE

*If a white sauce came out too thin, my grandmother always added a little bit of instant mashed potatoes until it became thicker. "Just use about a teaspoon at a time and wait a minute or two before adding more," she'd say.*

# Cajun Shrimp

CYNTHIA STRUBE, MARION CHEESE

*Makes 3 large servings*
*Prep. Time: 20 minutes*
*Cooking Time: about 10 minutes*

I lb. shrimp
¼ tsp. ground cayenne pepper
¼ tsp. black pepper
½ tsp. salt
½ tsp. crushed red pepper
½ tsp. dried thyme
I tsp. dried basil
½ tsp. dried oregano
⅓ cup (5⅓ Tbsp.) butter
3 cloves garlic, minced
I tsp. Worcestershire sauce
2 cups diced tomatoes
¼ cup beer, room temperature

1. Peel and devein shrimp under cold running water. Drain well.

2. Combine all dry seasonings.

3. In a large skillet or wok, combine butter, garlic, Worcestershire sauce, and dry seasonings. Stir over high heat until butter is melted.

4. Add the tomatoes and the shrimp. Cook for approximately 3 minutes (until shrimp is almost cooked), stirring constantly.

5. Add the beer. Cover and cook for 1 minute longer.

6. Serve over rice with crusty French bread.

NOTE

*Great to serve to friends, but be sure the friends enjoy hot and spicy food!*

# Baked Salmon

JEAN RISSER, HOFFMASTER AND WIKE, THE WOODEN CAOUSEL

*Makes 4 servings*
Prep. Time: 15 minutes    ❦    Baking Time: 40 minutes

2 cups fresh salmon, broken into pieces
2 cups cracker crumbs
2 eggs, beaten
2 cups hot milk
butter and salt to taste

1. Put alternate layers of salmon and cracker crumbs into a greased baking dish.

2. Beat eggs and slowly add hot milk, stirring.

3. Pour over salmon and crumbs. Add butter and salt.

4. Bake at 375° for 40 minutes.

# Poached Salmon

PAM GRIFFE, THE GOODIE SHOPPE

*Makes 4 servings*
Prep. Time: 15 minutes    ❦    Cooling Time: about 30 minutes    ❦    Cooking Time: 15 minutes

4 salmon steaks, 1" thick, skinned
½ cup white wine
½ cup water
dill sprigs
1 lemon, sliced

**Sauce:**
1 cup mayonnaise
1 cup crème fraiche
2 Tbsp. lemon juice
1 tsp. white wine
½ tsp. salt
½ tsp. white pepper
3 Tbsp. fresh dill
dash of cayenne pepper
lemon slices and dill sprigs, for garnish

1. Poach salmon steaks in ½ cup wine and ½ cup water for 15 minutes.

2. Mix sauce ingredients together to make dill sauce.

3. Let salmon cool to room temperature. Cover with dill sauce.

4. Just before serving, garnish with lemon slices and dill sprigs.

NOTE

*A cool, refreshing dish for summer entertaining!*

# Mr. Bill's Lobster Rolls

MR. BILL'S SEAFOOD

*Makes 3 servings*
*Prep. Time: 10 minutes*

I lb. steamed, chilled lobster
meat

4 ribs celery

½ cup mayonnaise

3 hot dog buns (Mr. Bill's uses
Pepperidge Farms)

lettuce, *optional*

1. Squeeze out excess juice from lobster.

2. Chop lobster meat medium coarse.

3. Chop celery crosswise into half-moons.

4. Add mayonnaise.

5. Fold ingredients together gently.

6. Fill buns with lettuce if desired, then mound
with lobster salad.

TIP

*For instructions about how to steam a lobster, see
page 66.*

# Long's Gourmet Seafood Sauce

CHARLES J. LONG, LONG'S HORSERADISH

*Makes 4–8 servings*
*Prep. Time: 5 minutes*

4 oz. chili sauce

I oz. Long's horseradish

I tsp. fresh lime juice

pinch Old Bay seasoning

I tsp. Worcestershire sauce

4 drops Tabasco sauce

1. Mix all ingredients thoroughly.

2. Store in tightly covered jar in refrigerator.

# Long's Cocktail Sauce

CHARLES J. LONG, LONG'S HORSERADISH

*Makes 4–8 servings*

2 cups ketchup
5-oz. jar Long's horseradish
1 Tbsp. Worcestershire sauce
1 Tbsp. lemon juice
5 drops Tabasco sauce
1 tsp. salt

1. Mix all ingredients thoroughly.

2. Store inverted in a tightly covered jar in refrigerator.

VARIATIONS

1. *Delete salt for no-salt diets.*

2. *If sauce is too hot, add more ketchup to make it milder.*

3. *If sauce is too thick, add equal parts water and vinegar to thin.*

NOTE

*Cocktail sauce is a favorite for shrimp, but it is also delicious on other seafood, hot dogs, and hamburgers.*

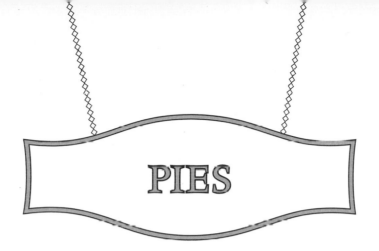

# Strawberry Snowbank Pie

ESTHER GROFF, KIEFER'S MEATS AND CHEESE

*Makes a 9" pie*
*Prep. Time: 20 minutes*
*Cooking Time: about 10 minutes*

1 quart fresh strawberries

1¼ cups sugar

½ cup water

½ tsp. cream of tartar

2 egg whites at room temperature

pinch of salt

¼ tsp. almond extract

1 9" baked pie shell

1. Wash, hull, and drain berries.

2. Fill pie shell with whole, unsweetened berries. Put the prettiest berries in the center.

3. Mix sugar, water, and cream of tartar in saucepan. Cover and bring to a boil.

4. Uncover and cook until syrup spins long threads (240° on candy thermometer).

5. Stiffly beat egg whites. Fold in salt.

6. Gradually pour sugar mixture into egg whites, beating constantly. Beat until mixture piles into peaks.

7. Add almond extract.

8. Pile "snowbank" egg white mixture onto pie around perimeter of pie, leaving center uncovered.

9. Chill before serving.

# Fresh Strawberry Pie

ROSE MECK, MECK'S PRODUCE

*Makes a 9" pie* ❧ *Prep. Time: 15 minutes* ❧ *Cooking Time: 10 minutes*

I quart fresh strawberries
I cup sugar
1 ¼ cups water, *divided*
4 Tbsp. cornstarch
¼ tsp. salt
I Tbsp. lemon juice
3-oz. pkg. strawberry gelatin
I 9" baked pie shell

1. Stem strawberries; then slice them. Set aside.

2. Dissolve sugar in ½ cup water and bring to a boil.

3. In separate container mix remaining ¾ cup water with cornstarch. Stir to form a smooth paste.

4. Add cornstarch mixture to boiling sugar water and stir.

5. Add all other ingredients except strawberries. Heat, stirring constantly, until mixture is thick and transparent.

6. Place strawberries in pie shell.

7. Pour glaze over berries.

8. Chill until ready to serve.

# Fresh Banana Rhubarb Pie

MABEL HAVERSTICK, VIV'S VARIETIES

*Makes a 9" pie* ❧ *Prep. Time: 20 minutes* ❧ *Baking Time: 35 minutes*

½ lb. fresh rhubarb
3 large, ripe bananas
I cup sugar
¼ cup freshly squeezed orange juice
3 Tbsp. flour
¼ tsp. salt
¼ tsp. cinnamon
I tsp. nutmeg
I Tbsp. butter
I 9" unbaked double pie crust

1. Slice rhubarb (should yield about 3 cups).

2. Slice bananas (should yield about 3 cups).

3. Gently combine rhubarb, bananas, sugar, orange juice, flour, salt, and spices.

4. Spread into pastry in pie plate. Dot with butter.

5. Place crust on top. Pinch edges together.

6. Bake at 450° for 15 minutes. Reduce oven temperature to 350° and bake 20 minutes longer, until golden brown.

# Rhubarb Meringue Pie

## MARGARET GROFF, FRIEND OF HELEN E. BITNER

*Makes a 9" pie* ❦ *Prep. Time: 20 minutes* ❦ *Baking Time: 1 hour 15 minutes*

3 cups sliced fresh rhubarb

I 9" unbaked pie shell

I cup + 4 Tbsp. sugar, *divided*

2 Tbsp. flour

I Tbsp. water

⅛ tsp. salt

3 egg yolks, well beaten

3 egg whites

1. Fill pie shell with sliced fresh rhubarb.

2. Thoroughly mix together 1 cup sugar, flour, water, salt, and egg yolks.

3. Pour over rhubarb. Bake at 400° for 30 minutes.

4. Reduce oven temperature to 350° and bake for 30 more minutes.

5. To prepare meringue, beat egg whites until stiff. Add 4 Tbsp. sugar and beat until well mixed.

6. Spread over pie.

7. Return pie to 350° oven until meringue is brown, about 15 minutes.

# Mother Stover's Peach Pie

## SAM NEFF, S. CLYDE WEAVER, INC.

*Makes 2 9" pies* ❦ *Prep. Time: 25 minutes* ❦ *Baking Time: about an hour*

8 fresh peaches

3 eggs

¾ cup sugar

4 Tbsp. flour

2 Tbsp. (¼ stick) butter, melted

cinnamon

2 9" unbaked pie shells

1. Peel and dice peaches. Separate the eggs.

2. Brush pie shells with some of the egg white. Bake shells (weighted with rice or dried beans) at 350° until lightly brown.

3. Blend sugar, flour, and butter. Add egg yolks.

4. Beat egg whites until stiff. Fold into mixture.

5. Put diced peaches into partially baked pie shells.

6. Pour mixture over peaches. Sprinkle with cinnamon.

7. Bake at 425° for 15 minutes.

8. Reduce oven temperature to 325° and bake for another 30 minutes.

# Orange Pie

DORIS REINHART, D. M. WEAVER AND SONS, INC.

*Makes 2 9" pies*  ❧  *Prep. Time: 20 minutes*  ❧  *Cooking/Baking Time: 35-40 minutes*

8 Tbsp. (I stick) butter
I orange, cut up fine
I cup sugar
2 egg yolks
2 cups milk
¼ cup flour
2 egg whites
2 9" unbaked pie shells

1. Melt butter and brown slightly.

2. Thoroughly mix all ingredients together except egg whites and pie shells.

3. Beat egg whites until stiff and fold into pie filling.

4. Pour into pie shells and bake at 350° for 30-35 minutes.


# Concord Grape Pie

DORIS SHENK, DONEGAL GARDENS
RUTH WIDDERS, IRWIN S. WIDDERS PRODUCE

*Makes a 9" pie*  ❧  *Prep. Time: 25 minutes*  ❧  *Cooking/Baking Time: 45 minutes*

4 cups Concord grapes
I cup sugar
⅓ cup flour
¼ tsp. salt
2 Tbsp. (¼ stick) butter, melted
I Tbsp. lemon juice
I 9" unbaked pie shell

***Crumb Topping:***
½ cup flour
½ cup sugar
¼ cup (½ stick) butter, softened

1. Slip skins from grapes. Set skins aside.

2. Bring pulp of grapes to a boil. Reduce heat and simmer for 5 minutes.

3. Remove from heat and put through food press to separate seeds from pulp.

4. Stir pulp and skins together.

5. In a large bowl, combine sugar, flour, and salt. Add melted butter and lemon juice to dry ingredients.

6. Add grapes and mix well.

7. Spoon into unbaked pie shell.

8. To prepare crumb topping, sift flour with sugar. Cut butter into mixture until it is crumbly. Sprinkle topping over pie filling.

9. Bake at 400° for 40 minutes.

Sticky Buns, page 42

Pecan Pie, page 200

Turkey Sliders, page 22

Baked Figs and Goat
Cheese, page 16

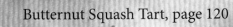

Butternut Squash Tart, page 120

# Blueberry Pie

JOYCE DEITER, EISENBERGER'S BAKED GOODS

*Makes a 9" pie* ❧ *Prep. Time: 15 minutes* ❧ *Cooking/Baking Time: about 45 minutes*

6 cups fresh blueberries
½ cup water
1 cup sugar
1 Tbsp. butter
4 Tbsp. cornstarch
1 9" unbaked pie shell

1. Wash and drain blueberries. Combine blueberries, water, sugar, and butter in saucepan and bring to a boil.

2. Add cornstarch and boil until mixture is clear.

3. Cool mixture and place in unbaked pie shell.

4. Bake at 425° for 10 minutes.

5. Reduce oven temperature to 375° and bake another 20 minutes. Cool and serve.

# Double Good Blueberry Pie

SALLIE Y. LAPP, FLOWER GARDEN CRAFTS

*Makes a 9" pie* ❧ *Prep. Time: 20 minutes* ❧ *Cooking Time: 10 minutes*

¾ cup sugar
3 Tbsp. cornstarch
⅛ tsp. salt
¼ cup water
4 cups fresh blueberries, *divided*
1 Tbsp. butter
1 Tbsp. lemon juice
1 9" baked pie shell
whipped cream

1. Combine sugar, cornstarch, and salt in saucepan.

2. Add water and 2 cups of blueberries.

3. Cook over medium heat, stirring constantly, until mixture comes to a boil and is thickened and clear. Mixture will be quite thick.

4. Remove from heat and stir in butter and lemon juice.

5. Cool.

6. Place remaining 2 cups of blueberries in baked 9" pie shell.

7. Top with cooked blueberry mixture. Chill.

8. Serve with whipped cream.

# Lemon Sponge Pie

### RUTH ESHLEMAN, GIVANT'S BAKERY

*Makes an 8" pie*   ❧   *Prep. Time: 20 minutes*   ❧   *Baking Time: 40-45 minutes*

2 Tbsp. (¼ stick) butter, softened
1 cup sugar
3 Tbsp. flour
½ tsp. salt
3 eggs, separated
juice and rind of 1 lemon
1½ cups milk
1 8" unbaked pie shell

1. Cream butter and sugar together. Add flour and salt.

2. Separate the eggs and add egg yolks to mixture.

3. Add lemon juice, grated rind, and milk.

4. Beat egg whites until stiff. Fold into mixture.

5. Pour into unbaked pie shell and bake at 325° for 40 to 45 minutes.

# Dried Snitz (Sliced Apple) Pie

### CHARLES HESS

*Makes a 9" pie*
*Prep. Time: 20 minutes*   ❧   *Cooking/Baking Time: about 1 hour*

2 cups dried tart apple slices
1½ cups warm water
⅔ cup sugar
½ tsp. ground cloves
½ tsp. cinnamon
1 9" unbaked double pie crust

1. Place apple slices and warm water in a saucepan. Cook over low heat until soft.

2. When apples are soft, drain in a colander, pressing them to remove water.

3. Add sugar and spices to apples. Put mixture in an unbaked pie shell.

4. Cover pie with a top crust. Pinch crusts together around the edges.

5. Bake at 425° for 15 minutes.

6. Reduce oven temperature to 375° and continue to bake for 35 minutes.

# Greatest Apple Pie

DORIS SHENK, DONEGAL GARDENS

*Makes a 9" pie* ❧ *Prep. Time: 20 minutes* ❧ *Baking Time: 55 minutes*

¾-1 cup sugar
2 Tbsp. flour
½-1 tsp. cinnamon
dash nutmeg and salt
6 cups sliced, peeled apples
2 Tbsp. (¼ stick) butter
1 9" unbaked double pie crust

1. Combine sugar, flour, cinnamon, nutmeg, and salt. Add sliced apples and mix well.

2. Fill pie plate with apple mixture and dot with butter.

3. Cover with a top crust.

4. Bake at 400° for 55 minutes. Serve warm.

### VARIATION

*Cover with crumb topping instead of top crust.*

# Pumpkin Delight Pie

ALICE SHENK, SHENK'S CHEESE CO.

*Makes a 9" pie* ❧ *Prep. Time: 15 minutes* ❧ *Baking Time: 45-50 minutes*

2 cups cooked, pureed pumpkin
½ cup brown sugar
¼ cup sugar
2 Tbsp. flour
½ tsp. salt
2 eggs, slightly beaten
1 cup evaporated milk
½ tsp. vanilla extract
½ -1 tsp. ground cinnamon, *optional*
1 9" unbaked pie shell
whipped topping, for serving

1. Combine pumpkin, both sugars, flour, and salt.

2. Add eggs and mix well. Stir in evaporated milk and vanilla. Also add cinnamon, if you wish.

3. Pour into pie shell and bake at 375° for 45-50 minutes.

4. Serve cold with whipped topping.

# Pumpkin Pie

ANN KREIDER, VIV'S VARIETIES

*Makes 2 9" pies* ❧ *Prep. Time: 15 minutes* ❧ *Baking Time: 40 minutes*

| | |
|---|---|
| I cup cooked pumpkin | 1. Mix pumpkin, sugar, and egg yolks. |
| I cup sugar | 2. Stir in flour and spice. Add melted butter and warm milk. Mix well. |
| 4 eggs, separated | |
| ½ cup flour | 3. Beat egg whites until stiff. Fold into pumpkin mixture. |
| 2 tsp. pumpkin pie spice | |
| 2 Tbsp. (¼ stick) butter, melted | 4. Pour into two unbaked pie shells. |
| 4 cups warm milk | 5. Bake at 450° for 10 minutes. |
| 2 9" unbaked pie shells | 6. Reduce oven temperature to 325° and bake for 30 more minutes. |

# Raisin Cream Pie

DORIS SHENK, DONEGAL GARDENS

*Makes an 8" pie* ❧ *Prep. Time: 20 minutes* ❧ *Cooking/Baking Time: about 20 minutes*

| | |
|---|---|
| ¾ cup brown sugar | 1. In a double boiler, mix brown sugar, cornstarch, and ¼ cup milk until smooth. |
| 5 Tbsp. cornstarch | |
| 2¼ cups milk, *divided* | 2. Then add remaining milk and bring mixture to a boil over boiling water. |
| 2 egg yolks | |
| I Tbsp. butter | 3. Add egg yolks, butter, vanilla, and raisins. |
| I Tbsp. vanilla | 4. Remove from heat and pour mixture into a baked pie shell. |
| I cup raisins | |
| I 8" baked pie shell | 5. Prepare meringue by beating egg whites with vanilla and cream of tartar. |
| **Meringue Ingredients:** | |
| 3 egg whites | 6. Gradually add sugar and beat until mixture forms peaks. |
| ½ tsp. vanilla | |
| ¼ tsp. cream of tartar | 7. Spread meringue over pie. |
| 6 Tbsp. sugar | 8. Broil just until meringue is brown. It happens fast, so watch carefully to prevent burning! |

# Raisin Pie

PATRICIA A. CARTER, MCCOMSEY FAMILY

*Makes 2 8" pies* ❦ *Prep. Time: 15 minutes* ❦ *Baking Time: 30 minutes*

I cup sugar
I cup raisins
I Tbsp. flour
I Tbsp. vinegar
I Tbsp. butter, softened
dash of salt
I ½ cups boiling water
2 8" unbaked pie shells

1. Mix all ingredients together except water and pie shells.

2. Pour boiling water over mixture and stir well. Let mixture stand while preparing pie shells.

3. Mixture will seem thin. Do not add anything to thicken as mixture will set up as it bakes.

4. Bake at 375° for 30 minutes.

# Butterscotch Pie

ELLA PORTER, HIDDEN ACRES FLOWERS

*Makes a 9" pie* ❦ *Prep. Time: 15 minutes* ❦ *Cooking/Baking Time: about 25 minutes*

2 Tbsp. (¼ stick) butter
2 cups milk
2 egg yolks
⅓ cup flour
⅛ tsp. salt
I cup brown sugar, firmly packed
½ tsp. vanilla
I 9" baked pie shell
2 egg whites
2 Tbsp. sugar
pinch of cream of tartar

1. Melt butter in a saucepan. Add milk, yolks, flour, salt, and brown sugar and bring to a boil, stirring constantly. Continue stirring until mixture thickens.

2. Pour into baked pie shell.

3. Cool.

4. Beat egg whites until they form peaks.

5. Fold in sugar and cream of tartar.

6. Spread meringue over pie and put into broiler to brown. Watch carefully since it can quickly burn!

NOTE

*I enjoy this recipe because I received it from a dear friend, and it is delicious.*

# Peanut Butter Pie

MARY LOU GRABY, SPRING GLEN FARM KITCHENS, INC.

*Makes a 9" pie*  ❧  *Prep. Time: 15 minutes*
*Freezing Time: at least 4 hours*  ❧  *Standing Time: 10 minutes*

4 oz. (half an 8-oz. pkg.) cream cheese

½-1 cup peanut butter, according to your taste preference

½ cup milk

I cup confectioners sugar

8 oz. whipped topping

9" graham cracker crust

shaved chocolate or chocolate syrup, *optional*

1. Soften cream cheese to room temperature. Beat cream cheese, peanut butter, milk, and sugar together with electric mixer. Mix until well blended.

2. Fold whipped topping into mixture.

3. Spoon into graham cracker crust.

4. Freeze for at least four hours.

5. Remove from freezer and let stand about 10 minutes before serving.

6. Garnish with shaved chocolate or chocolate syrup, if you wish.

# Shoo-Fly Pie

MARIAN SWEIGART, S. CLYDE WEAVER, INC.
BARBIE KING, SHREINER'S FLOWERS

*Makes a 9" pie*  ❧  *Prep. Time: 20 minutes*  ❧  *Baking Time: 40 minutes*

I cup flour

⅔ cup brown sugar

I Tbsp. vegetable shortening

I egg

I cup molasses

¾ cup boiling water

I tsp. baking soda

I 9" unbaked pie shell

1. Mix flour and brown sugar together. Cut in shortening. Reserve ½ cup of this crumb mixture for topping.

2. To the remaining crumb mixture, add the egg, molasses, boiling water, and baking soda.

3. Spread mixture into unbaked pie shell.

4. Spread reserved crumbs over pie.

5. Bake at 375° for 10 minutes.

6. Reduce oven temperature to 350° and bake for 30 minutes longer.

# Wet-Bottom Shoo-Fly Pie

SALLIE Y. LAPP, SALLIE Y. LAPP

*Makes 5 8" pies* ❦ *Prep. Time: 20 minutes* ❦ *Baking Time: 55 minutes*

**Filling:**
2 tsp. baking soda
3 cups boiling water
3 cups molasses
1 cup brown sugar
8 eggs
5 8" unbaked pie shells

**Crumbs:**
6 cups flour
2 cups brown sugar
1 tsp. baking soda
1½ cups shortening

1. Dissolve 2 tsp. soda in boiling water. Add remaining filling ingredients and mix well.

2. Mix dry ingredients for crumbs.

3. Cut in shortening.

4. Beat 4 cups of crumbs into filling mixture. Save remaining crumbs.

5. Divide filling evenly into 5 unbaked pie shells. Use remaining crumbs to cover each pie.

6. Bake at 425° for 10 minutes.

7. Reduce oven temperature to 350° and bake 45 minutes longer.

# Sunday Pie

VIV HUNT, VIV'S VARIETIES

*Makes a 9" pie*

*Prep. Time: 15 minutes* ❦ *Cooking Time: about 15 minutes* ❦ *Chilling Time: 3 hours*

3½-oz. pkg. lemon pudding and pie filling

1 pkg. unflavored gelatin

1 cup sugar

2¼ cups water, *divided*

2 Tbsp. lemon juice

3 egg yolks

1 tsp. grated lemon rind

1 Tbsp. butter, melted

3 egg whites

1 cup whipped topping

1 9" baked pie shell

1. Combine pie filling mix, gelatin, sugar, ¼ cup water, and lemon juice in saucepan.

2. Blend in egg yolks and add remaining water. Cook and stir over medium heat until mixture comes to a full boil. Remove from heat.

3. Add lemon rind and butter.

4. Beat egg whites until peaks form. Gradually fold into hot pie filling.

5. Cover with wax paper. Chill.

6. Fold whipped topping into chilled pie filling. Pour into pie shell.

7. Chill pie until set (about 3 hours).

8. Garnish with remaining topping and lemon slices just before serving, if you wish.

NOTE

*Refreshing and delicious!*

# Coconut Pie

RUTH L. MELLINGER, E. H. THOMAS AND SON

*Makes a 9" pie* ❦ *Prep. Time: 20 minutes* ❦ *Baking Time: 45 minutes*

2 eggs, beaten

¾ cup sugar

1½ Tbsp. flour

1½ Tbsp. milk

1½ cups milk

1½ cups shredded fresh coconut, *divided*

1 tsp. vanilla

1 9" unbaked pie shell

1. Beat eggs and add sugar.

2. Mix flour with 1½ Tbsp. milk to make a smooth paste. Beat flour mixture into egg and sugar mixture.

3. Heat 1½ cups milk to near boiling point.

4. Add milk, 1 cup coconut, and vanilla to flour and egg mixture. Mix well.

5. Spoon into unbaked pie shell. Spread remaining ½ cup coconut over top of pie.

6. Bake at 400° for 15 minutes.

7. Reduce oven temperature to 350° and bake 30 minutes longer or until pie is set in the middle.

# Amish Pie

LOIS THOMAS, C. H. THOMAS AND SON

*Makes 2 9" pies* ❦ *Prep. Time: 15 minutes* ❦ *Baking Time: 45 minutes*

2 cups sugar

1 cup flour

1 cup molasses

3 cups buttermilk

2 eggs

1 tsp. baking soda

1 tsp. vanilla

½ cup shredded coconut

2 9" unbaked pie shells

1. Mix all ingredients together.

2. Pour into 2 unbaked pie shells.

3. Bake at 425° for 15 minutes.

4. Reduce oven temperature to 350° and bake another 30 minutes or until pie is set in the middle.

# Vanilla Pie

REBECCA KING, JOHN R. STONER VEGETABLES

*Makes 4 8" pies*

*Prep. Time: 20 minutes* ❧ *Cooking/Baking Time: 50 minutes*

1 cup sugar

1 cup molasses

3 cups water

1 heaping Tbsp. flour

1 egg, beaten

1 Tbsp. vanilla

4 8" unbaked pie shells

***Crumb Topping:***

2½ cups flour

1½ cups brown sugar

½ cup lard

1 tsp. baking soda

1 tsp. cream of tartar

1. Mix sugar, molasses, water, flour, egg, and vanilla and cook over medium heat until smooth and well mixed.

2. Pour into unbaked pie shells.

3. Mix all dry crumb ingredients together. Cut in lard until mixture forms crumbs.

4. Spread over vanilla pie filling.

5. Bake at 350° for 40 minutes.

**From the other side of the Market stand . . .**

# WENDY JO HESS OF
# WENDY JO'S HOMEMADE

Wendy Jo Hess's mother and grandmothers worked on Central Market. Wendy Jo hadn't planned to do that, but when she finished college and wasn't sure what she wanted to do next, she followed her love of baking, bid on a market stand, and started selling her extraordinary, made-from-scratch cookies and pies.

"The hours are longer than when I was growing up and working on my parents' dairy farm. But I get to meet people I'd never talk to otherwise.

"The socio-economic differences among my customers really interest me. *Everybody* shops here. Where else do you find that?

"One evening I was walking on the east side of the city with some friends, headed to dinner. We passed by a couple of girls jumping rope, when one of them said to the others, 'That's Wendy Jo. She bakes my cookies.' I was so warmed to be recognized outside of Market—and by a child!

"We say it often, but the relationships that form between customers and standholders are truly unique and special.

"My customers give me Christmas gifts and cards. They worry if I'm not at my stand. They invite me to parties. One author who buys my baked things encourages me to write and offers to proof my work. He even gave me the pen he used to write his first book! Jessica, the Market Manager, invited me to join a book club she's part of.

"Central Market is about more than selling my freshly baked treats!"

# Pecan Pie

WENDY HESS, WENDY JO'S HOMEMADE

*Makes a 9" pie, serves 6–8*  ❧  *Prep. Time: 20 minutes*  ❧  *Baking Time: 40 minutes*

3 eggs

1 scant cup light corn syrup

1 cup light brown sugar

⅔ tsp. salt

½ cup (1 stick) butter, melted

1 tsp. vanilla

1 heaping cup pecans

unbaked 9" pie shell

1. Beat eggs for a few minutes.

2. Mix all ingredients except pecans and crusts. Mix until completely combined.

3. Sprinkle pecans into pie shell.

4. Pour filling on top.

5. Bake at 375° for 10 minutes.

6. Then bake at 350° for 25-30 minutes until firm in the middle. If the pie is browning on top before it's finished, create an aluminum foil tent over the pie.

7. Cool and serve, perhaps with vanilla ice cream!

# Frozen Yogurt Pie

JOYCE FAIR, UTZ'S POTATO CHIPS

*Makes 1 small pie* ❦ *Prep. Time: 10 minutes* ❦ *Freezing Time: 4 hours or overnight*

2 8-oz. containers fruit-flavored yogurt

1 9-oz. container whipped topping, thawed

1 6-oz. graham cracker pie crust

1. Fold yogurt into whipped topping, blending well.

2. Spoon mixture into crust. Freeze until firm (4 hours or overnight).

3. Before serving, move to refrigerator for at least 30 minutes, or longer for softer texture.

VARIATIONS

1. Cool and light, this can be made with your favorite yogurt.

2. Garnish with any choice of topping.

3. Fold diced fruit in with yogurt and whipped topping to give added texture.

# Rice Krispie Pie

### SALLIE Y. LAPP, FLOWER GARDEN CRAFT

*Makes 1 pie* ❧ *Prep. Time: 15 minutes* ❧ *Chilling Time: 1 hour or more*

1 cup peanut butter
1 cup corn syrup
4 cups Rice Krispies
ice cream, softened

1. Blend peanut butter and corn syrup.

2. Add Rice Krispies.

3. Press mixture into pie pan.

4. Fill with ice cream. Smooth top. Freeze at least an hour before serving.

# Never-Fail Pastry

### ETHEL STONER, JOHN R. STONER VEGETABLES

*Makes 4 9" pie shells* ❧ *Prep. Time: 20 minutes*

3 cups flour
1 tsp. salt
1 cup vegetable shortening
1 egg, beaten
¼ cup cold water
1 Tbsp. vinegar

1. Mix flour and salt. Cut in shortening.

2. Combine remaining ingredients and stir into shortening mixture.

3. Knead until flour is thoroughly mixed into shortening and dough forms a ball.

4. With a rolling pin, roll dough onto floured board to desired thickness and size.

# Crumbs for Top of Pie

### ETHEL STONER, JOHN R. STONER VEGETABLES

*Covers a 9" pie* ❧ *Prep. Time: 10 minutes*

¼ cup brown sugar
¼ cup white sugar
¾ cup flour
scant ⅓ cup shortening

1. Mix sugar and flour together. Cut in shortening, mixing until crumbly.

2. Crumble over top of pie before baking.

# CAKES

# Chocolate Cake with Peanut Butter Icing

LISA MAE KNIGHT, WINDOWS ON STEINMAN PARK

*Makes 12–16 servings*
*Prep. Time: 20 minutes*
*Baking Time: 30-35 minutes*

1 tsp. baking powder

2 tsp. baking soda

2 cups all-purpose flour

pinch of salt, *optional*

2 cups sugar

¾ cup unsweetened cocoa powder

2 eggs

½ cup vegetable oil

1 cup hot, strong gourmet coffee

1 cup milk

2 tsp. vanilla

*Icing:*

2 cups chunky peanut butter

¾ cup confectioners sugar

1 tsp. butter, softened

1 Tbsp. milk

1. In a large bowl combine baking powder, baking soda, flour, and salt if you wish.

2. Stir in sugar and cocoa.

3. Beat in the eggs. Add oil, coffee, milk, and vanilla. Batter should be thin and runny.

4. Pour into a greased and floured 9"x13" baking pan.

5. Bake at 350° for 30-35 minutes. Do not overbake.

6. To prepare icing, mix peanut butter and confectioners sugar on high speed until smooth. Add milk and butter to incorporate more smoothness.

7. Spread icing on cake after cake has cooled.

TIP

*This cake is a sure dessert pleaser. I usually bake the cake the day before a family get-together and spread the icing just before leaving for the event.*

# Chocolate Cake

FANNIE S. FISHER, TOM'S FLOWER GARDEN

*Makes 12–15 servings* ❧ *Prep. Time: 20 minutes* ❧ *Baking Time: 35 minutes*

3 eggs
1¾ cups sugar
2¼ cups cake flour
¾ cup unsweetened cocoa
powder
2 tsp. baking soda
1½ tsp. salt
1 cup canola oil
2 tsp. vanilla
1½ cups buttermilk *or* sour milk

1. Beat eggs and sugar in small bowl until thickened.

2. In large bowl, sift together flour, cocoa, baking soda, and salt. Separately mix oil and vanilla. Add some oil mixture to the large bowl and mix. Add some milk and mix again. Repeat until oil and milk are used up.

3. Combine chocolate mixture with sugar mixture.

4. Pour into two greased and floured 8"-square pans or one 9"x13" baking pan.

5. Bake at 350° for 35 minutes.

### HINTS

*If you don't have cake flour on hand, put 2 Tbsp. cornstarch in a 1-cup measure. Fill rest of cup with all-purpose flour. This is a homemade substitute for cake flour.*

*A friend passed this recipe on to me as an excellent way to use up sour milk, which collects from time to time.*

# Marble Cake

NANCY GEIB, NANCY'S GOODIES

*Makes 12–14 servings* ❧ *Prep. Time: 25 minutes* ❧ *Baking Time: 40-45 minutes*

¾ cup shortening
2 cups sugar
1½ cups milk *or* water, *divided*
4 egg whites
3½ cups flour

1. Cream shortening, sugar, and 2 Tbsp. milk or water until light and fluffy.

2. Add unbeaten egg whites to mixture one at a time, beating well after each addition.

½ tsp. salt
3 tsp. baking powder
3 tsp. vanilla
2 oz. unsweetened chocolate
¼ tsp. baking soda

3. Sift flour and measure it. Sift it again with salt and baking powder.

4. Add sifted dry ingredients alternately with remaining milk or water to creamed mixture. Add vanilla.

5. Divide batter into two equal parts.

6. Melt chocolate and combine with baking soda.

7. Pour chocolate into one part of the batter and mix well.

8. Drop batter by large spoonfuls into a greased and floured 9"x13" baking pan, alternating the white and chocolate batters until all is used. Draw a knife through the batter to create marbling effect.

9. Bake at 350° for 40-45 minutes, until tester inserted in middle comes out clean.

# Strawberry Shortcake

ROSE MECK, MECK'S PRODUCE

*Makes 10–12 servings* ❦ *Prep. Time: 20 minutes* ❦ *Baking Time: 25 minutes*

2 eggs
1 cup sugar
2 Tbsp. butter, melted
2½ cups flour
½ tsp. salt
2 tsp. baking powder
1 cup milk
1 tsp. vanilla

1. In a mixing bowl, beat together eggs, sugar, and melted butter.

2. Add all remaining ingredients and beat until thoroughly blended.

3. Pour into two greased 8" cake pans or one 9"x13" baking pan.

4. Bake at 375° for 25 minutes, or until tester inserted in middle comes out clean.

5. Serve warm with fresh strawberries and milk.

# Orange-Glazed Shortcake

ANNA MARY NEFF, S. CLYDE WEAVER, INC.

*Makes 12–18 servings* ❦ *Prep. Time: 20 minutes* ❦ *Baking Time: 12-15 minutes*

1¼ cups boiling water
1½ cups raisins
½ cup (1 stick) butter, softened
2 cups brown sugar
2 eggs
3 cups flour
1 tsp. baking soda
2 tsp. ground cinnamon
1 tsp. ground allspice

**Frosting:**
3 cups confectioners sugar
3 Tbsp. butter, softened
3 Tbsp. orange juice concentrate
2 Tbsp. cold water

1. Soak raisins in boiling water for 5 minutes.

2. In a mixing bowl, cream butter and sugar together. Add eggs and mix. Add undrained raisins and mix well.

3. Separately, sift together dry ingredients. Mix with batter. Do not overmix. Batter should be thin.

4. Pour mixture into two jelly roll (10"x14") pans. Spread to edges.

5. Bake at 350° for 12-15 minutes, until tester inserted in middle comes out clean.

6. Mix all frosting ingredients. Spread over shortcake while still warm.

# Blueberry Cake

MARILYN DENLINGER, IRWIN S. WIDDERS PRODUCE

*Makes 8 servings* ❦ *Prep. Time: 20 minutes* ❦ *Baking Time: 40 minutes*

1 egg
1 cup sugar
3 Tbsp. butter, melted
½ cup milk
2 cups flour
1 tsp. baking powder
pinch of salt
1 pint fresh blueberries

1. In a mixing bowl, cream together egg, sugar, and butter.

2. Add milk and mix well.

3. Add flour, baking powder, and salt and mix again.

4. Fold blueberries into this stiff batter.

5. Pour into a greased 8"-square baking dish.

6. Bake at 350° for about 40 minutes, until tester inserted in middle comes out clean.

# The Market Boys and their Wagons

Shoppers leaving the farmer's markets with full baskets often found their burdens too great to bear. Enterprising boys and a few girls waited with their express wagons (or sometimes sleds in winter) around the market houses to offer their assistance. Few of these youngsters were older than 12 years old.

Many market-goers had favorite wagon boys whom they patronized regularly. Some people reserved a boy and his wagon when going into the market. If the boy was still waiting when the person was finished shopping, an extra tip was in order. Elderly shoppers often asked boys to carry their baskets through the market as they shopped. Those who could not be early birds but still wanted to get the proverbial worm made arrangements with boys to go to the market as early as possible and have the cream of the crop set aside until they arrived.

In the 1920s, the fee for transporting a basket ranged from 10 cents to 25 cents depending on the length of the trip. For carrying a basket around as a person shopped, a youngster was paid 10 cents. A boy might make as many as a dozen trips in a day. The distance could range from a short walk to the trolley or bus stop, to going more than a mile. A few boys specialized in long-distance traveling and equipped their bicycles to carry baskets. Some shoppers did not accompany the delivery boy home but arranged to have their market baskets deposited on back-door steps while they did additional shopping. Boys could also earn extra money helping standholders to unload and load their wares.

Of course, it was in the summertime, on Saturday mornings and during evening market hours, that the school boys had their greatest opportunity to earn money. Some of the more energetic youth managed to get in a few trips early in the mornings and during lunch breaks throughout the school year. Truant officers kept a special lookout for industrious hooky-players at the market houses. A speedy youth could earn a decent day's wages, but he needed to be steady and agile. Being in too much of a hurry often meant an upset wagon, with apples, oranges, and potatoes rolling down the street.

# Fresh Apple Cake

RUTH B. WHITE, BRENNEMAN FARM

*Makes 6–8 servings*
Prep. Time: 20 minutes ❦ Standing Time: 20 minutes ❦ Baking Time: 50-55 minutes

2 cups peeled, coarsely chopped apples
1 cup sugar
1½ cups flour
1 tsp. baking soda
½ tsp. salt
1 tsp. ground cinnamon
½ tsp. ground nutmeg
½ tsp. ground allspice
½ cup vegetable oil
1 egg
½ cup raisins
½ cup chopped walnuts
confectioners sugar

1. Combine sugar and apples in large mixing bowl. Let stand 10 minutes.

2. In another bowl, sift flour and add soda, salt, cinnamon, nutmeg, and allspice.

3. Blend oil and egg into apple mixture. Add dry ingredients, stirring until blended. Fold in raisins and walnuts.

4. Spread evenly into greased 8"-square pan.

5. Bake at 350° for 50-55 minutes.

6. Cool for 10 minutes. Sprinkle with confectioners sugar.

TIP

*Easy to prepare and wonderful for a family who loves apples.*

# Apple Cake

MRS. MARTHA FORRY, JOHN M. MARKLEY MEATS

*Makes 8 servings* ❦ Prep. Time: 15 minutes ❦ Baking Time: 35 minutes

¼ cup (half stick) butter, melted
1 cup sugar
1 egg, beaten
1 cup flour
½ tsp. baking soda
½ tsp. baking powder
½ tsp. ground cinnamon

1. Cream butter, sugar, and egg together in a mixing bowl.

2. Separately, mix all dry ingredients and add to sugar mixture. Fold in apples, walnuts, and vanilla.

¼ tsp. salt
2 cups chopped apples
½ cup chopped walnuts
1 tsp. vanilla

3. Pour batter into greased 8"-square baking dish.

4. Bake at 350° for 35 minutes or until tester inserted in middle comes out clean.

VARIATION

*Dust lightly with confectioners sugar when cake is cooled to create a more festive appearance.*

# Rhubarb Sour Cream Cake

MRS. JILL RAUCH, CUSTOMER OF ETHEL STONER

*Makes 12–14 servings*
*Prep. Time: 20 minutes    Baking Time: 40 minutes*

4 Tbsp. (half stick) unsalted butter, softened
1½ cups brown sugar, firmly packed
1 egg
1 Tbsp. vanilla
2½ cups flour
1 tsp. baking soda
1 tsp. salt
1 cup sour cream
4 cups red rhubarb, cut into ½" inch pieces
½ cup sugar
½ tsp. ground nutmeg

1. In a mixing bowl, cream butter and brown sugar until fluffy. Beat in egg and vanilla.

2. Sift flour with baking soda and salt. Add to mixture.

3. Fold in sour cream and rhubarb.

4. Spoon batter into greased 9"x13" baking pan.

5. Mix sugar and nutmeg and sprinkle over batter.

6. Bake at 350° for 40 minutes or until tester inserted in middle comes out clean.

# Carrot Cake

JOANNE MYLIN, IRWIN S. WIDDERS PRODUCE

*Makes 24 servings*
Prep. Time: 20 minutes    ✣    Baking Time: 40-50 minutes

4 eggs
I cup vegetable oil
2 cups sugar
2 cups flour
2 tsp. baking soda
2 tsp. ground cinnamon
I tsp. salt
3 cups grated raw carrots

*Frosting:*
6 oz. cream cheese, softened
4 Tbsp. (half stick) butter, softened
4 cups confectioners sugar
I ½ tsp. vanilla
½ tsp. maple flavoring

1. In a large bowl, beat eggs and add vegetable oil.

2. Mix all dry ingredients and add to egg mixture.

3. Fold carrots into mixture.

4. Pour batter into greased and floured 9"x13" baking pan.

5. Bake at 350° for 40-50 minutes or until tester inserted in middle comes out clean. Cool.

6. To prepare frosting, beat cream cheese and butter together. Add confectioners sugar, vanilla, and flavoring. Beat well and spread over cooled cake.

# Best Pineapple Cake

ETHEL STONER, JOHN R. STONER VEGETABLES

*Makes 12–16 servings*
Prep. Time: 20 minutes
Baking Time: 45 minutes

2 cups flour
2 cups sugar
2 tsp. baking powder
2 eggs
I tsp. vanilla
20-oz. can crushed pineapple
I cup chopped nuts

1. Mix flour, sugar, and baking powder in mixing bowl.

2. Add eggs, vanilla, and undrained pineapple. Blend well. Add nuts.

3. Pour batter into greased 9"x13" baking pan.

**Frosting Ingredients:**
8-oz. pkg. cream cheese
8 Tbsp. (1 stick) butter, softened
1½ cups confectioners sugar
½ tsp. vanilla
½ cup chopped nuts

4. Bake at 350° for 45 minutes or until tester inserted in middle comes out clean.

5. Remove from oven and let cool before frosting.

6. To prepare frosting, mix cream cheese, butter, sugar, and vanilla and spread over cake. Sprinkle chopped nuts over top.

# Pineapple Zucchini Cake

RACHIE HOWARD, CUSTOMER OF IRWIN S. WIDDERS PRODUCE

*Makes 24 servings*
*Prep. Time: 20 minutes*
*Baking Time: 18-60 minutes*

3 eggs
2 cups sugar
2 tsp. vanilla
1 cup vegetable oil
2 cups peeled, grated zucchini
3 cups flour
1 tsp. baking powder
1 tsp. baking soda
1 tsp. salt
½ cup crushed pineapple, undrained
1 cup raisins
1 cup chopped nuts

**Cream Cheese Frosting:**
2 cups confectioners sugar
3-oz. pkg. cream cheese, softened
½ cup (1 stick) butter, softened

1. Beat eggs, sugar, vanilla, and oil until fluffy.

2. Add zucchini, flour, baking powder, baking soda, and salt.

3. Stir in pineapple, raisins, and nuts and mix well.

4. Spoon into a greased 9"x13" baking pan. Bake at 350° for 1 hour or until tester inserted in middle comes out clean.

5. Mix all frosting ingredients and frost cooled cake or cupcakes.

VARIATION

*Put batter in lined or greased cupcake tins and bake for 18-20 minutes.*

# Date Nut Cake

FANNIE ESH, FRANK WEAVER GREENHOUSES

*Makes 12–14 servings*
Prep. Time: 30 minutes  ❦  Baking Time: 25-30 minutes

2 cups chopped dates
2 cups very warm water
2 tsp. baking soda
2 Tbsp. butter, softened
2 eggs
2 cups brown sugar
3 cups flour
2 tsp. vanilla
1 cup chopped nuts

1. Dissolve soda in very warm water and pour over dates. Set aside.

2. In a mixing bowl, cream butter, eggs, and sugar together. Add flour and vanilla.

3. Fold in nuts and date mixture.

4. Pour into 9"x13" baking pan and bake at 375° for 25-30 minutes or until tester inserted in middle comes out clean.

# Matrimony Cake

LABERTA MINNEY, SHENK'S CHEESE CO.

*Makes 12 servings*
Prep. Time: 20 minutes  ❦  Baking Time: 15-20 minutes

3 cups quick oats
2 cups flour
1¼ cups brown sugar
½ tsp. baking soda
pinch of salt
1 cup (2 sticks) butter, softened

**Filling:**
1 lb. dates, chopped
1 cup white sugar
1½ cups water

1. To prepare batter, mix oats, flour, brown sugar, baking soda, and salt. Use a pastry cutter to work butter into dry ingredients.

2. Put about ¾ of mixture into well-greased and floured 9"x13" baking pan. Press it down firmly.

3. Mix all filling ingredients in a saucepan and boil until thickened. Spread over batter in pan.

4. Sprinkle reserved crumbs over date mixture.

5. Bake at 375° for 15-20 minutes or until lightly browned.

# Pumpkin Roll

DEBBIE BUHAY, SHENK'S CHEESE CO.

*Makes 8–10 servings*
*Prep time: 20 minutes ❧ Baking Time: 15-20 minutes*
*Standing Time: 35 minutes ❧ Chilling Time: several hours*

3 eggs
1 cup sugar
¼ cup brown sugar
⅔ cup cooked pumpkin
¾ cup flour
1 tsp. baking soda
2 tsp. ground cinnamon

**Filling:**

1 cup confectioners sugar, plus extra for dusting
8-oz. pkg. cream cheese, softened
4 Tbsp. (half stick) butter
½ tsp. vanilla

1. Beat eggs for 5 minutes in a mixing bowl. Add sugar, brown sugar, pumpkin, flour, baking soda, and cinnamon. Mix well.

2. Spread mixture into a generously greased and floured 10"x14" jelly roll pan.

3. Bake at 350° for 15-20 minutes or until tester inserted in middle comes out clean. Cool about 5 minutes.

4. Dust two paper towels with confectioners sugar and gently lift cake from pan onto paper towels.

5. Cool 5 more minutes. Roll cake, paper towels and all, starting with a long edge. Let stand ½ hour.

6. Meanwhile, beat together all filling ingredients until smooth.

7. Unroll cake and spread with filling.

8. Reroll cake without paper towels.

9. Refrigerate until firm, several hours.

# Oatmeal Cake

DEB MARTIN, MARTIN'S HOME-BAKED GOODS

*Makes 20 servings*
*Prep. Time: 20 minutes* ❧ *Baking Time: 45-50 minutes*

1 cup dry quick oats
1 ½ cups boiling water
½ cup shortening
1 cup brown sugar, packed
1 cup sugar
2 eggs
1 ⅓ cups flour
1 tsp. ground cinnamon
1 tsp. baking soda
½ tsp. salt
½ tsp. ground nutmeg
1 tsp. vanilla

**Topping:**
½ cup (1 stick) butter
½ cup brown sugar
½ cup milk
½ cup chopped nuts
1 cup grated coconut

1. Pour boiling water over quick oats and set aside.

2. In a mixing bowl, cream shortening and sugars until fluffy. Add eggs and beat well.

3. Separately, mix all dry ingredients and add to batter. Add soaked oats and vanilla and mix well.

4. Pour into a greased and floured 9"x13" baking pan and bake at 350° for 40-45 minutes, or until tester inserted in middle comes out clean.

5. To prepare topping, melt butter in saucepan. Add sugar and milk, and cream together.

6. Bring mixture to a boil and cool slightly.

7. Add nuts and coconut and spread over hot cake.

8. Place under broiler until topping bubbles, watching carefully to prevent burning.

# Angel Food Cake

MARY KING, SHREINER'S FLOWERS

*Makes 10–12 servings*
*Prep. Time: 25 minutes  ❧  Baking Time: 40 minutes*

1½ cups cake flour
1½ cups sugar, *divided*
1½ cups egg whites (10-12)
1¼ tsp. cream of tartar
¼ tsp. salt
¼ tsp. almond extract
1 tsp. vanilla extract

1. Sift flour and ½ cup sugar together four times. Set aside.

2. In a large mixing bowl, beat egg whites until foamy. Add cream of tartar and salt. Beat until peaks form.

3. Add remaining sugar to egg whites, about 2 Tbsp. at a time, beating after each addition. Add almond and vanilla extracts.

4. Fold flour into egg whites, about ¼ cup at a time. Fold in until no flour shows. Do not beat.

5. Spoon batter into an ungreased angel food cake pan and bake at 350° for about 40 minutes, until tester inserted in middle comes out clean.

**From the other side of the Market stand . . .**

# ROGER GODFREY OF RAFIKI'S DELI

When Roger Godfrey and Dorothy Dulo first opened their Central Market stand, Rafiki's Deli, they sold "Amish food," as Roger calls it. The former owners were Amish, so the couple assumed that's what their customers expected.

"But that wasn't us," smiles Roger. He's from Uganda, and his wife, Dorothy, is from Kenya. "We wanted to make healthier foods, fresher foods, our own from-scratch foods.

"The City was running the Market then, and they said, 'You're from Africa. It makes sense that you'd sell African food.'

"In the spring of 2006, when we first started offering African dishes, it took a while for people to be willing to try what we were selling. Some of the locals tend to eat bland food. But we cook with native spices from our home countries—and that's a big plus!

"People travel more, and they're looking for dishes they've eaten in South Africa or Kenya." So Roger and Dorothy accommodate them with samosas, chickpea cakes, sweet potato salad with plantains, spicy potato cakes, their signature falafel sandwiches, and Kajiji salad.

"Rafiki" means "friend" in Swahili. "We have formed strong friendships and bonds with many of our customers," says Roger. "Some have gone to Africa with us, too, where we help to support a school with profits from our Market stand."

# Feather Cake

LABERTA MINNEY, SHENK'S CHEESE CO.

*Makes 12–15 servings*
Prep. Time: 20 minutes ❧ Baking Time: 35-40 minutes

2 cups sugar
½ cup (1 stick) butter, softened
3 eggs
3 cups flour
2 tsp. baking powder
1 cup milk

1. Cream sugar and butter in a large bowl. Add eggs and beat until well mixed.

2. Separately, mix flour and baking powder. Alternately add flour and milk to creamed mixture. Mix well.

3. Pour into two greased 8" cake pans.

4. Bake at 350° for 35-40 minutes, until tester inserted in middle comes out clean.

TIP

*Great with chocolate icing!*

# Sponge Cake Receipt

THOMAS L. MARTIN, WILLOW VALLEY FARMS

*Original receipt from 1880s:*

1 lb. sugar
½ lb. flour
10 eggs
juice and rind of 1 lemon

*Recipe as you would make it today:*
10 eggs
2 cups sugar
juice and rind of 1 lemon
2 cups cake flour

1. Separate eggs. In a mixing bowl, beat yolks until thick and lemon-colored.

2. Gradually beat in sugar and add lemon juice and rind.

3. Separately, beat egg whites until stiff. Fold egg whites into egg yolk mixture. Fold in the flour.

4. Turn into a greased and floured bundt pan. Bake at 350° for about 50 minutes, until tester inserted in middle comes out clean.

NOTE

*This recipe was taken from a hand-written cookbook that I own. It was written by a woman from Strasburg between 1872 and 1903, around the time when Central Market was built. In the 1800s, recipes were called "receipts" and, as you can see, most only listed ingredients. The mixing and baking was left to the skill of the cook. You were expected to know how to mix and bake cakes, cookies, and breads.*

# Molasses Crumb Cake

BARBARA J. WEAVER, D. M. WEAVER AND SONS, INC.

*Makes 9 servings*
*Prep. Time: 20 minutes* ❧ *Baking Time: 25 minutes*

**Crumbs:**
1 cup sugar
½ cup shortening
2 cups flour
½ tsp. ground cinnamon
½ tsp. ground cloves
½ tsp. salt

**Batter:**
1 tsp. baking soda
1 cup buttermilk *or* sour milk
4 Tbsp. baking molasses

1. Mix all crumb ingredients and set aside ¾ cup of crumbs.

2. To prepare batter, pour milk over baking soda. Pour this mixture over molasses in a mixing bowl. Mix. Add all crumbs except the reserved ¾ cup, and mix well.

3. Pour into greased and floured 9"-square cake pan. Sprinkle reserved crumbs evenly over batter.

4. Bake at 350° for 25 minutes or until a tester inserted in middle comes out clean.

NOTE

*This was my Grandmother Wooding's recipe.*

# Shoo-Fly Cake

HELEN E. BITNER, BITNERS

*Makes 15–20 servings*
*Prep. Time: 20 minutes   Baking Time: 45 minutes*

4 cups flour
I lb. dark brown sugar
I cup (2 sticks) butter, softened
I cup mild molasses, or King
Syrup
2 cups boiling water
2 tsp. baking soda

1. Combine flour, sugar, and butter. Work into fine crumbs with a pastry cutter or two knives. Reserve 1½ cups crumbs for topping.

2. Mix all remaining ingredients and the rest of the crumbs until batter is thin. Pour into greased and floured 9"x13" baking pan. Sprinkle reserved crumbs on top.

3. Bake at 350° for 45 minutes or until a tester inserted in middle comes out clean.

# Yum-Yum Coffee Cake

MARY E. HESS, CHARLES HESS

*Makes 12 servings*
*Prep. Time: 20 minutes   Baking Time: 40 minutes*

½ cup (I stick) butter, softened
I cup sugar
2 eggs
I tsp. vanilla
I cup sour cream
2 cups flour
I tsp. baking soda
I tsp. baking powder
½ tsp. salt

1. In a mixing bowl, cream butter until soft. Add sugar and mix until fluffy.

2. Add eggs, one at a time, beating after each addition. Add vanilla and sour cream.

3. Separately, sift flour, baking soda, baking powder, and salt. Add dry ingredients to creamed mixture.

4. Mix topping ingredients and set aside.

**Topping:**

½ cup brown sugar

½ cup white sugar

1 tsp. ground cinnamon

1 cup chopped nuts

5. Spoon half of batter into a lightly greased 9"x13" baking pan. Cover with half the topping. Add remaining batter and cover with remaining topping.

6. Bake at 325° for 40 minutes or until tester inserted in middle comes out clean.

# Cinnamon Flop Coffee Cake

### CINDY COVER, MARION CHEESE

*Makes 2 9" cakes*

*Prep. Time: 20 minutes  ❧  Baking Time: 30 minutes*

2 cups sugar

4 Tbsp. (half stick) butter, softened, *divided*

3 eggs

2 tsp. lemon extract

4 cups flour

4 tsp. baking powder

2 cups milk

2 tart apples, peeled and sliced thinly

1 tsp. ground cinnamon

½ cup brown sugar

1 cup sliced almonds

1. Cream 2 Tbsp. butter and sugar in a mixing bowl. Beat in eggs, one at a time. Beat mixture until fluffy. Add lemon extract.

2. Separately, sift flour, measure, and combine with baking powder.

3. Add dry ingredients alternately with milk into creamed mixture.

4. Divide mixture between two greased and floured 9" layer pans. Press apple slices on top. Sprinkle with almonds, cinnamon, and brown sugar. Dot with remaining 2 Tbsp. butter.

5. Bake at 375° for 30 minutes or until the cakes test done. Serve warm or at room temperature.

NOTE

*The original recipe is from my maternal grandmother. I add apples, lemon, and almonds because I enjoy the added flavors.*

# Yummy Cupcakes

DONNA BETANCOURT, EISENBERGER'S BAKED GOODS

*Makes 30 cupcakes*
*Prep. Time: 25 minutes*
*Baking Time: 15-20 minutes*

2 cups sugar *or* less, as you wish

3 cups flour

½ cup unsweetened cocoa powder

2 tsp. baking soda

2 Tbsp. vinegar

⅔ cup vegetable oil

2 cups water

2 tsp. vanilla

**Filling:**

8-oz. pkg. cream cheese, softened

1 egg

½ cup sugar

dash of salt

12-oz. pkg. chocolate chips

1. Combine all batter ingredients and mix thoroughly.

2. To prepare filling, combine cream cheese, egg, sugar, and salt. Add chocolate chips and blend well.

3. Fill greased or lined muffin tins ½ full of batter. Top with 1 heaping tsp. filling.

4. Bake 15-20 minutes at 350°, until cake part just springs back to a light touch.

# Banana Cupcakes

RUTH WIDDERS, IRWIN S. WIDDERS PRODUCE

*Makes 24–30 cupcakes*
*Prep. Time: 20 minutes*
*Baking Time: 15-20 minutes*

½ cup shortening
1 ½ cups sugar
2 eggs
1 tsp. vanilla
1 cup ripe, mashed bananas
2 cups flour
½ tsp. salt
1 tsp. baking powder
¼ cup sour milk *or* buttermilk
¾ tsp. baking soda

1. Cream shortening and sugar together in a mixing bowl and beat until fluffy. Add eggs, vanilla, and mashed bananas. Mix well.

2. Separately, mix together flour, salt, and baking powder. Mix together sour milk and baking soda.

3. Alternately add flour mixture and sour milk mixture to shortening mixture. Mix thoroughly.

4. Fill greased or lined muffin pans ½ full.

5. Bake at 350° for 15-20 minutes.

---

TIP

*Wonderful topped with peanut butter icing and a few ground black walnuts.*

# Ganache Icing

PETER KOVALEC, WINDOWS ON STEINMAN PARK

*Frosts a 9-square cake*

*Prep. Time: 15 minutes* ❦ *Cooking Time: about 15 minutes* ❦ *Standing Time: 8-12 hours*

**7½-oz. pkg. semi-sweet chocolate**

**¾ cup heavy cream**

**1½ Tbsp. butter, softened**

1. Melt chocolate in double boiler, stirring constantly.

2. Separately, bring cream to a boil.

3. Stir hot cream into melted chocolate in double boiler a little at a time. Make sure mixture stays smooth.

4. Stir in butter until completely melted.

5. Let set overnight, or for at least 8-12 hours, until stiff enough to use.

---

### HINT

*To coat cake with a thin layer, allow ganache to cool only slightly, about 1 hour. Pour frosting over cake.*

*Very rich and very silky!*

# Pumpkin Cookies

ETHEL STONER, JOHN R. STONER VEGETABLES

*Makes 7–8 dozen cookies*
*Prep. Time: 30 minutes*
*Baking Time: 10-15 minutes*

3 cups sugar

1 cup oil

3 cups cooked pumpkin

3 tsp. ground cinnamon

2 tsp. ground cloves

3 tsp. vanilla

6 cups flour

3 tsp. baking soda

3 tsp. baking powder

2 cups raisins

1 cup chopped nuts, *optional*

**Caramel Frosting:**

3 Tbsp. butter

4 tsp. milk

½ cup brown sugar

¾ tsp. vanilla

1-1¼ cups confectioners sugar

1. Mix sugar, oil, and pumpkin. Gradually stir in spices, flour, baking soda, and baking powder. Mix thoroughly. Fold in raisins and nuts.

2. Drop by spoonfuls on greased baking sheets. Bake at 375° 10-15 minutes, until just set in the middle. Do not overbake.

3. Remove from oven. Cool slightly and frost with caramel frosting.

4. To prepare frosting, cook butter, milk, brown sugar, and vanilla over low heat until mixture is smooth. Remove from heat and add confectioners sugar. Stir until very smooth. Keep frosting warm, and frost each tray of cookies as soon as it can be handled.

NOTE

*All you have to do is taste one: you will be hooked!*

# Potato Chip Cookies

CUSTOMER OF JOYCE FAIR, UTZ'S POTATO CHIPS

*Makes 3½ dozen cookies*

*Prep. Time: 20 minutes* ✤ *Chilling Time: overnight* ✤ *Baking Time: 15 minutes*

1 lb. (4 sticks) butter, softened

1 cup sugar

3½ cups flour

1 cup crushed potato chips

1 tsp. vanilla

1 cup confectioners sugar

1. Mix butter, sugar, and flour in a mixing bowl.

2. Stir in potato chips and vanilla.

3. Chill overnight.

4. Roll into small balls, about 1 rounded tsp. each. Flatten on baking sheet with fork.

5. Bake at 350° for 15 minutes.

6. Lay cookies out on paper towels or rack to drain any excess shortening.

7. Sprinkle cookies with confectioners sugar while still warm.

# Hermits

ESTHER EISENBERGER, EISENBERGER'S BAKED GOODS

*Makes 5 dozen cookies* ✤ *Prep. Time: 20 minutes* ✤ *Baking Time: 12-15 minutes*

½ cup shortening

½ cup (1 stick) butter, softened

2 cups brown sugar

2 eggs

2⅔ cups flour

½ tsp. salt

2 tsp. baking powder

½ tsp. baking soda

½ tsp. ground cinnamon

½ tsp. ground cloves

½ tsp. ground nutmeg

⅓ cup milk

⅔ cup raisins, chopped

⅔ cup chopped nuts

1. In a mixing bowl, cream shortening, butter, and sugar together. Add eggs and beat until fluffy.

2. Separately, sift flour. Measure and add salt, baking soda, baking powder, and spices to flour. Sift again.

3. Add dry ingredients alternately with milk to shortening mixture. Beat after each addition.

4. Add chopped nuts and raisins and blend into mixture.

5. Drop by teaspoonfuls onto greased baking sheet, placing about 2" inches apart.

6. Bake at 350° for 12-15 minutes, until cookies are barely set in middle.

# Banana Cookies

RUTH WIDDERS, IRWIN S. WIDDERS PRODUCE

*Makes 4 dozen cookies* ❧ *Prep. Time: 20 minutes* ❧ *Baking Time: 12 minutes*

½ cup (1 stick) butter, softened

1 cup sugar

2 eggs

1 tsp. vanilla

2½ cups flour

2½ tsp. baking powder

½ tsp. salt

1 cup ripe, mashed bananas

1. Cream butter and sugar until fluffy.

2. Add eggs, vanilla, flour, baking powder, and salt.

3. Fold in mashed bananas.

4. Drop by teaspoonfuls onto greased baking sheet and bake at 350° for 12 minutes.

NOTE

*Wonderfully tasty and moist cookies!*

# Molasses Cookies

MRS. AARON Z. KING, KAUFFMAN'S FRUIT FARM

*Makes 6–7 dozen cookies* ❧ *Prep. Time: 20 minutes* ❧ *Baking Time: 10-15 minutes*

1½ cups lard *or* vegetable shortening, melted

1 cup sugar, plus more for sprinkling

½ cup dark brown sugar

2 cups New Orleans molasses, *or* substitute 1 cup mild table molasses, plus 1 cup blackstrap molasses

2 Tbsp. baking soda

½ cup boiling water

1 tsp. ground ginger

1 tsp. ground cinnamon

10 cups flour

1. Melt lard over low heat. In large mixing bowl, mix melted lard well with granulated and brown sugar. Add molasses and mix well.

2. Bring water to a boil and add baking soda to boiling water. Add to molasses mixture.

3. In a separate bowl, add ginger and cinnamon to flour. Then add flour to molasses mixture and mix well.

4. Roll dough into balls and place on greased baking sheet. Press down lightly with fork and sprinkle with granulated sugar.

5. Bake at 375° 10-15 minutes or until just set in the middle.

NOTE

*This recipe came from one of my husband's aunts at least 50 years ago.*

**Cookies** ❧ **227**

# Sugar Cookies

## LOIS THOMAS, C. H. THOMAS AND SON

*Makes 6 dozen cookies*  ✣  *Prep. Time: 20 minutes*
*Chilling Time: several hours or overnight*  ✣  *Baking Time: 8-10 minutes*

7 Tbsp. butter, softened
2 cups sugar
3 eggs, beaten
1 cup cultured sour cream
4 cups all-purpose flour, sifted
1 tsp. baking soda
1 tsp. baking powder
¾ tsp. salt

1. In mixing bowl, cream together butter and sugar. Add beaten eggs and sour cream.

2. Separately, sift together flour, soda, baking powder, and salt. Stir into batter.

3. Chill batter several hours or overnight.

4. Drop by teaspoonfuls onto greased baking sheet and bake at 375° for 8-10 minutes, until just set in the middle.

# Butter Pecan Cookies

## JANICE KREIDER, EISENBERGER'S BAKED GOODS

*Makes 3–4 dozen cookies*
*Prep. Time: 20 minutes*  ✣  *Baking Time: 8-10 minutes*

2 Tbsp. + ½ cup (1 stick) butter, softened, *divided*
1¾ cups brown sugar, *divided*
1 cup chopped pecans
2 cups flour
½ tsp. baking powder
1 egg
½ tsp. vanilla extract

1. Combine 2 Tbsp. butter, ½ cup brown sugar, and pecans. Mix until blended together. Set aside.

2. In large mixing bowl, combine ½ cup butter, 1¼ cups brown sugar, and all remaining ingredients. Blend well with mixer. Stir pecan mixture into this until evenly distributed.

3. Shape dough into walnut-sized balls and place on ungreased baking sheet. Flatten balls slightly with the bottom of a glass that has been greased and dipped into flour.

4. Bake cookies at 375° for 8-10 minutes. Allow to cool about 2-3 minutes before removing from baking sheet.

# Crescent Nut Rolls

JOYCE DEITER, EISENBERGER'S BAKED GOODS

*Makes 3 dozen rolls*
*Prep. Time: 20 minutes*
*Chilling Time: overnight*
*Baking Time: 12 minutes*

**2 cups flour**
**1 cup (2 sticks) butter, softened**
**¾ cup sour cream**
**1 egg yolk**

**Filling:**
**¾ cup finely chopped pecans**
**¾ cup sugar**
**1 tsp. ground cinnamon**

1. Cut butter into flour with a pastry cutter until crumbs are pea-sized.

2. Add sour cream and egg yolk, and mix just until dough comes together into a ball.

3. Divide into 6 balls.

4. Wrap each ball in plastic wrap and refrigerate overnight.

5. On a lightly floured board, roll dough like pie dough. Then use pastry wheel to cut the circle in half, then each half in thirds. Each ball of dough will make 6 crescents.

6. Mix all filling ingredients and spread over each crescent shape. Roll up, starting at the wide end and ending with the narrow end.

7. Place on greased baking sheet. Bake at 375° for 12 minutes or until golden brown. Be careful not to let the bottoms get too dark.

8. When cool, dust with confectioners sugar, using a small strainer and shaking it.

HINT

*All the crescents may be rolled and prepared before starting to bake.*

*These cookies may be frozen. They are a family favorite at Christmastime.*

# Tea Cookies

BARBARA J. WEAVER, D. M. WEAVER AND SONS, INC.

*Makes 12–24 cookies*  ❧  *Prep. Time: 15 minutes*  ❧  *Baking Time: 5-10 minutes*

⅔ cup confectioners sugar

½ cup shortening

I egg

I tsp. lemon rind *or* vanilla extract *or* Amaretto

I ½ cups flour

1. In a mixing bowl, whip confectioners sugar, shortening, and egg until they become light in color and very creamy.

2. Add flavoring and stir.

3. While stirring, gently sprinkle in the flour. Continue to fold in flour until well mixed.

4. Drop batter by tablespoonfuls onto greased baking sheet.

5. Bake at 325° for 5-10 minutes or until peaks of dough just begin to toast.

# Kourabiedes

KOULA VAKIOS, KOULA'S GREEK PASTRIES

*Makes 4 dozen*  ❧  *Prep. Time: 40 minutes*  ❧  *Baking Time: 25 minutes*

I lb. (4 sticks) butter, softened

½ cup confectioners sugar, plus more for finished cookies

2 lbs. flour, *or* a little less

1. In mixing bowl, cream butter about 20 minutes or until very fluffy. Add sugar and cream, mixing another 20-25 minutes. (You have to work for these!)

2. Sift flour. Add gradually to creamed mixture by hand. Do not use a mixer. Work until dough is fluffy, never clumpy.

3. Grease hands. With a teaspoon, take a lump and roll in your hands. Form into oval or ball.

4. Place on greased baking sheet. Bake at 350° for 25 minutes.

5. Let cool and then dip into confectioners sugar.

# Raisin-Filled Cookies

MIRIAM M. HESS, FRANK WEAVER GREENHOUSES

*Makes 2 dozen cookies* ❧ *Prep. Time: 20 minutes*
*Chilling Time: several hours* ❧ *Baking Time: 10-15 minutes*

2 cups light brown sugar
1 cup (2 sticks) butter, softened
3 eggs
4 cups flour
1 tsp. baking soda
1 tsp. vanilla

**Filling:**
1 cup raisins
1 cup light brown sugar
1 cup water
2 Tbsp. flour

1. Cream sugar, butter, and eggs in a mixing bowl. Stir in flour, baking soda, and vanilla.

2. Chill until dough is stiff enough to roll, several hours.

3. Mix together all filling ingredients in a saucepan and bring to a boil. Cook over low heat, stirring often, until thickened. Let filling cool.

4. On lightly floured board, roll out dough to 1/8" thickness.

5. Cut out rounds of dough with a cookie cutter and lay 1" apart on greased baking sheet.

6. Top each round of dough with 1 tsp. filling. Cover with another round of dough. Then pinch edges together to prevent filling from cooking out.

7. Bake at 375° for 10-15 minutes, until edges are lightly brown and tops are barely set.

NOTE

*My mother, Florence Heiney, said this was her favorite cookie recipe. She and her husband, Samuel Heiney, had a stand on Central Market for 25 years.*

# Mincemeat-Filled Cookies

PAUL B. MARTIN, SPRING GLEN FARM KITCHEN, INC.

*Makes 5–6 dozen cookies*
Prep. Time: 25 minutes ❧ Baking Time: 10-12 minutes

1 cup shortening
2 cups brown sugar, packed
3 eggs
½ cup water
1 tsp. vanilla
3½ cups flour, sifted
½ tsp. salt
1 tsp. baking soda
⅛ tsp. ground cinnamon
1½ cups mincemeat

1. In a large mixing bowl, cream together shortening, brown sugar, and eggs. Stir in water and vanilla.

2. Separately, sift together flour, salt, baking soda, and cinnamon. Stir into batter.

3. Drop by teaspoonfuls onto ungreased baking sheet.

4. Put about 1 tsp. mincemeat on dough. Cover mincemeat with another teaspoonful of dough.

5. Bake at 375° for 10-12 minutes or until lightly browned.

# Omar Al Saife of Saife's Middle Eastern Food

Omar Al Saife bought his family's stand on Central Market in 1991. "When my family left Kuwait during the Gulf War, we needed a source of income. My degree is in urban planning and political science. But my dad was a chef, and I had always watched him cook."

So Omar and his wife, Nadia, drew on their love of food and began making the dishes they knew and cherished. They still prepare what they sell.

"We're famous for our falafel sandwiches and our vegan items—cardamom cookies, baklava, salads, pita breads. I try to keep all of my customers healthy!

"Our first customer was Big Bill. He bought a baklava. Bill disposes of empty boxes around the market, sweeps the aisles, helps carry things—and he wanted to help us. It was such a small thing, but so touching to us.

"The media took care of bringing us curious shoppers. Here was someone from a hot spot in the world! People came in then just to support us.

"A lot of our customers have become our friends. We're like a big family here. We stand by each other, whether things are good or bad."

# Hungarian Kiffles

SWEETHEARTS CELERY

*Makes 3½ dozen cookies*
*Prep. Time: 30 minutes*
*Chilling Time: 3-4 hours or overnight*
*Baking Time: 20 minutes*

**Dough:**
4½-5 cups (I lb.) flour
4 sticks (I lb.) butter
2 8-oz. pkgs. (I lb.) cream cheese
confectioners sugar

**Nut Filling:**
2 egg whites
¾ cup confectioners *sugar*
I lb. ground walnuts
2 tsp. milk

1. Place flour, butter, and cream cheese in a large bowl and mix well.

2. Shape dough into walnut-size balls and refrigerate 3-4 hours or overnight.

3. To make nut filling, beat egg whites.

4. Add confectioners sugar, nuts, and milk.

5. Roll chilled dough balls in confectioners sugar on a board, and then roll out into small circles.

6. Place a dab of nut filling on each circle.

7. Roll into crescent shape and pinch edges.

8. Place on greased baking sheet and bake at 350° for 20 minutes, or until light brown and fluffy.

TIPS

1. *We line the baking sheets with tin foil. That way you don't need to grease the pans.*

2. *Instead of nut filling, you can use lekvar or apricot filling.*

# Sand Tarts

HELEN THOMAS, HELEN THOMAS PRODUCE

*Makes 6 dozen cookies*

*Prep. Time: 30 minutes* ❦ *Chilling Time: several hours* ❦ *Baking Time: 10-12 minutes*

**Cookies:**

1½ cups sugar

1 cup (2 sticks) butter, melted

3 eggs

4 cups flour

2 tsp. cream of tartar

1 tsp. baking soda

1 tsp. vanilla

**Topping:**

3 eggs, beaten

2-3 tsp. ground cinnamon

2-3 cups chopped peanuts

1. In large mixing bowl, cream together sugar and melted butter. Add eggs. Beat well.

2. Separately, sift together flour, cream of tartar, and baking soda. Add to batter. Add vanilla and mix well.

3. Chill until stiff, several hours.

4. Roll out batter in a thin layer about ⅛" thick and cut out sand tarts into any shape desired. Place on greased baking sheet.

5. Spread small amount of beaten egg on each cookie and sprinkle with cinnamon and chopped peanuts.

6. Bake at 300° for 10-12 minutes.

# Brownies

FRANCES KIEFER, KIEFER'S MEATS AND CHEESE

*Makes 24 brownies*

*Prep. Time: 15 minutes* ❦ *Baking Time: 20 minutes*

4 squares (4 oz.) baking chocolate

1 cup (2 sticks) butter

4 eggs, beaten

1 tsp. baking powder

2 cups sugar

2 Tbsp. vanilla

dash of salt

1 cup flour

2 cups chopped pecans *or* walnuts

1. Melt chocolate and butter in large saucepan.

2. Remove from stove. Add all other ingredients. Stir well until blended.

3. Pour into 9"x13" baking pan.

4. Bake 20 minutes at 350° until just set in the middle.

# Magic Cookie Bars

RUTH ANN KAUFFMAN, SALLIE Y. LAPP

*Makes 36 cookies* ❦ *Prep. Time: 15 minutes* ❦ *Baking Time: 25-30 minutes*

½ cup (1 stick) butter
1½ cups graham cracker crumbs
14-oz. can sweetened condensed milk
6-oz. pkg. semi-sweet chocolate chips
3½-oz. can flaked coconut
1 cup chopped nuts

1. Melt butter in 8"x12" baking pan.

2. Sprinkle cracker crumbs evenly over butter.

3. Pour condensed milk evenly over crumbs.

4. Combine chocolate chips, coconut, and nuts, then sprinkle evenly over mixture in pan.

5. Bake at 350° for 25-30 minutes.

# White Brownies

MARY ELLEN SPEICHER, SALLIE Y. LAPP

*Makes 35 brownies*
*Prep. Time: 20 minutes* ❦ *Baking Time: 35-40 minutes*

**Brownies:**
¾ cup (1½ sticks) butter, melted
½ cup brown sugar
½ cup white sugar
3 egg yolks
1 tsp. vanilla
1 tsp. baking powder
2 cups flour
¼ tsp. salt

**Topping:**
3 egg whites
1 cup brown sugar
½ cup chopped nuts
½ cup chocolate chips

1. Thoroughly mix together all ingredients for the brownie mixture. Spread batter in a 12"x17" baking pan.

2. Beat egg whites until stiff. Fold in brown sugar. Spread this mixture over brownies.

3. Sprinkle with nuts and chocolate chips.

4. Bake at 350° for 35-40 minutes.

# Chocolate Chip Squares

JUDITH E. MARTIN, PAUL L. SENSENIG AND SONS

*Makes 20–24 servings*
*Prep. Time: 15 minutes* ❦ *Baking Time: 30 minutes*

⅔ cup shortening
2¼ cups brown sugar
3 eggs
2¼ cups flour
2½ tsp. baking powder
½ tsp. salt
12-oz. pkg. chocolate chips
1 tsp. vanilla

1. In mixing bowl, cream shortening and sugar. Add eggs. Cream again.

2. Separately, combine flour with baking powder and salt. Mix slowly into creamed mixture.

3. Stir in chocolate chips and vanilla.

4. Spread in greased 9"x13" baking pan.

5. Bake 30 minutes at 350° until center is barely set. Cut while still warm.

# Marble Squares

JOYCE DEITER, EISENBERGER'S BAKED GOODS

*Makes 4 dozen squares* ❦ *Prep. Time: 20 minutes* ❦ *Baking Time: 25-30 minutes*

*Topping:*
8-oz. pkg. cream cheese, softened
⅓ cup sugar
1 egg

*Batter:*
¾ cup water
1-1½ oz. unsweetened chocolate squares
½ cup (1 stick) butter
2 cups flour

1. Mix topping by beating softened cream cheese and sugar until well blended. Add egg and mix well until smooth. Set aside.

2. For batter, combine water, unsweetened chocolate, and butter in large saucepan. Bring to boil. Remove from heat.

3. Combine flour and sugar and stir into mixture.

4. Add eggs, sour cream, baking soda, and salt. Mix well.

5. Pour into greased and floured 10"x15" jelly-roll pan.

2 cups sugar

2 eggs

½ cup sour cream

1 tsp. baking soda

½ tsp. salt

1 cup semi-sweet chocolate chips

6. Spoon topping over chocolate batter. Cut through batter several times for marbled effect. Sprinkle with chocolate chips.

7. Bake at 375° for 25-30 minutes or until toothpick inserted in center comes out clean.

8. Cool and cut into squares before serving.

# Nellie Blythes

MARY E. HESS, CHARLES HESS

**Makes 10 dozen cookies**

*Prep. Time: 20 minutes* ❦ *Baking Time: several minutes per batch*

4 eggs

2 cups sugar

2 cups buttermilk

2 tsp. baking soda

7 cups flour

2-3 cups shortening, for frying

2 cups confectioners sugar

1. Mix together eggs, sugar, buttermilk, baking soda, and flour.

2. Drop by scant teaspoonfuls into hot lard or shortening. Deep fry until light brown, several minutes per batch.

3. Drain in colander.

4. Shake in a bag of confectioners sugar and serve.

TIP

*These little desserts are best eaten when they are freshly made and still warm. If preparing to serve later, let them cool before dusting with confectioners sugar.*

# English Lemon Tarts

JACKIE PARKER, THE GOODIE SHOPPE

**Makes 4 dozen tarts**

Prep. Time: 30 minutes  ❧  Chilling Time: several hours  ❧  Baking Time: 12 minutes

**Pastry:**

2 cups flour

½ cup sugar

grated rind of 1 lemon

¾ cup (1½ sticks) butter, softened

3 egg yolks

**Lemon Curd Filling:**

5 eggs

2 cups sugar

½ cup (1 stick) plus 2 Tbsp. butter, melted

grated rind and juice of 2 lemons

confectioners sugar

candied violets

1. Make the pastry. Mix flour, sugar, and rind of one lemon in food processor.

2. Cut in butter. Add egg yolks one at a time. Mix until dough clings together.

3. Roll pastry on floured board until it is ⅛" thick.

4. Fit pastry into greased tart shells.

5. Bake shells at 375° for 12 minutes. Cool before filling.

6. Make filling. In top of double boiler, over briskly boiling water, beat eggs and add sugar gradually.

7. Add remaining ingredients and mix well. Cook and stir until thick

8. Chill.

9. Assemble. Using pastry bag or spoon, fill tart shells with chilled lemon curd.

10. Sift confectioners sugar over top and garnish with candied violets.

TIP

*Great for an afternoon tea!*

Thomas Produce opened at Central Market in 1927. Today, Ruth and Wilmer Thomas are third-generation standholders, growing their in-season vegetables and many flowers on their 65-acre farm in northern Lancaster County.

"Marketing teaches valuable lessons," Ruth reflects. "As we raised our seven children, they all helped grow, prepare, and sell our vegetables. None of us used calculators—and it was a great way for them to learn math by doing it in their heads! Customers were always amazed. And now our grandchildren do the same thing."

—Ruth Thomas, Thomas Produce

# DESSERTS AND CANDIES

## Espresso Mousse

REGINE IBOLD, THE SPICE STAND

*Makes 10–12 servings*

*Prep. Time: 25 minutes* ❧ *Cooking Time: about 10 minutes* ❧ *Chilling Time: overnight*

**6 egg yolks**

**½ cup sugar**

**1½ cups espresso, French roast**

**2 pkgs. unflavored gelatin**

**½ cup cold water**

**1½ pints heavy cream**

***Sauce:***

**⅔ cup sugar**

**1 cup espresso, French roast, hot**

**1 Tbsp. arrowroot**

**1 Tbsp. Cognac**

**shaved chocolate,** *optional*

1. Beat egg yolks with ½ cup sugar in a saucepan.

2. Beat in espresso and cook over low heat, stirring constantly, until mixture forms a thin custard.

3. Remove from heat. Soften gelatin in cold water and blend thoroughly into espresso custard. Let cool.

4. Whip cream and fold into the cooled custard.

5. Rinse a 2-quart mold with cold water, scrape the mousse into it and cover with plastic wrap. Chill overnight.

6. Dissolve ⅔ cup sugar in hot espresso in a saucepan. Mix arrowroot to thin paste with cold water and stir into the espresso.

7. Cook over low heat, stirring constantly, until clear and thickened. Add cognac.

8. Chill, covered with plastic wrap.

9. To serve, unmold mousse and top with sauce and shaved chocolate, if desired.

NOTE

*Light as a cloud, this lovely rich dessert uses French roast espresso beans in a new way!*

# Spanish Cream

ANNA MARIE GROFF, RUTH S. NOLT

*Makes 8–10 servings*
*Prep. Time: 25 minutes    ❧    Cooking Time: about 15 minutes    ❧    Chilling Time: several hours*

2 pkgs. unflavored gelatin
3 cups cold milk
½ cup sugar
3 eggs, separated
¼ tsp. salt
1 tsp. vanilla
fresh fruit

1. Dissolve gelatin in cold milk.

2. Add sugar, beaten egg yolks, salt, and vanilla.

3. Cook over low heat, stirring constantly. When mixture starts to boil, immediately remove from heat.

4. Beat egg whites until stiff. Gently fold into mixture. Do not cook after adding egg whites.

5. Pour into mold immediately. Chill until firm, several hours.

6. Unmold. Garnish around the edges with alternating slices of bananas and strawberries, or fill center of mold with raspberries, pineapples, peaches, or apricots.

# Graham Cracker Fluff

MRS. MARTHA FORRY, JOHN M. MARKLEY MEATS

*Makes 6–8 servings*

*Prep. Time: 25 minutes* ❧ *Cooking Time: about 15 minutes* ❧ *Chilling Time: several hours*

2 egg yolks

½ cup sugar

⅔ cup milk

1 pkg. unflavored gelatin

½ cup cold water

2 egg whites, stiffly beaten

1 tsp. vanilla

1 cup heavy cream

3 Tbsp. butter, melted

3 Tbsp. sugar

12 graham crackers, crushed

1. Beat egg yolks and add sugar.

2. Add milk and cook in top of double boiler over boiling water, stirring, until slightly thickened.

3. Soak gelatin in cold water.

4. Pour hot mixture over softened gelatin. Stir until smooth.

5. Chill until slightly thickened.

6. Add egg whites, vanilla, and heavy cream to chilled mixture.

7. Combine melted butter, sugar, and cracker crumbs to make crumbs.

8. Sprinkle half of crumbs into bottom of serving dish. Spread chilled mixture over crumbs. Sprinkle remaining crumbs over top.

9. Chill in refrigerator until set.

# Butterscotch Supreme

MRS. ROBERT FUNK, FUNK BROTHERS, INC.

*Makes 15 servings*
*Prep. Time: 25 minutes*
*Baking Time: 15 minutes*
*Chilling Time: several hours*

**First Layer:**

1½ cups flour

12 Tbsp. (1½ sticks) butter, melted

¾ cup chopped walnuts

**Second Layer**

8-oz. pkg. cream cheese, softened

1 cup confectioners sugar

1 cup whipped topping, thawed

**Third Layer:**

2 3-oz. pkgs. butterscotch pudding

3 cups milk

1 tsp. vanilla

**Fourth Layer:**

2 cups whipped topping, thawed

½ cup chopped walnuts

1. Mix together all ingredients for first layer.

2. Press into 9"x13" baking pan. Bake at 350° for 15 minutes. Cool.

3. Beat together all ingredients for second layer. Pour onto cooled first layer.

4. Mix together all ingredients for third layer. Pour over second layer.

5. Cover with whipped topping. Sprinkle with chopped walnuts.

6. Chill before serving.

VARIATION

*Use any flavor pudding you wish.*

# OTHER FARMERS MARKETS IN LANCASTER CITY

Lancaster Central Market is now the only farmers market in Lancaster City. But at least nine other markets, including the Curb Market, once operated within the city. Lancaster Central Market has by far the longest history; only two other city markets lasted more than a hundred years. Three Lancaster markets endured for fewer than 40 years. From 1882 to 1965 there were at least five farmer's markets operating simultaneously within Lancaster. The high point was between 1907 and 1918 when there were seven markets in the city. It was not uncommon for the standholders to sell at several different markets on different days of the week.

**The Northern Market** was located on the northwest corner of Queen and Walnut Streets. Built in 1872, it was the first of the large market houses. The building measured 80 feet by 240 feet and contained 250 stalls. The relatively new market building suffered a great tragedy in 1883, when the roof collapsed from the weight of snow. When the market closed in 1953, there were only 15 occupied stands. The building was demolished in 1958.

**The Eastern Market** was built in 1882 at the southeast corner of King and Shippen Streets. It had about 200 stalls. The unique Second-Empire-style architecture featured towers that could be viewed over a large part of the city. The market closed in 1918. The building has been renovated and is now used for offices.

**The Western Market** occupied the southeast corner of Orange and Pine Streets. It was built in 1882 and contained about 180 stalls. Like the Eastern Market, it enjoyed a rather brief existence and closed about 1920. The building still survives, but the second floor was destroyed by fire in 1942 (it was then being used as a roller-skating rink).

**The Southern Market** was built in the elaborate Queen Anne style in 1888 at the southwest corner of Queen and Vine Streets. It survived until 1986, but from the 1950s on, it suffered a dwindling trade. The building was most recently used by the Lancaster Chamber of Commerce.

**The Fulton Market,** located east of Frederick Street between Plum and Hand Streets in the northeastern part of town, was rather detached from the other Lancaster markets. The 1907 building originally had 150 standholders. When the market closed in 1971, there were only six stands. The building has been occupied by several different businesses.

**The Arcade Market** began in 1927 in the block between Orange and Marion Streets and Prince and Market Streets. The farmer's market continued until 1965; the entire building was demolished in 1969. The Prince Street parking garage now occupies the site.

**The West End Market,** the smallest and most recent of the markets, began in 1954 in a building that had been a car dealership. The building at the corner of Lemon and Mary Streets ceased to be a farmers' market in 1985 but is still occupied by a grocery store.

# Strawberry Pretzel Dessert

MIRIAM M. HESS, FRANK WEAVER GREENHOUSES

*Makes 12–16 servings*
*Prep. Time: 20 minutes*
*Cooking/Baking Time: about 10 minutes*
*Chilling Time: 2 hours*

**Crust:**

2 cups crushed pretzels

3 Tbsp. sugar

¾ cup (1½ sticks) butter, melted

**Filling:**

8-oz. pkg. cream cheese, softened

1 cup sugar

8-oz. container whipped topping, thawed

**Topping:**

6-oz. pkg. strawberry gelatin

2 cups boiling water

10-oz. pkg. frozen strawberries

8-oz. can crushed pineapple, drained

1. Mix crust ingredients and press into a 9"x13" baking pan. Bake at 400° for 7 minutes. Let cool.

2. Blend all filling ingredients and spread over crust.

3. To prepare topping, dissolve gelatin in boiling water. Add frozen strawberries and pineapple.

4. Chill about 45 minutes until mixture has thickened but not set. Pour over cream cheese layer.

5. Chill until set and ready to serve.

# Cranberry Dessert

JOANNE MYLIN, IRWIN S. WIDDERS PRODUCE

*Makes 16 servings*
Prep. Time: 15 minutes
Cooking Time: about 15 minutes
Chilling Time: 4 hours or more

1 lb. fresh cranberries

2 cups water

1 cup sugar

6-oz. pkg. cherry gelatin

2 cups halved, seedless red grapes

20-oz. can crushed pineapple, undrained

1 cup chopped nuts, *optional*

***Topping:***

8-oz. pkg. cream cheese, softened

¼ cup milk

1 tsp. vanilla

2 cups whipped topping, thawed

1. Combine cranberries, water, and sugar. Cook until cranberries pop. Remove from heat and add gelatin.

2. Add grapes, pineapple, and optional nuts. Pour into a large bowl and chill at least 4 hours. Do not use a mold.

3. To prepare topping, beat cream cheese, milk, and vanilla until smooth. Fold in whipped topping.

4. Spread topping over cranberry mixture. Serve.

### VARIATION

*Instead of fresh cranberries use two 16-oz. cans whole-berry cranberry sauce. Omit sugar and reduce water to 1 cup. Instead of Step 1, pour 1 cup boiling water over gelatin, stirring until dissolved. Add cranberry sauce, one can at a time, and stir until well mixed. Continue with Step 2.*

# Pumpkin Custard

MARY K. BRIEGHNER, RUDOLPH BREIGHNER

*Makes 6 servings*
*Prep. Time: 10 minutes* ❧ *Baking Time: 35-40 minutes*

2 cups cooked, mashed pumpkin
⅔ cup sugar
1 Tbsp. flour
½ tsp. salt
½ tsp. ground ginger
½ tsp. ground cinnamon
½ tsp. ground cloves
2 eggs
1 cup milk

1. Combine all ingredients and mix well.

2. Pour into baking dish. Bake at 350° about 35-40 minutes or until set in the middle.

### VARIATION

*Add vanilla and ½ cup coconut instead of spices.*

# Baked Apples

KATHLEEN PIANKA, MARION CHEESE

*Makes 4 servings*
*Prep. Time: 20 minutes* ❧ *Baking Time: 40 minutes*

2 tsp. ground cinnamon
¼ cup brown sugar
¼ cup raisins
8 dried apricots, chopped
4 Granny Smith, *or another tart variety,* apples
¼ cup brandy *or* Grand Marnier, heated slightly
2 Tbsp. butter, melted
1 tsp. ground nutmeg

1. Combine cinnamon, brown sugar, raisins, and apricots to make filling.

2. Core apples. Stuff apples with filling. Place in greased baking dish.

3. Combine brandy, butter, and nutmeg and pour over apples.

4. Bake at 350° for 40 minutes.

# Apple Dumplings

SUSIE BEILER, KAUFFMAN'S FRUIT FARM

*Makes 6 servings*
*Prep. Time: 30 minutes*
*Baking Time: 40-45 minutes*

6 baking apples

enough sugar to fill centers of 6 apples

cinnamon

**Dough Ingredients:**
2 cups flour

2½ tsp. baking powder

½ tsp. salt

⅔ cup shortening

¼ cup milk

**Sauce Ingredients:**
2 cups brown sugar

¼ tsp. ground cinnamon

2 cups water

¼ cup (half stick) butter, softened

1. Pare and core apples and cut in half. Fill centers with sugar and sprinkle with cinnamon. Put apples back together.

2. Make pastry by sifting flour, baking powder, and salt. Cut in shortening and add milk.

3. Roll dough as for pie crust and cut into 6 squares.

4. Place an apple on each square and wrap pastry around the apple.

5. Place apples into a greased baking pan.

6. To make sauce, combine sugar, cinnamon, and water. Cook 5 minutes.

7. Remove from heat and add butter. Mix well. Pour sauce over the apple dumplings.

8. Bake at 375° for 40-45 minutes. Serve hot with milk.

**From the other side of the Market stand . . .**

# RUTH THOMAS OF THOMAS PRODUCE

Thomas Produce opened at Central Market in 1927. Today, Ruth and Wilmer Thomas are third-generation standholders, growing their in-season vegetables and many flowers on their 65-acre farm in northern Lancaster County.

"Marketing teaches valuable lessons," Ruth reflects. "As we raised our seven children, they all helped grow, prepare, and sell our vegetables. None of us used calculators—and it was a great way for them to learn math by doing it in their heads! Customers were always amazed. And now our grandchildren do the same thing.

"Our granddaughters have commented that many of their friends know so little about fruits and vegetables and how to prepare them. We need more parents to *show* how to fix and eat fresh, local produce!"

Ruth indulges her customers, telling them her favorite ways of making the bok choy she sells, and the kohlrabi. And she even makes fresh pumpkin puree for those who are intimidated by a butternut squash or don't take time to prepare it from scratch themselves.

"I had a customer walk up to our stand showing signs of exhaustion. She called out, "Thank God! I found it! I've been all over the County, going to many markets looking for fresh pumpkin." When she told me where all she had been, she had not exaggerated the extent of her search. I was anticipating a large purchase of pumpkin puree, but instead, she bought one pint.

"I was happy I had it for her, but I couldn't help thinking, For $1.50, you could have purchased a nice-sized neck or butternut at any one of the markets you visited, and you'd have saved time and fuel in the process!

"But I enjoy our customers!"

# Quick Apple Cobbler

RUTH THOMAS, THOMAS PRODUCE

*Makes 8 servings*
*Prep. Time: 20 minutes*
*Baking Time: 45 minutes*

**Batter:**

1 cup sugar

1 cup flour

2 tsp. baking powder

1 cup milk

½ tsp. salt

½ tsp. ground cinnamon

**Other Ingredients:**

8 Tbsp. (1 stick) butter

4 cups peeled, diced apples

1. Mix all ingredients for batter. Set aside.

2. Melt butter in 7"x12" baking dish. Pour batter over melted butter. Do not stir.

3. Scatter apples over batter without stirring. Bake at 375° for 40 minutes.

4. Serve warm with milk or vanilla ice cream.

VARIATION

*Substitute any fruit that is in season.*

# Granny's Apple Crisp

SUSIE BARR, BARR'S FARMS

*Makes 4–6 servings*
*Prep. Time: 20 minutes     Baking Time: 30-35 minutes*

7 apples *or* 7 peaches, peeled and chopped

¼ tsp. ground cinnamon

¼ tsp. salt

¼ cup water

1 Tbsp. lemon juice

1 cup sugar

¼ cup brown sugar

½ cup flour

½ cup (1 stick) butter

1. Place apples or peaches in buttered casserole dish.

2. Mix cinnamon, salt, water, and lemon juice. Pour over top.

3. Mix sugar, brown sugar, flour, and butter to make crumbs. Spread over apples or peaches.

4. Bake at 400° for 30-35 minutes until fruit is soft and juice is bubbling at edges.

# Gourmet Apple Crisp

BRAD LOERCHER, PARSLEY PORCH

*Makes 6 servings*
*Prep. Time: 20 minutes*
*Baking Time: 50 minutes*

9 apples, peeled and sliced
1 cup flour
1 cup sugar
1 tsp. baking powder
pinch of salt
1 egg
4 Tbsp. (half stick) butter
gourmet cinnamon
dash of cardamom, *optional*

1. Place apples in a greased 7"x11" baking dish.

2. Mix flour, sugar, baking powder, and salt. Break egg into mixture and mix with your hands.

3. Sprinkle mixture evenly over apples.

4. Melt butter and pour over all. Liberally sprinkle with gourmet cinnamon. Add cardamom for a slightly different flavor.

5. Bake at 350° for 50 minutes, until apples are soft and top is browned.

NOTE

*A family favorite for years!*

# Blueberry Buckle

MARIAN EISENBERGER, SPRING GLEN FARM KITCHENS, INC.

*Makes 9–12 servings*
*Prep. Time: 20 minutes*
*Baking Time: 45-50 minutes*

**Batter:**

2 cups flour

¾ cup sugar

2½ tsp. baking powder

¾ tsp. salt

¼ cup shortening

¾ cup milk

I egg

2 cups blueberries, well-drained if thawed

**Topping:**

½ cup sugar

⅓ cup flour

½ tsp. ground cinnamon

¼ cup (half stick) butter, softened

1. Blend all batter ingredients except blueberries in blender for about half a minute.

2. Carefully stir in blueberries.

3. Spread mixture into a greased 9"-square baking pan.

4. Mix together all topping ingredients. Sprinkle over batter in pan.

5. Bake at 375° for 45-50 minutes or until juice is bubbling at edges.

# Christmas Plum Pudding

ANNA MARY NEFF, S. CLYDE WEAVER, INC.

*Makes 8–10 servings*
*Prep. Time: 15 minutes*
*Cooking/Baking Time: 2½ hours*

**Pudding:**
1 cup ground beef suet
1 cup raisins
½ cup chopped nuts
½ cup dried currants
⅔ cup milk
1 egg
1 scant cup sugar
1 cup flour
1 tsp. baking soda
½ tsp. ground cinnamon
½ tsp. ground nutmeg

**Sauce:**
1 cup water
½ cup sugar
1 Tbsp. cornstarch
1 Tbsp. butter
pinch of salt
1 tsp. vanilla

1. Mix all pudding ingredients thoroughly.

2. Pour into 2-quart casserole. Cover casserole and set into a 9"x13" baking dish. Pour as much water as possible into the 9"x 13" baking dish.

3. Bake at 300° for 2 hours. Check occasionally to make sure baking dish has not dried, adding water if needed.

4. Mix all sauce ingredients except vanilla. Bring to a boil and cook until thickened. Remove from heat, add vanilla, and stir.

5. Serve warm sauce over warm pudding.

# Rhubarb Pudding

RUTH ESHLEMAN, GIVANT'S BAKERY

*Makes 6 servings*
*Prep. Time: 20 minutes*
*Baking Time: 35-50 minutes*

2 egg yolks
½ cup sugar
2 cups milk
2 cups cubed bread
2 cups chopped rhubarb
2 Tbsp. butter
2 egg whites plus 2 Tbsp. sugar

1. Beat egg yolks in mixing bowl. Add sugar, milk, and bread cubes. Mix well.

2. Fold in rhubarb.

3. Put in greased baking dish and dot with butter.

4. Bake at 350° until knife comes out clean when inserted in middle of casserole, about 30-45 minutes.

5. Prepare a meringue by beating egg whites until stiff. Fold in sugar.

6. Spread over casserole and return to oven to brown meringue. Watch carefully to be sure the meringue does not get too dark!

NOTE

*This old dessert receipe came from my home.*

# Rhubarb Crunch

HELEN CRAUL, S. CLYDE WEAVER, INC.

*Makes 6–8 servings*
*Prep. Time: 20 minutes*
*Baking Time: 40 minutes*

I quart rhubarb, cut in I" pieces
¾ cup sugar
2 Tbsp. flour
I tsp. ground cinnamon
⅛ tsp. salt

*Topping:*
¾ cup quick oats *or* rolled oats
¾ cup brown sugar
¼ cup (half stick) butter, melted

1. Combine rhubarb, sugar, flour, cinnamon, and salt.

2. Spoon into greased 9-square baking dish.

3. Combine oats, brown sugar, and butter to make topping.

4. Sprinkle over rhubarb and pat down evenly.

5. Bake at 375° about 40 minutes, until juice is bubbling at edges.

6. Serve warm with milk or whipped cream.

# Orange Rhubarb

MRS. DOROTHY MARTIN, MARTIN'S HOME-BAKED GOODS

*Makes 10–12 servings*    *Prep. Time: 10 minutes*
*Cooking Time: about 15 minutes*    *Chilling time: several hours*

4 cups chopped rhubarb
½ cup water
I cup sugar
3-oz. pkg. orange gelatin
II-oz. can mandarin oranges

1. Boil rhubarb in water until it is soft, about 10 minutes.

2. Add sugar and gelatin. Stir in oranges and continue stirring until gelatin is completely dissolved.

3. Chill until thickened and serve.

**Desserts and Candies**    257

# Rhubarb Sauce

ETHEL STONER, JOHN R. STONER VEGETABLES

*Makes 8–10 servings*
*Prep. Time: 10 minutes    ❦    Cooking Time: about 15 minutes*

6-8 cups rhubarb sliced into
1"-thick pieces
1 cup water
1½-2 cups sugar
2-3 Tbsp. minute tapioca

1. Put rhubarb pieces in saucepan with water and sugar and bring to a boil. Simmer until tender, about 10 minutes.

2. Add tapioca and stir until well mixed. Simmer an additional 5 minutes.

3. Cool and serve.

### VARIATION

*Substitute 3-oz. pkg. strawberry gelatin for tapioca.*

# Rhubarb Tapioca Pudding

RUTH WIDDERS, IRWIN S. WIDDERS PRODUCE

*Makes 6–8 servings*
*Prep. Time: 15 minutes    ❦    Cooking Time: about 15 minutes*

2 cups chopped rhubarb
2 cups water
¼ tsp. salt
1 cup sugar, *or less, as you wish*
¼ cup quick-cooking tapioca
8-oz. can crushed pineapple,
drained, *or* 1 cup fresh
strawberries, sliced or mashed
1 cup heavy whipping cream

1. Combine rhubarb, water, salt, sugar, and tapioca in saucepan.

2. Cook over medium heat until mixture comes to a full boil, stirring constantly. Remove from heat.

3. Add crushed pineapple or strawberries and chill.

4. Whip the heavy cream in a chilled bowl until it is fluffy and holds its shape. Spread over chilled pudding.

### HINT

*I like to make this pudding (Steps 1 and 2) in the microwave, stirring several times.*

# Apple Tapioca

MRS. DOROTHY MARTIN, MARTIN'S HOME-BAKED GOODS

*Makes 4–6 servings*
*Prep. Time: 10 minutes*  ❧  *Cooking Time: about 15 minutes*

⅓ cup minute tapioca
1 cup brown sugar, packed
4 cups peeled, chopped apples
2 cups water
1 Tbsp. lemon juice
2 Tbsp. butter, softened
½ tsp. ground cinnamon
½ tsp. salt

1. Mix all ingredients together in a saucepan and let stand 5 minutes.

2. Over medium heat, bring to a boil, stirring frequently.

3. Simmer until apples are tender, about 12 minutes.

4. Serve at room temperature or chilled.

# Strawberry Tapioca

LOIS THOMAS, E. H. THOMAS AND SON

*Makes 6 servings*
*Prep. Time: 10 minutes*  ❧  *Cooking Time: about 15 minutes*

2 cups water
⅓ cup minute tapioca
½ cup sugar
2 cups crushed fresh *or* frozen strawberries
1 cup whipped topping, thawed

1. Boil water, tapioca and sugar until mixture begins to thicken, about 10 minutes. Remove from stove.

2. Add strawberries. Cool.

3. Serve with whipped topping.

### VARIATION

*Substitute ¼ cup lemon juice and grated rind from 2 lemons in place of strawberries.*

# Caramel Pudding

JOYCE DEITER, EISENBERGER'S BAKED GOODS

*Makes 6 servings* ❧ *Prep. Time: 10 minutes*
*Cooking Time: about 15 minutes* ❧ *Chilling Time: overnight*

4 Tbsp. (half stick) butter

4 cups milk

1 cup brown sugar

¼ tsp. salt

⅔ cup flour

2 tsp. vanilla

frozen whipped topping,
thawed, *optional*

1. Melt butter in large saucepan over low heat.

2. Add milk and heat until milk is scalding.

3. Add sugar, salt, and flour and cook until thickened, stirring frequently. Remove from heat.

4. Stir in vanilla and refrigerate overnight.

5. Serve with whipped topping, if you wish.

# Grape-Nut Pudding

JOYCE FAIR, UTZ'S POTATO CHIPS

*Makes 6 servings*
*Prep. Time: 15 minutes* ❧ *Baking Time: 1 hour*

½ cup brown sugar

⅛ tsp. salt

1 Tbsp. cornstarch

1 egg, beaten

½ cup Grape-Nuts

2 cups milk

½ cup raisins

⅓ cup chopped nuts

1 Tbsp. flour

1 tsp. vanilla

1. Combine brown sugar, salt, and cornstarch. Stir in the beaten egg.

2. Add Grape-Nuts and milk and beat thoroughly.

3. Dust raisins and chopped nuts with flour. Fold into mixture. Add vanilla.

4. Pour into greased 7"x11" baking dish. Bake at 350° for about 1 hour or until firm.

# Nut Pudding

GRACE E. BAKER, S. CLYDE WEAVER, INC.

*Makes 10–12 servings* ❧ *Prep. Time: 15 minutes* ❧ *Baking Time: about 30 minutes*

1 quart milk
2 cups bread crumbs
1 cup sugar
3 eggs, separated
½ tsp. ground nutmeg, *optional*
1 cup chopped walnuts

1. Mix milk with bread crumbs in a saucepan and cook, bringing to a boil.

2. Mix sugar, egg yolks, and nutmeg, as you wish. Add to bread mixture. Remove from heat.

3. Add walnuts to mixture and mix well. Place in lightly greased baking dish.

4. Beat egg whites until stiff and spread over bread mixture. Bake at 400° for about 8-10 minutes or until egg whites brown. Watch carefully!

NOTE

*This old recipe is a real conversation piece.*

# Bread Pudding

WILLOW VALLEY FARMS

*Makes 12–14 servings* ❧ *Prep. Time: 15 minutes* ❧ *Baking Time: 1½ hours*

1 loaf bread
6 cups milk, *divided*
10 eggs, beaten
2¾ cups sugar
1 tsp. ground cinnamon
1 tsp. vanilla

1. Break bread into mixing bowl. Pour 3 cups milk over bread and fold together.

2. Spoon into greased 9"x13" baking dish.

3. Mix remaining 3 cups milk with eggs, sugar, cinnamon, and vanilla. Mix well and pour over bread mixture using a spatula to push mixture down on bread.

4. Bake 1½ hours at 325° until set in the middle.

# Cracker Pudding

MARY K. BREIGHNER, RUDOLPH BREIGHNER

*Makes 8–10 servings* ❧ *Prep. Time: 15 minutes* ❧ *Cooking Time: about 20 minutes*

1 quart milk

2 egg yolks

1¼ cups sugar, *divided*

1 cup crumbled saltine crackers

¾ cup grated coconut

1 tsp. vanilla

2 egg whites

1. Scald milk in saucepan until steaming. Whisk in egg yolks, ¾ cup sugar, cracker crumbs, and coconut.

2. Mix well, cooking and stirring constantly until thickened. Remove from heat and stir in vanilla.

3. Pour into a baking dish.

4. Beat egg whites until stiff. Fold in remaining ½ cup sugar to make a meringue. Spread over pudding and put in oven long enough for meringue to brown. Watch carefully!

# Creamy Rice Pudding

LENA KING, SHREINER'S FLOWERS

*Makes 4–6 servings* ❧ *Prep. Time: 15 minutes* ❧ *Cooking Time: 1-1½ hours*

1 quart milk

1 cup uncooked rice

1 egg, well beaten

ground cinnamon

1 cup sugar

½ tsp. salt

½ tsp. vanilla

1. Cook rice in milk in double boiler over rapidly boiling water until soft, about 1-1½ hours. Stir occasionally and add more milk if needed. (Check bottom pan occasionally and add more water if needed so pan doesn't cook dry.)

2. Remove 1 cup hot rice and milk from heat and gradually whisk in the egg.

3. Then stir back into the rest of the hot rice and milk, along with the sugar, salt, and vanilla. Cook and stir briefly.

4. Sprinkle with cinnamon and serve warm.

# Pineapple Dessert

LOIS THOMAS, C. H. THOMAS AND SON

*Makes 6 servings*
*Prep. Time: 15 minutes*

6-oz. pkg. vanilla pudding

1¾ cups pineapple juice

8-oz. can crushed pineapple, undrained

4 apples, finely diced

miniature marshmallows, *optional*

1. Follow directions on box of pudding, but substitute pineapple juice for water.

2. Fold undrained pineapples and apples into pudding.

3. Add miniature marshmallows, if you wish.

# Orange Fluff Dessert

MILDRED BRACKBILL, UTZ'S POTATO CHIPS

*Makes 4 servings*
*Prep. Time: 20 minutes*
*Chilling Time: 20-60 minutes*

1 pkg. unflavored gelatin

¼ cup cold water

½ cup boiling water

1 cup frozen orange juice concentrate

2 egg whites

1 cup fresh orange slices

1. Mix gelatin with cold water. Add boiling water and stir until dissolved.

2. Add undiluted frozen orange juice concentrate. Stir and chill until thickened.

3. Beat egg whites at high speed until frothy. Fold into mixture.

4. Beat again until frothy.

5. Decorate with fresh oranges and serve.

NOTE

*This fresh, fluffy dish is good for the diet-conscious—it has no added sugar or egg yolks.*

# Orange Custard Fondue

ETHEL STONER, JOHN R. STONER VEGETABLES

*Makes 3½ cups*
*Prep. Time: 15 minutes*
*Chilling Time: 2 hours*

3-oz. pkg. vanilla pudding
1¾ cups milk
2 cups whipped topping, thawed
2 Tbsp. orange juice
1 tsp. grated orange peel

**Dippers:**
strawberries, pineapple chunks,
cantaloupe, honeydew, melon,
pear, peach slices, apples, bananas

pound cake cubes

1. Prepare pudding according to package directions using 1¾ cups milk.

2. Cover with plastic wrap and chill about 2 hours until thickened.

3. Beat pudding with rotary beater until smooth.

4. Fold in whipped topping and orange juice. Top with orange peel.

5. Serve fondue with fresh fruit and cake cubes.

# Cheese Cake

SUSIE BEILER, KAUFFMAN'S FRUIT FARM

*Makes 16 servings*
*Prep. Time: 20 minutes*
*Cooking/Baking Time: about 20 minutes*
*Chilling Time: several hours*

**Crust:**

2 cups crushed graham crackers

½ cup (1 stick) butter, melted

⅓-½ cup sugar, according to
your taste preference

**Cheese Cake:**

2 pkgs. unflavored gelatin

½ cup cold water

2 eggs

½-¾ cup sugar, according to
your taste preference

¾ cup water

2 8-oz. pkgs. cream cheese,
softened

12-oz. container whipped
topping, thawed

1. Mix all ingredients for the crust. Press firmly into bottom of 9"x13" baking dish.

2. Bake at 350° about 5-8 minutes. Cool.

3. Dissolve gelatin in cold water. Set aside.

4. Over low heat, mix egg yolks, sugar, and water. Cook and stir until mixed well and boiling. Let cool.

5. Beat egg whites until stiff.

6. Mix cream cheese with egg yolk mixture and gelatin. Fold in egg whites and whipped topping. Beat for a few minutes.

7. Pour cheese cake mixture over graham cracker crust. Refrigerate several hours before serving.

VARIATIONS

1. *Use ⅔ cup water and juice from ½ fresh lemon in egg yolk and sugar mixture.*

2. *Stir zest from 1 lemon (about 1 Tbsp.) into cream cheese, egg yolk, and gelatin mixture.*

# Chèvre Cheesecake

ANDREW AND MARY MELLINGER, LINDEN DALE FARMS

*Makes 6 servings*
*Prep. Time: 30 minutes*
*Baking Time: 50 minutes*

9 graham crackers (about 1 sleeve), crushed

1 ¼ cups sugar, *divided*

¼ cup (half stick) butter, melted

16 oz. Linden Dale Farm chèvre

3 eggs

2 tsp. real vanilla

1. Mix crushed crackers, ½ cup sugar, and butter. Pack into greased 9″ springform pan.

2. Beat chèvre, remaining ¾ cup sugar, eggs, and vanilla together using an electric mixer until well blended.

3. Pour mixture into springform pan on top of cracker crust.

4. Bake at 300° for 45-55 minutes, until set in the middle.

5. Allow to cool to warm and serve, or chill first before serving. The flavors are different—but delicious!

---

TIP

*You can also mix in lemon zest or orange zest if you wish. Fresh berries are an awesome topping to this cake, such as blueberries, raspberries, and strawberries. Substitute buttery crackers instead of graham crackers for a different flavor.*

---

NOTE

*Since this is a homemade recipe, I want to draw attention to the nutritional value of this cake. The chèvre has fewer calories and more nutritional value than the cream cheese traditionally used in cheesecake, since chèvre is made from whole goat's milk as compared to cow's milk cream in cream cheese.*

# Oreo Cookie Dessert

DONNA BETANCOURT, EISENBERGER'S BAKED GOODS

*Makes 12–14 servings*
*Prep. Time: 20 minutes*
*Chilling Time: several hours*

15-oz. pkg. Oreo cookies
8 Tbsp. (1 stick) butter, melted
2 3-oz. pkgs. vanilla pudding
8-oz. pkg. cream cheese, softened
3½ cups milk, *divided*
2 cups whipped topping, thawed

1. Crunch up cookies with a rolling pin.

2. Pour melted butter over cookie crumbs. Mix.

3. Press half of crumbs into the bottom of a 9"x13" baking dish. Reserve remaining crumbs for topping.

4. Beat ½ cup milk with cream cheese until fluffy.

5. Add pudding and remaining milk and mix well. Fold whipped topping into pudding mixture.

6. Spread pudding mixture over cookie crumbs. Spread reserved crumbs over pudding layer.

7. Chill and serve.

# Frozen Banana Split Dessert

JOY WADEL, IRWIN S. WIDDERS PRODUCE

*Makes 15 servings*
*Prep. Time: 20 minutes*
*Freezing Time: several hours*

3 cups crushed graham crackers, *divided*

⅓ cup butter, melted

2-3 bananas

2 quarts ice cream

1 cup chopped nuts

1 cup chocolate chips

½ cup (1 stick) butter

2 cups confectioners sugar

1½ cups evaporated milk

1 tsp. vanilla

2 cups whipped cream

1. Prepare graham cracker crust by pouring ⅓ cup melted butter over 2 cups graham crackers. Mix well.

2. Spoon this crust into bottom of 9"x13" pan. Press down firmly with spoon.

3. Slice bananas and lay over crust.

4. Cut ice cream into ½" thick slices and create a layer on top of bananas.

5. Sprinkle nuts over ice cream. Freeze until firm, at least 1 hour.

6. Melt chocolate chips and ½ cup butter over low heat. Add confectioners sugar and evaporated milk to chocolate mixture. Cook until thickened, stirring constantly.

7. Remove from heat and add vanilla. Cool slightly (not too long or it will become stiff).

8. Pour over the ice cream. Freeze until ready to serve, at least 1 hour.

9. Before serving spread whipped cream over top. Sprinkle reserved 1 cup of graham cracker crumbs over all.

TIP

*This cool, refreshing dessert is great for special events.*

# Cream Topping for Fresh Fruit

ETHEL STONER, JOHN R. STONER VEGETABLES

*Makes 3 cups topping*
*Prep. Time: 5 minutes*

I cup vanilla ice cream, softened
½ cup sour cream
¼ cup sugar
I tsp. vanilla
I cup whipped topping, thawed

1. Combine all ingredients except whipped topping, stirring well.

2. Fold in whipped topping.

3. Serve with fruit and angel food cake.

# Fruit Pizza

DEB WARFEL, S. CLYDE WEAVER, INC.

*Makes 8 servings   Prep. Time: 30 minutes*
*Baking Time: 10-20 minutes   Chilling Time: several hours*

**Filling:**
8-oz. pkg. cream cheese, softened
½ cup sugar
8 oz. whipped topping, thawed
I tsp. lemon juice

**Topping:**
any variety of fresh or canned fruits

**Glaze:**
½ cup sugar
2 Tbsp. cornstarch
I cup orange juice
¼ cup lemon juice

**Crust:**
favorite sugar cookie recipe or Fruit Pizza crust recipe found on page 270

1. Mix ingredients for crust according to directions. Press into greased pizza pan and bake 10-20 minutes at 325° or until slightly brown.

2. Cream all ingredients for filling together and spread over cooled crust.

3. Arrange fruit over pizza as desired. Different colors make it more attractive.

4. Mix ingredients for glaze together in a saucepan. Stir constantly over medium heat until thickened. Spoon over fruit while glaze is hot. This glaze helps prevent fruit from turning brown.

5. Chill pizza several hours before serving.

NOTE

*Attractive and very delicious!*

# Fruit Pizza Crust

VIV HUNT, VIV'S VARIETIES

*Makes crust for one pizza pan*
*Prep. Time: 20 minutes*
*Baking Time: 8-10 minutes*

2 cups flour

1 tsp. salt

⅔ cup shortening

3-4 Tbsp. ice water

⅔ cup sharp cheddar cheese, grated

1. Mix together flour and salt. Cut in shortening with two knives or a pastry cutter.

2. Add ice water until mixture forms a ball.

3. Work in the grated cheese with a fork or your fingers until well mixed.

4. Press into greased pizza pan.

5. Bake crust 8-10 minutes at 475°. Prick throughout baking time with a fork.

# Diplos

KOULA VAKIOS, KOULA'S GREEK PASTRIES

*Makes about 35 diplos*
*Prep. Time: 20 minutes*
*Cooking Time: several minutes per diplo*

1 cup milk

2 eggs, beaten

1 tsp. lemon juice

½ tsp. salt

1 cup plus 1 Tbsp. flour

1 tsp. sugar, *optional*

**Syrup:**

2 cups sugar

1 cup water

1-1½ cups honey

2-3 whole cloves

1 cinnamon stick

**Other Tools and Ingredients:**

diplo mold

enough oil for deep-frying

1 cup finely ground walnuts

1. Mix milk and eggs together. Add lemon juice.

2. Stir in dry ingredients and mix until smooth. Batter should be runny.

3. Pour oil into deep-frying pan. Heat until very hot.

4. Place diplo mold into hot oil until it is hot. Carefully remove from oil and dip into batter. Do not immerse; rather, dip into batter about ¾ of way.

5. Place mold, covered with batter, into hot oil. Batter will drop into oil. Fry until golden brown.

6. Let cool on paper towels.

7. Mix all syrup ingredients in a saucepan. Cook until it thickens like honey. Let cool.

8. Drizzle syrup over diplos. Sprinkle with ground walnuts and serve.

NOTE

*Koula Vakios sold this delicate pastry on Central Market. To make her diplos, she uses a mold that she received from her Greek mother-in-law at least 25 years ago.*

# Peanut Butter Fudge

JOHNNIE YOUNG, PA FUDGE COMPANY

*Makes 24 servings*
*Prep. Time: 30 minutes*
*Cooking Time: 4 minutes*
*Chilling Time: several hours*

1½ cups sugar
6 Tbsp. (¾ stick) butter
⅓ cup evaporated milk
½ cup peanut butter
1 cup marshmallow creme

1. In a saucepan, mix together sugar, butter, and evaporated milk.

2. Bring to a boil. Boil for 4 minutes, stirring constantly.

3. Remove from heat. Add peanut butter and marshmallow creme.

4. Stir well. Pour into a 13"x9"pan.

5. Let cool. Chill in refrigerator.

NOTE

*This is a family recipe that I have made at holidays for years. It is a favorite of the children and now grandchildren.*

# Chocolate Fudge

ANNA F. KREIDER, VIV'S VARIETIES

*Makes 60 pieces*
*Prep. Time: 15 minutes*
*Cooking Time: about 10 minutes*
*Chilling Time: 2 hours*

3 6-oz. pkgs. semi-sweet chocolate chips

14-oz. can sweetened condensed milk

dash of salt

½-1 cup chopped nuts

1½ tsp. vanilla

1. In a double boiler over medium heat, melt chocolate chips with condensed milk. Remove from heat.

2. Stir in remaining ingredients. Spread evenly into a wax-paper-lined 8"- or 9"-square pan.

3. Chill 2 hours or until firm.

4. Turn fudge onto cutting board. Peel off paper and cut into squares. Store loosely covered in refrigerator.

VARIATIONS

1. *Melt chocolate chips with condensed milk in microwave for 4 minutes on medium high.*

2. *Use peanut butter chips or mint chocolate chips instead of chocolate chips.*

NOTE

*Very creamy and rich!*

# Chocolate Potato Fudge

JOHNNIE YOUNG, PA FUDGE COMPANY

*Makes 10 servings*
*Prep. Time: 45 minutes*
*Cooking Time: 20 minutes*

3 squares bittersweet baking chocolate

3 Tbsp. butter

⅓ cup mashed potatoes

⅛ tsp. salt

I tsp. vanilla

I lb. confectioners sugar

1. Melt the butter and chocolate together.

2. Add mashed potatoes, salt, and vanilla. Mix.

3. Add confectioners sugar. Mix with hands until smooth.

4. Press into an 8"-square pan. Chill. Cut into pieces.

NOTE

*Sometimes we would make this fudge if we had leftover mashed potatoes.*

# Peanut Brittle Candy

HELEN THOMAS, HELEN THOMAS PRODUCE

*Makes about 4 cups*
*Prep. Time: 15 minutes*
*Cooking Time: about 10 minutes*

I cup sugar

½ cup dark corn syrup

½ cup light corn syrup

I Tbsp. water

2 cups raw peanuts

½ tsp. ground cinnamon

½ tsp. salt

¾ tsp. baking soda

1. Mix sugar, dark and light corn syrup, and water in a saucepan. Bring to a boil over medium heat. Boil for 2 minutes.

2. Add peanuts and continue to boil until peanuts look like they are roasted brown.

3. Remove from heat. Add cinnamon, salt, and baking soda, and mix. Pour onto greased baking sheet. Cool.

4. Break peanut brittle into pieces and store in an airtight container.

# Potato Butter Mints

RUTH THOMAS, THOMAS PRODUCE

*Makes 3 dozen mints* ❦ *Prep. Time: 15 minutes* ❦ *Cooking Time: about 15 minutes*

¼ cup warm mashed potatoes

¼ cup (half stick) butter, softened

1 lb. confectioners sugar

any flavoring *or* coloring that you wish

small amount of sugar

1. Cook peeled, chopped potatoes. Mash, but do not add any milk, salt, or butter.

2. Cream warm mashed potatoes and butter with mixer. Add confectioners sugar slowly, eventually mixing with hands. Add a few drops of water or a little more confectioners sugar, whichever is needed, to make dough workable.

3. Add flavoring or coloring, as you wish. Mixture should be consistency of play dough.

4. Roll dough into balls or any shape desired. Roll each mint in sugar.

# Vanilla Extract

BRAD LOERCHER, PARSLEY PORCH

*Makes 1 cup*
*Prep. Time: 5 minutes*
*Standing Time: 2 months*

1 vanilla bean, Tahitian preferred

1 cup vodka, *or* unflavored rum, brandy, or grain alcohol

1. Take kitchen scissors and cut vanilla bean in half to expose seeds.

2. Put alcohol into a bottle with a cap. Add split vanilla bean and shake.

3. Let sit for at least 2 months before using. The longer it sits, the better it will be.

### NOTE

*This vanilla extract is pure. Vanilla extracts purchased at supermarkets contain water, alcohol, corn syrup, caramel coloring, and often only a small amount of vanilla bean.*

# Index

# About the Author

Phyllis Good is a *New York Times* bestselling author whose books have sold more than 11 million copies. Good is a native of Lancaster County, Pennsylvania. As a teenager, she worked on Central Market, and today as a resident of Lancaster City, she shops on Market regularly.

Good authored the national bestselling *Fix-It and Forget-It* cookbook series, as well as numerous other cookbooks and nonfiction titles.

Good spends her time writing, editing books, and cooking new recipes.